An
Elusive
Presence

An
Elusive
Presence:

The Discovery of
John H. Finley
and His America

Marvin E. Gettleman

Nelson-Hall nh Chicago

Library of Congress Cataloging in Publication Data

Gettleman, Marvin E
    An elusive presence.

    Bibliography: p.
    Includes index.
    1. Finley, John Huston, 1863–1940. 2. College
presidents—United States—Biography. 3. Intellectuals
—United States—Biography. 4. United States—
Intellectual life. I. Title.
LD3816 1903. G47   370'.92'4 [B]   79-10547
ISBN 0-88229-312-5

Manufactured in the United States of America

10   9   8   7   6   5   4   3   2   1

dedicated to my sisters,
Mildred Garza and Roslyn Jacobs,
and to their niece,
Rebecca Lenore Gettleman-Braiman

Contents

Preface

A recent issue of the newsletter of a historian's organization in New York City carried the following satirical announcement of a dissertation prize contest:

> The Mid-Atlantic Radical Historians Organization [MARHO] Coordinating Committee proudly announces the awarding of the Nostabush P. Bryant Prize for Ph.D. Candidates in History. For too long, our colleagues on the left have labored under the illusion that moral incentives can inspire great achievements. Young radicals have been encouraged to view poverty, unemployment, and poor physical and mental health as necessary by-products of the quest for intellectual excellence, and they have lived their lives accordingly. But such discipline and asceticism, while inspiring to the innocent, has not loosened the foothold of the Capitalist State. Hungry people do not make revolutions. As its own contribution to the cause of American Socialism, MARHO has decided to offer material rewards for its members who have proven their commitment to revolutionary struggle through the medium of their craft.
>
> These awards, though conventional to the careless observer, will differ sharply in meaning from the Bancroft Prize, the National Book Award, and other symbols of bourgeois academic excellence. These prizes are given for the best finished product. The minute by minute agony of creation, the deep ambivalences, the broken marriages and strained friendships, only appear as cryptic references in prefaces. But those experiences are the embodiment of the social process of writing a dissertation. If we are to reward people justly, we must reward them for how they live, not simply what they produce. Hence the Nostabush P. Bryant Prize will be offered for the most radical dissertation *experience*. Members who wish to compete for this award are required to submit, in written or oral form, all evidence that they can amass proving that their dissertation experience demonstrates "the disorder of life under capitalism." In addition to the dissertation itself, contestants are encouraged to submit cancelled checks to psychiatrists, suicide notes, divorce proceedings, insulting letters from supervisors, and letters announcing that the time limit for their dissertation has run out. Materials will be carefully sifted over the next month and a half and a winner and a runner up will be selected and honored at the

MARHO Spring Conference. Please rush your dissertation and supporting materials to MARHO. . . .

While certain allusions in this satire (published in the Spring,
1975, number of the *Radical History Review*) will be best
understood by leftist cognoscenti, it touches on some of the
little-explored agonies of American academic life shared by
many who pursue graduate studies in the universities. This
book is a product of such study and in a much earlier form was a
rejected Ph.D. dissertation at a major Eastern university. Subsequently, it was rewritten twice, once for publication in article
form, and again for this book. Meanwhile, the author finally did
earn his doctorate with a thesis on early American radicalism,
which was published within a year of its completion.

Told about the rejection of the first completed book-length
dissertation, friends and acquaintances have promptly declared this to be one of the classic academic horror stories. In a
way, they are right. Something is wrong with a system that
permits senior professors in graduate schools the unchecked
power they now possess. That the rejection involved factors
other than merely the adverse judgment of a recognized scholar
on the inferior work of an apprentice was made painfully clear
when the placement service of the university inadvertently
sent a copy of my confidential record to my home instead of to
the school where I was applying for a teaching position. My
dissertation adviser, without informing me, was sending out the
kind of letter that ensured I would never get the job I was
seeking, and whatever modest academic advancement I subsequently achieved came only when I requested that the of-
fending letter be removed from my file. While he conceded that
I might do an adequate job of teaching undergraduates in
elementary courses, my adviser went on to write (in a letter that
would certainly win me the MARHO prize):

> Mr. Gettleman's economic origins were humble, and he has had his
> difficulties to master sufficiently the languages and other incidental re-
> quirements for the doctorate in history, all in pace with his peers of more
> cultivated background and training. Yet he won the Woodrow Wilson
> Fellowship, and maintaining a family meanwhile, he has kept up his
> work. No one would attribute to him an overly refined intellectual equip-
> ment, but it is a strong one, and the man has a great deal of fortitude. He
> will make a college teacher, or the heavens will fall.

The message was clear: here is an uncultivated upstart determined to shoulder his way into the society of his betters.

This appraisal was, in part, accurate, even insightful. My lower middle-class family had just recently emerged from the poverty of New York's Jewish ghettos, and to my knowledge I am the first Gettleman to earn a doctorate of any kind. Perhaps my graduate school professor exaggerated my "humble" origins somewhat, since during my early childhood my father was a fairly prosperous pharmacist. But the professor descended (as he was careful to inform his students) from distinguished personages in the early cultural history of colonial New England, and from such lofty genealogical heights the Gettlemans must have looked lowly enough. My former adviser knew too that I had had a tough time passing the French and German sight-reading examinations required for the Ph.D., and part of that problem might very well have been the lack, until years later, of any European travel—a "deprivation" suffered by few of my "peers of more cultivated background." On the basis of these defects, he may well have been surprised that I won a prestigious fellowship.

As for "maintaining a family," the outward forms certainly were kept intact, but those graduate school years marked the beginning of the end of my first marriage. A son was born then, and his mother never quite got over the indignity of being an impecunious (the fellowship paid some $2,400 a year) graduate student's wife. At certain crisis moments in the downward drift of the marriage, the dissertation itself became the focus of contention, and the rejection of the thesis exactly coincided with our final separation; the coincidence was, as my Trotskyist friends are sometimes fond of saying, no accident.

Neither rejection of the thesis nor divorce prevented continuation of my work on John Finley. In the subsequent years the subject of this book, John Huston Finley, or his persona, has virtually become a member of the household. As the various articles on aspects of Finley's career appeared in scholarly journals between 1969 and 1971, a real figure began to take shape; at the same time, a familiar pseudo-Finley became a local scapegoat, taking the blame for spilt milk, lost keys, and other minor domestic disasters. Confusion between the two was bound to develop, and I have overheard learned debates among the children as to whether Finley was real or a mythical figure akin to the tooth fairy or Santa Claus.

No uncritical subscriber to the notion that babes have special access to wisdom, I do nevertheless find substance in the debate over Finley's reality. Moving among the great and near great, associated with powerful educational and journalistic institutions, Finley was an elusive figure. Chronicling his long and involved career has been possible because of the extensive archival material in the New York Public Library, the Knox College Library (Galesburg, Illinois) and other depositories. But sifting, ordering, and comprehending the data posed a number of serious interpretative problems, some of a general nature and others more specifically rooted in this particular subject. Finley's life and career were marked by a near-total identification with the dominant trends in his society; it has been sometimes difficult to determine where Finley leaves off and where the climate of opinion begins. This is not to imply that he had a weak or unimpressive personality. Every scrap of surviving evidence testifies to precisely the opposite: Finley was a warm, genial, and forceful man, but these qualities were put at the service of a conventionality so profound as to almost swallow up the man. The consequent tasks of historical reconstruction, in my opinion, necessitate the somewhat unorthodox format of this book, combining history, biography, and autobiography in what I hope readers will find an enlightening and entertaining mixture.

Some of these readers, my friends who in the past have good-naturedly criticized me for a pedantic obsession with footnotes and scholarly apparatus, will doubtless wonder what has gotten into me when they notice the absence of such material in this book. Other readers too will probably be thankful that the pages that follow are not loaded with formal impedimentia. But let me at the same time assure one and all that I have been scrupulous in the search for and examination of every scrap of data I could lay my hands on relating to Finley's life and career. Usually the context of my narrative will make clear the source of each datum, whether manuscript letter, book, or magazine article. A brief bibliography at the end of this book

will tell even the most suspicious critic how to verify every fact
I invoke. If there is still anyone wishing to check further into
the documentation underlying this study, that person is invited
to read my heavily footnoted published articles (listed in the
bibliography) or to consult my own elaborately organized research notes now open to scholars in the Manuscript Division
of the New York Public Library (Annex).

Now comes the conventional section where in the "front
matter" of a book the author offers up thanks to all those who
helped his project, or refrained from hindering it. In the latter
category are those two wonderful women, my sisters, to whom
this book is lovingly dedicated. I can't say that either of them
provided essential data on John Finley; probably neither ever
heard of Finley before their brother began sending them articles on him. But in their support, their sympathy, and their love
over the decades, I have found part of what I needed to sustain
my ventures, including the present study. Not to be denied
credit either is my ex-wife, Marge, who appears as a minor
character in the autobiographical passages of this book. Though
our marriage eventually dissolved in bitterness and misun-
derstanding, there were some good moments when it was possible to do things like work on a Ph.D. thesis.

Among the others who provided various degrees of aid, support, and sympathy for this study were the late Dean Morton
Gottschall of the City College of New York, (CCNY), who
helped me obtain small research grants from the City College
Fund in 1962 and 1963; Knox College librarians Warren Morris
and Lucius Elder; Mrs. Wolf Frank, former curator of the Spe-
cial Collections, Morris R. Cohen Library, CCNY; Dean Her-
mann Muelder of Knox College; Freda Theiss of the Johns
Hopkins University Library; the late Frederick A. Morse, for-
merly Secretary to the Regents, State University of New York;
Professor Hugh Hawkins of Amherst College; Professor David
Mermelstein, Polytechnic Institute of New York; Helen
Matthews Smith, State University of New York, College at
Purchase; and Professor Charles A. Barker, Wonalancet, New
Hampshire. Special mention must be made of the sympathetic,
helpful, and efficient staff of the Manuscript Division, New
York Public Library, especially Paul R. Rugen and Jean R.

McNiece. Carol Gorski copy edited the manuscript with sympathy and intelligence; the author and all readers of this book are in debt to her.

Members of the Finley family have also been wonderfully cooperative and helpful. Professor John H. Finley, Jr., recently retired from a distinguished career of research and teaching at Harvard College, wrote repeatedly in answer to my requests for information. Dr. Ellen Finley Kiser, of Atlanta, Georgia, shared with me important portions of an autobiographical memoir, "Memories of My Married Life," prepared in 1950 by her mother, Martha Boyden Finley. (I have deposited my copy of this document with the Finley Papers, New York Public Library.) Robert J. Finley of Tamworth, New Hampshire, has been more than a delightful correspondent; he graciously took me to parts of John Finley's New York that would otherwise have been terra incognita to me. In their capacities as their father's heirs, the Finley children have given me authorization to use the vast depository of Finley manuscripts in the New York Public Library, for which I am extremely grateful. This aid from the second generation of Finleys, while deeply appreciated, did not result in the composition of anything resembling an authorized biography, as readers of these pages will soon discover.

Ocean Bay Park
Fire Island,
New York
August, 1978

Introduction

The substance of this introduction was originally written for presentation at an American Studies Association seminar on Problems in American Biography held at Adelphi College a decade ago. At that time, my aged parents were still alive, and it was the first and last time they heard their only son give a public talk. They were very proud. Also, the Johnson administration was actively heating up the war in Vietnam, and I had just published a book that was one of the earliest efforts at penetrating the dense screen of lies and deceptions about the struggle in Indochina. With the book came invitations to speak, including one that exactly coincided with the talk on problems in biography. I was barely finished with the pleasantries after the Finley talk when the radical students who had invited me were clamoring at the door, waiting for me to deliver what I had planned as a low-keyed but scathing indictment of U.S. imperial policy. Finley would not have approved of that latter talk.

The day after John H. Finley's inauguration as commissioner of education and president of the University of the State of New York in early 1914, his desk in Albany was covered with congratulatory letters. One of these was from the 'muckraking' editor S. S. McClure, who, like Finley, came out of Galesburg, Illinois, and Knox College. McClure commended Finley on his elevation to "the most responsible and influential educational work in the world." Year by year he had "watched with pleasure" Finley's "progress and achievement. There is no limit to where you may go. Privately," McClure confided, "I think you will become governor of this state and most likely President of the United States." The journalist immodestly added: "I am accustomed to judge the future rather successfully too."

Although no other correspondents at the time discerned the White House in Finley's future, many besides McClure did marvel at his prominence and success. Hamilton Mabie, editor of the *Century* in New York, declared it "good for young men to have an example of your climbing; no pull, no special privilege, but a sound heart, clear head, sure foot and the upward glance." A school official who had seen his early progress in Illinois wondered on Finley's latest elevation: "Pray where is he to stop? All summits seem accessible to him." If

additional testimony on John Finley's achievements in the
second decade of the twentieth century were needed, it was
forthcoming from the world's acknowledged expert on success,
Andrew Carnegie. The retired industrialist wrote that his
friend Finley "richly deserved promotion to the highest position." Carnegie professed to see "no further heits [*sic*]" for the
Albany educator to ascend. "But who knows what may later be
revealed [?] He is a climber, sure."

Contemporaries saw John Finley as one of the luminaries of
his age and were sure upon his death that it would not be "long
before a suitable biography will be written to record in our
literature the story of this most admirable career." Such a eulogy and prediction was delivered by Columbia University
president Nicholas Murray Butler in 1940. But almost four
decades later, no one but I had attempted a biography, and it is
sure that, if the stodgy, conservative Butler had lived, he would
not have found this book "suitable" at all.

Before explaining what may be distinctive about this biography of John Finley, besides the fact that it is the first, let me
trace what prompted me to undertake it. On one level, Finley
posthumously chose me, illustrating what John Garraty, in his
book *The Nature of Biography* (1957), called the tendency of
subjects, even from the grave, to appear to select their biog-
raphers. In my case, I simply stumbled over Finley's biographical footprints so often that I sometimes felt that it was not
quite accidental. During my undergraduate days at CCNY, I
had a speech course in a dilapidated building named Finley
Hall. Later, when the CCNY campus expanded, the appellation
'Finley Hall' was transferred to the new student center, in
which much of my junior and senior years was spent. One
learned as if by osmosis that Finley was a figure in the early
history of the college. I next encountered his traces at The
Johns Hopkins University, where I enrolled for graduate study
some seventy years after he had arrived at the same school in
Baltimore for the same purpose. In preparing my Johns Hopkins master's degree essay ("Social Ideas in the Era of Organized Charity" [1959]) I encountered the documentary records of Finley's early career as a social worker, a phase of his life
I discuss in book two of this biography. When I was casting

about for a fit topic for the doctoral thesis, I discovered the vast, unexploited depository of Finley manuscripts at the New York Public Library. By that time, I had returned to my alma mater, CCNY, as an instructor in government. Here, I thought, is the perfect topic for me, and I began work unaware of the awaiting pitfalls.

Some of these had to do with Finley's undeniable status as a "minor" figure. There seem to be two competing schools of thought about writing on such persons. According to some authorities, the only suitable subject for a full-scale biography is an influential personage who can be credited with notable innovation or who left behind a substantial institutional edifice indelibly stamped with his or her name. As the celebrated biographer Edmund Goose put it, there must be "some relationship between the size of [a subject's] portrait and the effect he produced in public life." On this basis, Finley, who held important posts and who knew famous people, but who had little discernible influence on public life, deserves only the kind of short biographical sketch Harry Carman supplied in the *Dictionary of American Biography.*

The other competing notion is to find significance in a biographical subject who reflects and reveals the larger context of the contemporary reality. Philosopher Philip Weiner (my former teacher), writing in the *Journal of the History of Ideas* (1961) has observed that the "intellectual biographer of an unknown or neglected minor figure may properly claim to find in his subject a revealing key to the opinions of a larger cross-section of the contemporary population than the more advanced thinkers of the same era." This clearly is a more fitting justification for writing about Finley than any effort to inflate him into a great mover and shaker. His genial character softly conformed to his status and to his era, and his life can be seen as a prism of the conventional ideals and convictions of his age. That is my justification for writing this book.

But what about the biographer's own relationship to these ideals and convictions? Must there be an affinity between author and subject? What about a radical who writes a study of a near contemporary whose views varied from tepid liberalism to nostalgic conservatism? And, depending upon the answers to these questions, what about the doctrine of scholarly objectivity?

Many studies have been written on the question of objectivity, and I have neither the intent nor the ability to make any original contribution here. Instead, I wish merely to associate myself with the methodological principles enunciated in such books as Marc Bloch's *The Historian's Craft* (1953), Robert Lynd's *Knowledge for What?* (1949), C. Wright Mills's *The Sociological Imagination* (1959), Edward Hallett Carr's *What Is History?* (1963), and Gunnar Myrdal's *Objectivity in Social Research* (1969). Whatever their differences of approach and subject matter, these writers agree that objectivity cannot be found by attempting to efface the researcher and to engage in some "pure" quest for limpid fact. It seems obvious that the number of "facts" is infinite and that any coherent statement involves a selection of relevant data according to some criteria of relevance, which may be implicit or explicit. If implicit, these criteria (and the value judgments and biases that shape them) may be hard to identify and may warp and distort understanding in ways that are difficult to correct. It seems obligatory for all future researchers to follow the example of the distinguished Swedish sociologist Gunnar Myrdal, who, in magnificent conformity with the principles enunciated in his above-mentioned book, *Objectivity,* prefaced his masterful study of economic underdevelopment in the Indian subcontinent (*Asian Drama: An Inquiry into the Poverty of Nations* [1968]) with a candid discussion of his own attitudes toward such key ideological concepts as imperialism, capitalism, and socialism. Can any of us who follow, even if our work is of more modest scope, fail to be open and explicit about the criteria of relevance that inform our scholarship? I think not.

In the case of Finley, whose life and career form something of an American saga, to achieve anything approaching objectivity demands clarification of the researcher's attitudes toward the whole congeries of political judgments and cultural attachments summed up by the word 'America.'

These views about the nature of historical analysis and its meaning might have remained my private convictions, to be shared only with students in a seminar, had not a bold and daring American scholar acted on the basis of his own similar views. (As impressive as Myrdal's example was, it apparently was insufficient to move me to emulation.) Martin Duberman, after a brilliant early career of teaching and of writing impeccable books on nineteenth-century politics and society in the United States, began in the 1960s to admit publicly of his disenchantment with conventional historical writing. He dealt creatively with his discontent, producing from standard documentary materials a moving theater presentation, *In White America* (1964). But Duberman's major challenge to the profession's pious pretentions to "objectivity" was his book *Black Mountain: An Exploration in Community* (1973), a history of the innovating college in North Carolina that nurtured a dazzling array of artistic and literary talents during the 1930s and '40s. By daringly injecting himself into the narrative as "participant" in faculty debates held before he was born, by including his own diary excerpts and records of his own efforts at innovative teaching, and by generally putting himself "up front," Duberman dares us to admit that we do not cease to be engaged human beings when we carry out inquiries in the past.

> *Whether from native timidity or some other motive, I often need relevant role models for my public actions. I might not have attempted this merger of biography and autobiography without Martin Duberman's example. Similarly, my earlier choice of an academic career was conditioned by admiration for those professors I saw in action. One of these was Jack Hexter, who taught history at Queens College in Flushing, New York, during the period when I was an art student in Philadelphia. Coming into New York often to see the young woman I would soon marry, I was occasionally smuggled into the overcrowded Queens College classroom of Marge's impressive "CC" (Contemporary Civilization) teacher. Indeed, I was impressed, perhaps more than she was, with Hexter's urbanity, wit, and erudition.*

Although Duberman's book was published to wide acclaim, the methodological principles on which it is based are not widely supported among the profession's mainstream historians, such as Jack Hexter. In 1954 Hexter published an autobiographical essay, "The Historian and His Day" (reprinted in Hexter's collection *Reappraisals in History* [1961]) which argues a position diametrically opposed to Duberman's, and to mine. His point of view must be respectfully examined. In the essay, Hexter presents an appealing picture of an unworldly

scholar relatively isolated from "the Great Crises of the Contemporary World," busy with his fifteen hours' teaching per
week about subjects "cobwebbed with age," and dedicated to
the "austere rule" that obliges him to keep "prejudices about present-day issues out of" the area of his scholarship, Europe from
1450 to 1650. Perhaps at the time of writing his essay in 1954,
Hexter had not set down any of his polemical thoughts on early
modern history but, when he unleashed a venomous attack on
the Marxist historian Christopher Hill in the *Times Literary
Supplement* in the fall of 1975, this former admirer began to
question Hexter's self-proclaimed objectivity. Attacking Hill as
a victim of "historiographic pathology," Hexter boldly pro-
claimed his intention to "venture forth [in polemical contest]. . .
as I have done before in similar circumstances, murmuring my
trusty old mandala: 'If you can't stand the heat, stay out of the
kitchen'." (*TLS*, October 25, November 28, 1975.) If there had
ever been any doubt of Hexter's occasional descent from the
exalted ivory tower of unsullied scholarship to the grubby
kitchen of politically charged historical controversy, this ex-
change would have silenced it. But in addition, when senior
history faculty at Yale University (where Hexter now teaches)
attempted to prevent Communist historian Herbert Aptheker
from obtaining a one-semester teaching position at the distinguished university in New Haven, Hexter's pose as a dis-
passionate scholar laboring chastely in fields far from the din of
political conflict became rather suspect. In a personal communication, Hexter claims that, since he was on leave from Yale
when the Aptheker issue erupted, he took no part, "either
active or passive," in the matter. But surely this is an extraordinary usage of the word *passive,* to cover the activity of a senior
faculty member who, even on leave, chooses not to participate
in urgent department decisions. (The Aptheker matter is now
under investigation by a national historians' committee of inquiry.) Without touching on the underlying philosophical issues, these data raise doubts about the adequacy (and even the
accuracy) of Hexter's disclaimer of political involvement in his
earlier essay "The Historian and His Day." And, by extension, the weaknesses of the doctrine of "pure objectivity" are

strongly suggested by the example of this distinguished historical exponent.

The position I am arguing for here—that the historian cannot
divest himself or herself of contemporary concerns when inves-
tigating the past—should not be understood as a call to abandon
"all standards" and transform historical study into narcissistic
introspection. In a brilliant series of recent essays (in the *New
York Review of Books, Partisian Review,* and elsewhere),
historian Christopher Lasch has identified narcissism as one of
the major psychological by-products of late capitalist culture,
by which narrow "self-awareness" and individualistic "self-
expression" are made to substitute for collective political action and for a healthy concern about posterity. At the very
moment when perhaps the need is greatest for a revival of
collective anticapitalist political striving, and for the reappear-
ance of a vigorous American left to challenge the grip of corporate power on people's lives, that grip is being strengthened
through deflection of discontent into sterile, narcissistic chan-
nels. As a product, and to some extent a victim, of these tendencies in modern American culture, I cannot be sure that in the
pages that follow I have purged myself of the narcissistic self-
indulgence that I find politically repugnant. Yet, I offer this
amalgam of biography and autobiography mainly to demonstrate that the John Finley I discovered in my research was a
real objective entity in the world out there, but that my evalua-
tions of his significance are to a considerable extent shaped by
who I am. Readers can thus have the opportunity to understand
where these judgments originate by learning something about
the situation and beliefs of the biographer, who may cut even
less of a swath through life than John Finley did—but, as the
poet said, a man's a man for all that.

Book 1.
The Prairie

Chapter 1

From Distinction to Obscurity

Usually oblivious to mail-order solicitations and other consumerist importunings, I had a near fit when a midwestern research outfit offered to supply "the Gettleman family coat of arms," for a substantial fee. What a blatant appeal to pseudosnobbery! What hucksterism! If there were such a thing as a family genealogy, it would more likely include peddlers, petty artisans, and horse thieves than feudal barons entitled to heraldic display of lions rampant. How absurd to contemplate a Jew with a coat of arms! Did the Rothschilds boast a coat of arms? Even Finley, whose concern for ancestry was nearly obsessive, never went so far as to sport a heraldic device.

Frequently and proudly did Finley allude to the accomplishments of his Scottish ancestors, a hardy race of martyrs, pioneers, and learned, pious preachers. Almost at his death, he was correcting proofs of his last book, *The Coming of the Scot* (1941), which chronicled the seventeenth-century migration from Scotland to Ireland, the tempering of the stock in Ulster, and the later "predestined" transplantation to America. It was a virile and robust genealogy that John Finley claimed, a family tree of such "tenacious root [that] no mathematician even, however skilled in the extraction of roots, could remove it against its will."

On September 28, 1734, one of these sturdy Scots-Irish immigrants, Michael Finley (1683–1747?), arrived at Philadelphia with a wife and nine children. He had seen to it even in Ulster that his children obtained the rudiments of an education. Before the family settled in backwoods Pennsylvania, Michael Finley's second son, Samuel (1715–66), decided while still a teenager to become a clergyman. The boy

3

was sent to study at the Reverend William Tennent's nearby Log College in Neshaminy, Bucks County.

The famous Log College was the spiritual center of the religious Great Awakening in the middle colonies. Even before his ordination as a Presbyterian minister in 1742, Samuel Finley threw his support behind the revival, contributing a fiery sermon, *Christ TRIUMPHING, AND Satan RAGING* (1741). He traveled with the great itinerant revivalist George Whitefield and carried the gospel even into unfriendly territory. Preaching once in New Haven without the invitation of the minister of the established church there, Samuel Finley was "seized as a vagrant by the civil authority, and carried beyond the limits of the colony." Much later, John Finley, who related the story, would express pride in this example of zeal and dedication by a family hero.

> *Perhaps having as much authenticity as Samuel Finley's expulsion from New Haven are the legends in my own family about my maternal uncle, Louis Antopol, who allegedly was forced to leave Czarist Russia because of his involvement in the revolution of 1905. After reaching New York as an impoverished immigrant, he worked as a sign painter, married unhappily, and died when I was a young child. Apparently a dreamy, artistic man, "Uncle Louey" was the center of many of my own childhood fantasies of fashionable revolutionary-bohemian squalor.*

In addition to his ministerial efforts, Samuel Finley was a noteworthy educator. In 1744, he was called to the pulpit of the New Side Presbyterian Church in Nottingham, Maryland, near the Pennsylvania border. There he established a classical academy that was described by its most distinguished graduate, Benjamin Rush, signer of the Declaration of Independence, as "the most respectable and flourishing of any in the middle provinces of America."

John Finley, whose own career began a century and a half later, might have taken pride in his forbear's educational work. Samuel Finley's Nottingham Academy prepared many other eminent men for useful lives as gospel ministers, lawyers, publicists, judges, and politicians. He was a strict and pious educator. He would not dispatch his own son to Philadelphia for medical study until he had been convinced that the boy's moral life would be guarded and "fortified against the temptations of this evil world." At the Nottingham Academy, good

manners, morality, religion, and learning were assiduously promoted, along with training in "practical agriculture." Samuel
Finley taught by precept and example to avoid "a life of
indolence or retirement." The most precious advice he would
offer to students taking leave of the academy was the injunc-
tion, "Learn to pronounce that bold word 'No'." Occasionally
he might enforce these lessons with a few well-placed blows,
Rush remembered.

As a minister and teacher in Nottingham, Samuel Finley
"laid up" a good deal of money. He continued to be deeply
involved in denominational affairs, including the founding of
the Presbyterian-connected College of New Jersey. The original board of trustees included him, and, when Samuel Davies
died in 1761, Finley was called from Nottingham to succeed
Davies as president of the institution. He served for five years
until his death, whereupon John Witherspoon was called from
Scotland to follow Samuel Finley in the presidency of what
was to become Princeton University.

John Finley descended from the younger brother of this
eminent eighteenth-century divine. Like his brother Samuel,
the Reverend James Finley (1725–95) was trained for the
ministry in a backwoods academy. James attended the school
of Samuel Blair at Faggs Manor, Chester County, Pennsylvania. His talents were reported to be "very inferior to those of
his brother . . . , yet he was reckoned to be eminently pious;
and continued laboriously to preach the gospel, until an advanced period of life." In 1752 he was called to the Rock
Presbyterian Church in Nottingham, Maryland, where he remained for thirty years, during nine of which the two Finley
brothers were pastors of adjacent congregations.

During his ministry at Nottingham, James Finley seemed
not to display his brother's interest in education, although he
did spend "much time going from house to house teaching and
catechising the young and old." Among those who received
such training were James Finley's slaves. He saw to it that
they were present at family worship and catechised them with
his own children. In his one extant printed sermon, James
Finley also continued a family and denominational tradition of
denouncing deviations from scriptural orthodoxy. This was

what John Finley had in mind when he remarked in 1915 that his ancestors were "accustomed to carry theological chips on their shoulders."

James Finley often traveled from Nottingham across the Appalachians into southwestern Pennsylvania. He was charged with the dual task of allaying "certain political troubles brewing among the settlers" and serving as supply minister. In this latter capacity, James Finley preached where he could, in barns, tents, and groves. He founded two congregations. But he also took care to look over the land and where possible buy up choice tracts. In 1772 he set up one of his sons on a farm in Fayette County, Pennsylvania. The lad, John Finley's great-grandfather, narrowly escaped death there in an Indian raid. Despite the dangers, other members of the family also began to migrate to Pennsylvania.

James Finley's own removal to join his sons was postponed by the reluctance of his Maryland Presbytery to let him go. After repeated appeals that he be allowed "to promote the kingdom of Christ" nearby to his kin, Finley's permission finally came in the spring of 1783. With his slaves, and accompanied by many of his parishioners, James Finley moved into the jurisdiction of the Redstone Presbytery, which, as his descendant described it, "reached from the Laurel Hills to the Pacific Ocean."

In the fertile southwestern corner of Pennsylvania, James Finley ministered to the two congregations he had himself established on earlier visits to the region. It was claimed that he was "the first Protestant clergyman to settle the other side of the Alleghenies." During his lifetime, James Finley freed many of his adult slaves. In his will, proved January 26, 1795, he freed their children, including one Plato, Jr. The land he owned was distributed among his nine children, who were already prosperous landowners in the vicinity.

Reverend James Finley's fourth son, Ebeneezer (1760–1849) participated in the bloody Indian warfare of the Pennsylvania frontier. He may also have been a captain in the revolutionary war. His prosperity and eminence among the farmers of Fayette County is revealed in the high taxes he paid and in the community responsibilities he discharged. Ebeneezer Finley outlived four wives and fathered twelve children. One of these inherited the name as well as part of the estate of his father.

Ebeneezer Finley, Jr. (1804–91), grandfather of John Finley, was, like his ancestors, a pillar of his community. He headed a local temperance society for forty years, served as ruling elder in the Dunlap Creek Presbyterian Church, and distinguished himself in other similar ways. Like his father before him, Ebeneezer Finley, Jr., sired twelve children.

The succession of prominent, prosperous, and learned Finleys was briefly interrupted in the next generation. It may have been that the prodigious production of offspring for three generations left little property to bequeath by the middle of the nineteenth century. Whether for this reason or some other, a number of the children of Ebeneezer Finley, Jr., sought opportunity in the West. Among them was a son born in 1836.

James Gibson Finley (1836–1913), as a young man in the 1850s, joined an earlier group of settlers from Fayette County, Pennsylvania, in north central Illinois. There he established a homestead on virgin prairie land in a region of La Salle County that had no name until the Chicago, Burlington and Quincy Railroad established a depot there in 1871. Long before that time, James Finley had brought a bride from Pennsylvania, and he soon began to raise a family. Four children were born in what was later called Grand Ridge. The eldest was a daughter, Mary. On October 19, 1863, a son was born and named John Huston. Another son, Robert, came in 1865, and the youngest was a girl, Anna.

John Finley's early life, and that of his brother and sisters, was rooted in the brute realities of prairie farming. He remembered learning to plow almost before he learned to read; being introduced to the drudgery of the fields before the awakening of childhood imagination and ambition. The literary work that best recaptured the spirit of his prairie childhood, Finley admitted, was Hamlin Garland's bitter *Main Travelled Roads* (1909). He wrote to a New York State politician who had had a similar Western upbringing, "That rather depressing book has a great many faithful pictures of the life that I knew as a boy and young man." Yet even in Grand Ridge there were influences capable of awakening and sustaining an urge for some other sort of life than that of farmer on the middle border.

Certainly one factor in John Finley's later ambition was the example of past generations of eminent Finleys. As we have seen, they stood for education, piety, and patriotism; but ancestry only reinforced more immediate tendencies impelling John Finley in these same directions.

Clear in its impact was the atmosphere of strict piety that pervaded the household at Grand Ridge. John Finley's earliest memories of prairie life (besides the fields, and nature generally) were of a small, lighted church at evening prayer meeting, "the only [light] in a square mile of darkness." He remembered that his father used to start the simple hymns in their rural Presbyterian church, and in later years could recall the picture of roughly clad farmers gathered by its door after Sunday services to discuss "free moral agency and predestination by an omniscient God." His father's "confident faith in a celestial destination" may have contributed to the soaring of the boy's hopes beyond the limits of the rude prairie.

The direction of his ambition all through Finley's long life was wholesome and respectable. This consequence may be better traced to his mother's influence than to his father's stern Calvinism. Lydia McCombs Finley was doubtless in her son's mind when he wrote in praise of the pioneer women, not "bowed down or embittered by hardship," who were able to retain something of Eastern culture and gentle religion in their rude prairie homesteads. There were cherished memories of her reading Bible stories to the children Sunday afternoons. "His memory of her was very vivid," wrote John Finley's wife, "and I feel he must have inherited his strong and fine character from her. . . . I've always felt it a wonderful testimonial to the kind of woman she must have been that she left such an impression on that young boy. . . ."

Reinforcing the influence of both parents were what Finley considered the spiritual enrichment and purifying effects of a rural upbringing. Country children, he observed, witness the seasonal changes that reveal the operation of "eternal forces"; their gaze is directed toward "God, the illimitable, the eternal." Later in life, and safely based in the city, Finley would celebrate the agrarian mythology. He rhapsodized then, in *New York Times* editorials, about "the poetry that lies at the heart of husbandry," and argued that "the prosperity and happiness of the country at large rest upon the shoulders of the farmer as the earth did in the ancient myth upon the shoulders of Atlas."

A city boy, brought up on the streets of the East Bronx, I had little in my childhood to echo Finley's rural upbringing. It seems almost absurd to compare an empty lot on the corner of Rosedale Avenue and East 176 Street with the boundless Illinois prairies; yet even that scrubby patch of ground represented much of what we called nature—caves to hide in, trees to climb, space to build what became a neighborhood social center: a pigeon coop, where our attention was fixed, however briefly, on one of nature's nonhuman creatures, its needs, patterns, rhythms, and mysteries.

It is doubtful whether such poetic fancies occurred to him while he was actually breaking the virgin prairie soil at Grand Ridge. But Finley's boyish dreams could find some early nourishment in the everyday occurrences of farm life. He remembered the thrill of finding an Indian arrowhead or stone hatchet in a newly plowed furrow. Living near rivers that had once carried the canoes of French explorers, watching westward-bound prairie schooners roll by, the excitement of the railroads "coming out of the unknown in one direction and passing on to the unknown in another"—all stirred his imagination.

John Finley could clearly remember in later life the occasional moments of happiness on the farm. But it obviously was the even more memorable drudgery and disasters of rural life that impelled him away from the farm, away from Grand Ridge, Illinois. When John and Rob were teenagers returning home from the fields flushed and exhausted in a wagon filled to the boards with stripped corn, their father met them in the yard. He put his hand on the older boy's shoulder, and said, "John, your mother has passed from us." The months that followed his mother's death were sad ones for John Finley; he never cared to talk about them even to his wife. A housekeeper was brought in, but the children did not like her. A few years later, his father remarried. John never became attached to his stepmother. He had little thereafter to do with his family of origin; his trajectory took him far out of their orbit.

Chapter 2

Prairie Awakenings

The dreams of ambition to transcend the family of origin often begin with the earliest knowledge of the outside world. In the East Bronx, we could find the art, the music, and the high culture of Manhattan at the other end of the Pelham Bay subway line. For prairie lads, the pull was eastward, back to the coastal cities, and to the professional careers that romantically beckoned.

For some it was the excitement and drama of the law; for others the intensity and prestige of medicine; for young John Finley and his brother Robert, journalism was the abiding early passion that enticed them away from the Grand Ridge homestead. Without ever having seen any original, the two prairie lads erected the replica of an editorial office in a corner of the family farmhouse. There they scribbled away to meet imaginary deadlines, mocked up front pages, drafted editorials, and no doubt counted revenues from subscription lists.

The first steps toward the realization of these prairie-born ambitions led the two brothers to the local district school in Grand Ridge. As Everett Dick describes them in his book *The Sod-House Frontier* (1954), these schools were often grim and cheerless places, the instruction was poor, and the discipline only as strict as the wretchedly paid teacher could enforce. John Finley admitted remembering only a few of the events of his grammar school days. Once, even before he was of age to attend, he approached the schoolhouse on an errand; "but when thirty yards from" there, he recalled, "I heard the teacher scolding someone and I dared not go nearer." His next vivid recollection was of being "severely rapped on the back

with a walnut ruler" when he was whispering to himself as he
tried to decipher the caption of a picture (of a Greek temple) in
his geography book. He also remembered a teacher once
bringing a flower into the otherwise desolate schoolroom one
spring morning. She wrote its Latin name on the blackboard,
wryly noting that all the pupils would forget it before the next
morning. Finley observed in 1892 that this teacher may have
"gone to her rest," but that he would never forget caryophyl-
lacous.

Supplementing the regular district school education was the
training in classical languages that John Finley sought outside
the classroom. At the age of ten, he induced a teacher to offer
him special instruction in the elements of Latin, which was
reinforced by lessons from a local Scotch parson. The boy
apparently was an apt student—and certainly a persistent one.
When one of his itinerant tutors (they came to Grand Ridge
from the student bodies of such nearby colleges as Knox) was
unequipped to carry young Finley further toward mastery of
the learned tongue, the boy and his teacher studied Latin
together.

It was likely that young Finley was aware that, to realize his
journalistic ambitions, he would certainly have to go to college. He could also hardly have been ignorant of the fact that
the general prerequisite for higher education included preparation in the classical languages. Such study on the prairie
would advance Finley's future ambitions; it also had immediate function. Antiquity was for him a fertile source of
imagery with which the harsh realities of farm life could be
connected, and thus more easily borne. He could imagine that
the croaking of frogs in the ponds, the chirp of "bloodless
grasshoppers" on the prairies, were like the sounds of Priam's
chieftains upon the walls of Troy. Vergil's *Georgics* and
Bucolics provided a continual classical commentary on his
everyday tasks. "Nothing has so glorified for me," Finley rem-
inisced at a Wisconsin gathering in 1919, "my youthful days
on these prairies, as the associations which the classics, including the Bible, gave to them on the farm."

Was it just a more genteel literary age in which Finley set down these
childhood memories, or was he speaking on these occasions to church

and educational audiences for which sexual allusions would have been inappropriate, or was Finley not in touch with feelings like those I remember from a comparable age—almost exclusively sexual and competitive?

But far from rendering him content to remain down on the farm—reading Vergil between corn husking and spring plowing or lashing a volume of Horace to the plow to be conned at the end of the furrow—the classics whetted Finley's ambition for another life altogether. For many keen-minded farm boys, such study "broadened the imagination, sharpened the vocabulary, and spurred ambition." John Finley and his brother, Rob, certainly reacted to their prairie education in this way.

Farm duties made it impossible for John Finley to enroll at nearby Ottawa Township High School until September, 1879, when he was almost sixteen years old. Rob Finley, a year younger, entered the next fall. The school was about eight miles from Grand Ridge. When weather permitted, Finley walked back and forth each day; other times he stayed with relatives in Ottawa. The route was level until a high bluff along the Illinois River was reached. A long bridge crossed the river near the confluence of the Fox and the Illinois. On his way to school, Finley passed a factory and mill run by water power, stores and saloons of the town of Ottawa, the LaSalle County Court House, and the State Supreme Court building. He also went daily through the park where Lincoln and Douglas debated. This walk, according to the Reverend George T. Scott, former resident of Ottawa, "gave much to think about and time for an imaginative youth to meditate." Finley's taste for long-distance walking probably also began in those days.

Ottawa High School was evidently a good one; Greek and Latin were taught, and full college-preparatory courses were offered. Young Finley, a bashful lad in a class of girls, slipped into the back row of the classrooms to partake of the educational treasures. In the four terms he spent at Ottawa High School, he did best in spelling and geometry and poorest in areas in which he was later to distinguish himself: rhetoric, social studies, and English literature. In Latin and Greek, he consistently scored in the high 80s. (The actual grades, supplied by Oledine Wood, registrar of Ottawa Township

High School, were: 76 percent in rhetoric, 91 in spelling, 81 in English literature, 87 and 89 in Latin, 86 in Greek, 94 in geometry, 83 in astronomy, 79 in history, and 80 in civil government.)

His special interest in classical languages is revealed in the lengths to which he would go to study them. When he was at home in the spring helping with the family's plowing, young Finley arranged to study in the fields. He described this in a characteristic bit of verse, written and published long afterward. Finley remembered the "sweet luring of the earth" on that youthful day when—

> . . . .
> The oat was springing in the green-fringed field
> That soon should furnish pipes for summer's winds;
> The solemn cranes went cronking overhead
> Through cloud-made aisles their glad processional,
> And I, my Horace strapped upon the beam,
> To read while resting at the furrow's end,
> Was happiness and hope impersonate.
> In that wide-circling amphitheater
> I strove along, while all about stood those
> Who'd come out from all time, from out all lands,
> To see what I would do with life.
>
> Finley, *Poems*, p. 6.

This engaging picture of the farm lad conning his Latin volume in the fields would be John Finley's most frequently used image; it seasoned his remarks in later life at innumerable college exercises and formal dinners. The bucolic image was significantly qualified by explicit reference to felt pressures in the prairie environment toward eminence and success.

Although his record at Ottawa High School was not an outstandingly brilliant one, John Finley was chosen valedictorian at graduation time. Returning to this school almost fifty years later, he revealed that "the reason I was accorded that honor was not because I had received the highest marks, but simply that the other ten members of our 11-member class were girls, who held a little election and chose me as class speaker." No text of the speech survives, although Finley did recall its opening: "Man is finite. . . ."

Even during his Ottawa High School days, John Finley may have been called upon to do some teaching in the rural school houses of La Salle County. But his major early experience in teaching came in the fall of 1882. Upon graduation from high school, he had been urged to seek higher education and, over his father's objection, did matriculate at a nearby college.

Before he could complete the freshman year, Finley was called back to Grand Ridge to take charge of the district school where he himself had studied. "There were two rooms in the schoolhouse," he remembered, "and another teacher beside myself—an asthmatic and cross-eyed French woman." Despite predictions that the big boys would run the school, Finley had few of the discipline problems that made life miserable for many real-life counterparts of the Hoosier Schoolmaster. He was able to teach English to illiterate Norwegian farmers; to French blacksmiths, United States history; Latin to American farm boys. In March many of his pupils were obliged to drop their studies for the urgencies of spring plowing. Finley thereupon "established night classes, which were well attended right along." Finley claimed to have instituted "the first continuation school by night" ever heard of on the prairies, and its teacher paid for the kerosene out of his own pocket.

In the fall of 1883, after almost a year of teaching, John Finley was financially better able to return to college. The prairie environment not only provided him with the modest resources with which he could pursue higher education, but also gave rise as we have seen to a professional ambition—journalism—that might demand college training. If his immediate family would not endorse these goals, Finley could allow himself to believe that ancestry somehow legitimized them. No decision made in his later life was as significant as the one to seek higher education on the prairie.

Chapter 3

Traditional Curriculum at Knox College
in the 1880s

Early in my college career, there was a grand convocation at CCNY on the question of "Whether a College Should Inculcate Values." Sitting in the audience as an impressionable sophomore, straining to find some point I could seize upon to make a clever pronouncement, I found nothing odd in the proceedings. But in an earlier age it would have been inconceivable to debate such a question. A college in John Finley's prairie days had no other function, or no other recognized function, than to inculcate values.

Knox College welcomed students who were prepared to travel a "rugged path" to academic success. The coeducational college on the prairie offered a stiff, classical curriculum as its standard of education. Knox College president Newton Bateman indicated that expenses in Galesburg were low but that students seeking higher education there could not expect anything but a "struggle," although a noble one.

Impelled by his prairie-born ambition to achieve, as his ancestors had done, a measure of eminence, John Finley came to the college in the fall of 1882. To gain admission to the classical course, the nineteen-year-old student had to demonstrate proficiency in a formidable body of knowledge, including Greek and Latin grammar and literature, ancient and modern history, and mathematics. Apparently he got past these requirements with little difficulty, for the faculty admitted Finley to the classical course on September 7. On the same day, Martha "Mattie" Boyden, a banker's daughter from nearby Sheffield, Illinois, was admitted conditionally to the abbreviated "literary" course also offered at Knox College. She had wanted to go to Wellesley, but her family was reluctant to send her so far from home. Later in life she often thought, "If I had gone to Wellesley as I had hoped, I never would have met John, and how different my life would have been."

During his freshman year, John Finley interrupted his studies at Knox College, as we have seen, to teach in the district school of Grand Ridge. The following fall he returned to Galesburg, bringing with him his younger brother, Rob. While John continued in the classical course, Rob enrolled in the somewhat easier scientific course.

The academic fare for freshmen in the classical course included, of course, heavy doses of Greek and Latin. The students received drill in classical authors as well as training in composition in the classical languages. John was well advanced in Latin because of his early study at Grand Ridge and Ottawa. He requested permission as a freshman to attend the sophomore Latin recitations as well. The professor "rather grudgingly gave consent," Martha Finley remembered.

> In a day or two when the person next to John had recited, Professor Hurd looked over his glasses at John, and said, "Are you the student who recited in the Freshman Latin yesterday?" John meekly replied, "Yes sir," to which the Professor responded, "You may recite." And from then on he was a regular member of the Sophomore Latin Class.

Finley also did well in freshman Greek, algebra, geometry, and rhetoric. Mattie Boyden and Rob Finley did almost as well in their somewhat easier programs.

The regular sophomore curriculum included more-advanced classical texts and an optional course in French, which John Finley did elect. He also enrolled in advanced mathematics (trigonometry and analytical geometry) as well as natural philosophy. Robert Finley, in the scientific course, also plunged into college mathematics, and began Latin. While the younger brother's record is marred by the appearance of a number of Bs, John continued to be a straight A student, as was Mattie Boyden. Listed in the catalogue as required only in the third term of the sophomore year was rhetoric. But the Finley brothers, and Martha Boyden too, continued to take the opportunity Knox College provided for extensive study of elocution and oratory. Oratorical ability, as we shall see, was a major factor in John Finley's later successes.

Martha left Knox College at the end of her sophomore year and continued studies in Chicago so as to obtain better medical attention for an eye ailment than could be gotten in Galesburg. But the Finley brothers stayed on and, in their junior year, continued the study of natural philosophy and also applied themselves to the mastery of English prose style. This latter subject was of great importance to boys already decided on journalistic careers.

The junior year at Knox College included courses in chemistry, anatomy, physiology, and botany for scientific as well as classical students. John Finley continued his A record, and Rob did almost as well. These courses in natural science were taught from textbooks written by the leading exponents of the evolutionary philosophy. Confidence abounded that Knox College could both promote liberal secular learning, "and proclaim the saving truths of the Christian faith" without doing violence to either science or piety. Student editors could express similar pride that "nowhere more" than in their college "is the student surrounded by religious influences."

In its dual emphasis on learning and Christian faith, Knox seems the very stereotype of an old-fashioned college dedicated to the unity of science and revelation. In later years Finley remembered that in his "college days the chronology of Ussher was followed in fixing the date of creation of man as the year 4004 B.C." In defending such a chronology, Finley's teachers would have had to ignore the clear implications of the evolutionary textbooks. It is easier to imagine that they could have done so in an age before college professors were supposed to be learned specialists. When John Finley arrived as a freshman, most of the college courses (as well as classes in the preparatory school connected with Knox College) were handled by a "Great Triumvirate" of venerable professors who had been at their posts since the early 1850s. An earlier Knox contemporary of Finley spoke eloquently of the "silent tragedies" of these dedicated, tireless men, tied to "the daily grind of class-work," and denied themselves the leisure to

study and achieve "self-development and self-expression."
Finley remembered fondly Professor Albert Hurd, one
member of the "Great Triumvirate," who was professor of
chemistry (but also taught geology, physiology, botany, and
Latin) at Knox College. Returning from a visit to some university laboratories, Hurd once announced to his colleagues
"with no mock modesty and with tears in his eyes that he
knew nothing of chemistry." In relating this story Finley intended no malice; he added that, although his teachers may
not have been learned in the modern sense, they "did know
the great truths."

At an old-fashioned college, the senior year was the period
of maximum exposure to these "great truths." The senior
course in moral philosophy taught by the president armed the
undergraduate with the last bits of the moral fortitude necessary in facing a sinful world. Knox president Newton Bateman's
teaching of moral philosophy was somewhat eclipsed by the
local fame of the "Great Triumvirate," and by other Knox
College influences that molded the Finley brothers. Yet in any
consideration of the evolution of John Finley's educational
career, Newton Bateman must occupy an important place, not
because he was some prairie Horace Mann or Frederick Bar-
nard, but because he first set before the young undergraduate
who was to be his successor a model of a college president. In
later years John Finley retained much from Newton Bateman's
example. A Galesburg friend informed him in 1920 that "not
only the mantle but the entire wardrobe of the good Dr. Bateman" had descended upon him.

In his senior courses on international law, evidences of
Christianity, and especially moral philosophy, Newton Bateman played the role of old-time college president—the last
Knox would have. To understand the precise nature of the
intellectual environment in which Finley was nurtured during
the 1880s, it is necessary to view the message that Newton
Bateman sought to transmit in perspective of the historical
development of Knox College.

Knox College was precipitated on the Illinois prairie by the
same tidal wave of evangelical enthusiasm that left in its wake
Illinois College, Oberlin, and a score of other colleges in the

old Northwest. The site chosen by a diverse group of settlers was in Knox County, named in honor of Revolutionary War General Henry Knox. The actual settlement was accomplished under a Plan of Union that allowed Presbyterians and Congregationalists to cooperate in the founding of Western colleges and communities. Thus, as Hermann Muelder shows in his admirable history of early Knox College, *Fighters For Freedom* (1959), a diverse group led in 1837 by the Reverend George Washington Gale, a key figure in the revivals of the "burned-over" district of New York, established a college community on the Illinois frontier.

At the outset Knox College was committed to the antislavery cause. Its first two presidents were militant abolitionists whose ardor defined the educational goals of the institution. The Reverend Jonathan Blanchard, fiery Congregationalist reformer, became second president of Knox College in 1845. In his inaugural address Blanchard called for a "martyr-age of Colleges and Seminaries, to send forth a host of young men, at the sound of whose goings the whole land shall tremble—men who will not rest while one way or practice in the community violates the law of God." He denounced that weaker sort of education that is "smitten with the common leprosy of the land," teaching "the great principles of morals feebly, and '*in the abstract*'." These views had wide support in Galesburg through the early 1850s.

Antislavery was only one among a number of reforms Blanchard championed. As a young man for temperance, he had smashed rum jars in his father's cellar, and he continued the offensive against Satan in all his guises at Knox. He warned students against attending "theaters, horse races, Methodist meetings, and other places of amusement." A Galesburg fair earned his denunciation, for it was to that town, he said, as the "bear garden to Paris, the cockpit to New Orleans, or gladiatorial shows to ancient Rome." When the Chicago, Burlington and Quincy railroad brought a line into Galesburg, Blanchard strode over to the yards one Sunday and, to the amazement of the workers there, forbade them to desecrate the Sabbath.

Despite, or perhaps partly because of, his uncompromising stand for righteousness, a number of forces were converging in the 1850s that would lead to the overthrow of Jonathan Blanchard and the educational philosophy for which he stood. Unresolved denominational and theological tensions began to drive a wedge between Presbyterians and Congregationalists, upon whose cooperation Knox College rested. The growing bitterness of national sectional controversy caused some of the more timid souls to retreat from the radical abolitionism that marked the college's early years. Even George Washington Gale, the founder, had abandoned much of the zeal that earlier had led him to risk imprisonment for violation of the Fugitive Slave Law. Gale's Presbyterian party on the Board of Trustees initiated in the early 1850s a fierce dispute known in Knox College annals as the "Blanchard War." The struggle extended beyond the trustees to involve students and the townspeople of Galesburg as well. Antiquarian questions (Whose influence was most substantial in the founding of the college? After whom was it named? etc.) masked a denominational struggle for control and unleashed a fierce pamphlet war. When the smoke of battle cleared in 1858, Blanchard had been removed as president, and Knox's "martyr-age" was at an end.

Blanchard's successor, the Reverend Harvey Curtis, signaled the change to a more genial and accommodating spirit. "The college is not the place," Curtis maintained in his inaugural address, "and this early stage of education is not the fitting time, in which to inculcate distinctive opinions on doubtful or contested points, either in religion or morals. . . ."

> Teachers in public institutions may form their own opinions on every question of religion, reform or politics; and may utter or publish those opinions at their discretion, in fitting ways and on appropriate occasions. But they should not compromise the character of the college by becoming propagandists of any individual or partisan peculiarities, nor should the college chapel, or lecture or recitation rooms be misappropriated to the inculcation of any such peculiarities.

What should teachers do? Simply ensure that the "principles and practical teachings of the Word of God" are made familiar to the students, inculcate a "high sense of honor," gentle manners, and other virtues; then, President Curtis happily concluded, "we may safely leave the rest to time and free individual action."

In dismissing its early abolitionist tradition as a mere "peculiarity," Knox College began its evolution into a modern college. By the time John Finley arrived at the Galesburg campus in the 1880s, the institution's radical past was a matter of historical nostalgia, and not ongoing policy. Rather than dispensing the fiery message of no compromise with evil, Knox College under Newton Bateman cultivated an inoffensive sort of piety in its students that would place few hurdles in the path of their drive toward success.

> Should college campuses be centers of militant radicalism or placid oases of quietistic scholarship? This was one of the burning questions in America during the years when this book took shape. My energies, such as they were, were thrown into this debate on the side of radical action. Not that I lacked sympathy for dispassionate scholarship; I have strong impulses toward quietism and passivity. But I took a stand that went against some of my deepest instincts because I perceived that the terms of the debate no longer reflected reality; the university in mid–twentieth century America had already become highly politicized as the state apparatus tapped the knowledge it produced for its war-making purposes and as the educational system became more and more of a processing for slots in an educated proletariat. To be a radical was in some sense a protest against the corruption of the promise and joy of learning.

Bateman's educational and social philosophy was expressed, not only in his senior courses in moral philosophy, but also in his frequent chapel talks at Knox College, and in his baccalaureate sermons. No document survives that specifically records Bateman's impact on John Finley, but all of Finley's later life seems an application of the doctrines that Bateman sought to inculcate in students. Bateman's baccalaureate sermon of 1887 was a representative sample of his views. Finley was certainly in the audience, for he was to deliver, later in the ceremonies, the valedictory address for that year. It is almost as certain that he shared much of Bateman's philosophy.

The venerable president preached on an appropriate text, Matt. 12:33: "The tree is known by its fruit." This is a divine criterion, "promulgated by the Son of God. . . . All systems of ethics, of religion, of education, of government," and such

institutions as Knox College, must be judged if at all by this
rule. Fifty years after the founding of the college, Newton
Bateman found its "fruit" commendable. Knox has stood for
"sound learning," a program of "systematic mastery of those
foundation principles upon which every science stands." So
trained, Knox graduates "go into the pursuits and professions
of life with an equipment of mental resources and power that
accounts for their successes—a success that is no exaggeration
to characterize as remarkable."

> On many a judicial bench, with the dignities of ample learning, and in
> unsullied ermine, men of Knox are sitting, honored and trusted for their
> abilities as jurists and for their virtues as men. In many a Christian pulpit
> are heralds of righteousness, strong and eloquent, whom the people
> delight to hear and whose work is significantly blest of God. . . . In
> not a few cities and towns of many States, the name of the physician to
> whom the afflicted look first for help when the shadow of death seems
> falling, will be found among the graduates of Knox. In scientific, literary,
> commercial and financial pursuits, Knox graduates have achieved pro-
> nounced and commanding success.

(Bateman then offered praise for teachers who, in "all grades,
from the primary to the collegiate," busily sow seeds of righteousness "in youthful minds and hearts." But, significantly, he
did not refer to the mission of teachers in the context of
"success.")

The enviable record of success compiled by graduates of the
college in Galesburg was credited not only to the soundness of
the learning available there. "The training of the moral and
religious faculties" also promoted at Knox College happily
increased "the chances for success in practical life." Bateman
also observed that "the relation of moral rectitude to success is
as close as that of scientific knowledge to success." Righteousness has a commercial as well as a heavenly value: "god-
liness is profitable in this world as well as in the next."

The physical side was not left out either. "Knox would send
forth her sons brawny as well as brainy, elastic in muscle as
well as alert in thought, prepared for physical endurance as
well as for spiritual, erect and manly in physical as well
as moral bearing." The importance of "gentle manners" was
also stressed by Newton Bateman:

> The supreme function of a Christian college is to produce a scholarly,
> Christian gentleman. The notion that a man may be rough in speech and

manners if only his principles are sound and his life without moral reproach, finds no countenance in Knox College. She is more grieved by trespasses against the unwritten rules of courtesy and refinement . . . than by infelicitous translations or bungling demonstrations in the class-room. She holds and teaches that true politeness is the beautiful flowering of the tree of life planted in the soul by the love and grace of God.

Bateman was evidently not voicing notions that were not widely shared in the college community of Galesburg. His baccalaureate sermons merely made explicit the reigning persuasion there. It is clear that, in championing worldly success, physical vigor, and genteel manners, Knox College was accommodating to secular forces that were transforming America.

But in embracing worldly goals, Knox College did not thereby abandon the realms of the mind and spirit. Bateman declared that "every fresh discovery in the realms of philosophy and science" would be welcomed. But important distinctions were drawn between theory and science, between mere hypothesis and true knowledge:

> When supposition ends in certainty, when theory culminates in knowledge, then, and surely not till then, Knox joyfully and reverently welcomes the advent of another star in the resplendent firmament of science. This is the respectful but cautious attitude of the College toward all new theories and systems challenging recognition and acceptance; an attitude at once both liberal and conservative.

Despite the claim that the pursuit of learning at Knox College was both liberal and conservative, during John Finley's student days emphasis fell clearly on the latter. Newton Bateman scoffed at such a thing as a "new education." He smugly concluded that the process by which knowledge is acquired was "settled and removed from the field of discussion."

> We know how a mental faculty, as memory or judgement, is trained, as well as we know how a muscle, as of the arm, is trained. . . . [Knox College] holds and teaches that knowledge, whether much or little, is not in itself power, seeing that many who have the most of the former have the least of the latter; but that power lies in the ability to use the mind, to wield the mental faculties with readiness, precision and force, whenever and however there may be call for such use and wielding, in the practical concerns of life.

Bateman was defending in 1887 the same sort of "faculty psychology" that had appeared in the famous Yale Report of

1828, and, as Frederick Rudolph shows in his standard history
of American higher education, *The American College and
University*, had confirmed much of American education even
then in a profound conservatism.

> *Although not exactly comparable to the nineteenth century doctrine
> of "faculty psychology," a widespread notion in contemporary America
> is that education—especially higher education—brings with it a measure
> of subtle but discernible sophistication. I certainly thought so in my
> college days, when my teachers (particularly one Harvard-educated
> historian) held out to me visions of exalted discourse possible when
> one's education had reached a kind of critical mass. Eagerly, I antici-
> pated the time when I too could converse about the intricacies of high
> culture, be one of the cognoscenti (people "come and go/Talking of
> Michelangelo," is the way T. S. Eliot put it). The sheer snobbery behind
> this notion is inextricably entwined with whatever validity it has. (For a
> recent restatement of the idea that university education should mainly
> train an esoteric elite of scholar-priests, see Philip Rieff, Fellow
> Teachers [1973].) Over time, reluctantly, I came to abandon this concep-
> tion of education as initiation into the inner circle of sophistication in
> favor of a view more in line with my socialist convictions—a view that
> sees knowledge as something not to be jealously guarded for the enjoy-
> ment of the chosen few, but to be used democratically in the construction
> of socialist societies.*

Yet Bateman on occasion spoke in behalf of an alternate
philosophy of education, less harsh and more sentimental
than the "vigorous, and steady, and systematic" discipline of
the mental and moral faculties. Stern intellectual discipline, of
course, was necessary for students of Knox College; but Bateman was convinced that students are best educated "not so
much by the contemplation of abstract truth, . . . as by truth
incarnate, as by moral beauty personified, illuminating human
lives, raying out from human hearts, inspiring human beneficence, speaking with human voices, ministering to human
joys and sorrows and needs." The beneficent *presence* of the
consecrated teacher was central to Bateman's educational outlook. Such a teacher not only radiates personal beneficence
but, by bringing students into "communion with the choicest
spirits of secular [and religious] history," their souls are made
"nobler, sweeter, [and] purer." Even his political philosophy
apparently amounted to a reverent belief in a moral presence
in political life. Since political morality in the American
Gilded Age did not exactly radiate purity, Bateman had to
turn for his political theory to the memory of his Illinois

friend, Abe Lincoln, who "recognized as did no other American statesman of this century, the *moral element* in politics." Whether it came to him from Newton Bateman or from some other source, this notion of *presence* was also to be the key element in John Finley's later educational and journalistic career.

In a baccalaureate sermon of 1885, Bateman confirmed Knox College in its dedication to Christian piety, if in a less spectacular form than during the "martyr-age" of Blanchard. Considering the growing secularism, President Bateman concluded that, even if Harvard had abandoned its traditional aims, Knox at least would remain devoted to *Christo et Ecclesiae*. (Table 1 suggests the extent to which Bateman's claims of special piety at Knox may be evaluated.) He perceived that the students needed religion; they cried "from the deeps of consciousness" and expressed an "inextinguishable yearning" for faith. The college years were the crucial time to satisfy this longing; it was then that "the illusions of life are the most seductive and the passions most insurgent and dangerous." Better to fill the need with sound Christian doctrine, or else "some chimera of the brain" would insinuate itself; better Jehovah than "Baal, or Fate, or Nature;" better "the Gospel of the Son of God, radiant with immortality" than "the dream of pantheism or the doom of annihilation and the shadow of despair." What inhumanity to launch a boy or girl into the world, "temptations assailing, the solemnities of choice inevitable, death drawing on, but no Rock of Ages in sight, no light ahead, no chart of the storm-swept seas, no foregleams of a haven of safety, a city of God."

But of course no one at Knox College had the slightest intention of depriving students of blessings of true faith, or of diminishing the college's dedication to Christian piety. Not only by the students' spiritual needs or by the college's tradition, emphasis on piety seemed to Newton Bateman to be called for by the essential inadequacy of scientific truth. Striking a Platonic note, Bateman maintained that science could only point the way, itself falling short of what he considered true knowledge. Scientific and philosophical inquiries, when pursued to their ultimate boundaries, were found to "abut upon celestial frontiers," to encounter "mysteries which only

the recognition of God as ultimate factor in the universe can
clear away."

> [Scientific and religious truth] cannot be sundered; they belong to-
> gether, they interblend inseparably; both are angels and interpreters of
> the everlasting God. Science is the nurse and servant of faith; along its
> solid gradients the believer climbs to sublimer ranges of cosmical
> knowledge, and so to grander outsweeps of faith, and higher conceptions
> of the divine glory. Christianity . . . floods with light whole districts of
> nature and being, which, to science alone are in impenetrable darkness.
> It solves problems which all the probings of science cannot reach; it
> moves in triumph over abysses which the utmost skill of science cannot
> bridge. . . . Yes, the kingdoms of Christ and culture are co-extensive
> and co-terminus.

The pattern of accommodation to the modern world that
began with the rejection of Jonathan Blanchard's reformist zeal
continued under President Newton Bateman. Knox College
attempted to reconcile the drive for worldly success with
Christian piety. Students like John and Robert Finley could
come to Knox and find nothing in the message of its president,
or in the atmosphere of the place, to interfere with their
legitimate ambition. But to account for the precise direction of
this ambition, one more Knox College influence needs to be
mentioned.

The senior course in English literature and political
economy taught by Professor Jeremiah W. Jenks temporarily
injected a novel element into the intellectual world of Knox
College. Jenks came to Galesburg in 1886, just after taking a
doctorate in economics at Halle. He was a representative of a
new and rising type in American academic life—the reform-
minded, university-trained social scientist with an exotic
European degree. Soon after their graduation from Knox College, the Finley brothers would be exposed to other such men
at Johns Hopkins University.

At Halle, Jenks had imbibed notions of economic efficiency
and public service, which he tried to transmit to students. He
confessed in a letter in 1901 that his greatest pleasure as a
teacher came from "turning in the right direction for future
usefulness men whose lives . . . are to be of distinguished
service to their fellows." Finley's life was so dedicated, and,
although there is no evidence that his devotion to public

service came primarily from Jenks's influence, the professor himself expressed satisfaction with his handiwork.

> I am sure [Jenks wrote to Finley in 1901] that you will let me say quietly to you what I have more than once said to others about you, that of the thousands of my pupils you are one of the three or four (and second to no one of them) in whom I have taken the greatest pride and comfort, and who have stood closest to me.

> *I am particularly touched by the sentiment expressed in Jenks's letter, as I have repeatedly longed for a close, warm relationship with my teachers. Occasionally we were able to achieve this; but more often I got hostility or cold correctness from these men and women. The exceptional teachers in my educational background will receive a small measure of the recognition they deserve: a listing on the dedication page of my next book—a study of the Johns Hopkins University in its late nineteenth century golden age.*

But, despite the novelty of Jeremiah Jenks's presence, and the inclusion in the curriculum of some modern courses, John Finley had the experience in the 1880s of being educated at an old-time college. The prominence of piety, the style of teaching, the role of the president clearly placed Knox in this category. But by the late nineteenth century, the content of education in such an institution was well on its way to becoming adapted to the realities of life in a capitalist society. The genial celebration of the success theme by President Newton Bateman was one sign of this adaptation. The extracurriculum was another.

Chapter 4

The Extracurriculum at Knox College:

Work and Journalism, 1882–87

*Often I remark to my students (in structured, formal classroom set-
tings) that the classroom is one of the worst places to obtain an education, and that informal processes outside the curriculum educate best.
In part, this viewpoint arises from perspectives such as that which Ivan
Illich expressed in his book* Deschooling Society *(1971). But I really
don't fully agree with this antiinstitutional perspective, or with the
political assumptions that underlie it. When I make such announce-
ments in class, they are intended as a device to stimulate student
attention, precisely to make my classroom teaching more effective. It
may be a dismal reflection on my teaching that I need these devices, and
I worry about such pedagogical matters far more than most of my students suspect.*

At least as important as the Latin recitations, the indoctrina-
tion in "evidences of Christianity," or the exposure to scientific truths were the activities generated by the students themselves. Many students may have found that the wide scope for
legitimate student enterprise and ambition afforded by the
old-time college was more relevant for their pursuit of worldly
success than the items of purely academic fare featured in the
college catalog. Certainly this was true for John Finley.

The first extracurricular problem Finley faced in Galesburg
was how to earn a living. The meager farm in Grand Ridge
could not support two boys, or even one, at college. Had he
come to Knox College two decades earlier, Finley might have
solved this problem by taking advantage of the college's manual labor system. But by the 1850s this system had disap-
peared from the Knox campus, and from campuses of most
other colleges that had tried it. Finley had to turn to the
growing community of Galesburg, in which he found ample

31

opportunity to practice the American ritual of Working One's
Way through College.

Opportunity came in a variety of ways, mostly from local
citizens willing to hire students at current rates. John Finley
lived at the home of Galesburg banker Albert Perry and did
chores in return. He dusted law books in the office of young
Edgar A. Bancroft (Knox '78), who later became U.S. ambassador to Japan. As an upperclassman whose spectacular
academic record marked him as a scholar of note, Finley was
allowed to conduct recitations in Horace for Knox freshmen.
His brother Rob had a flair for drawing, and he attempted to
earn extra cash by doing portraits. Others took to the road
selling notions, as S. S. McClure ('82) had done during his
student days at Knox. Carl Sandburg as a college student in the
nineties worked for the Galesburg fire department and occasionally had to leap from his classroom in response to the fire
alarm. Possibilities were endless, and doubtless even today
new variations are being tested in Galesburg. The pattern of
poor students working for a living was so prevalent at Knox
that it interfered with the military program. Army officers in
charge of the cadet corps at the college filed frequent reports
in Washington complaining that, because "many students at
this institution are poor and have to work their way[s] through
college," cadet enrollment suffered.

In the light of his earlier journalistic ambitions, and his later
career, the most significant job John Finley held during his
student days at Knox College was at George Colville's printing
plant on Galesburg's Main Street. There he learned the typog-
rapher's craft and practiced it by setting up his daily Greek
assignment in type. In plate 2, I reprint a few withered
pages of Finley's translation of *Prometheus Bound*. In later
years, after he had achieved prominence as an educator, Finley indulged his memories of that dark and dingy print shop.
In the moments when the Aeschylus text was being set up, he
said, the shop became transformed into the world of the titan
who "manward sent Art's mighty means." After he became a
Princeton professor in 1900, Finley attributed what success he
had enjoyed until then to his "knowledge of setting type and
reading proof." This knowledge, and the journalistic experi-

ence Finley gradually accumulated, served him well in the middle stages of his career. The casual thread leading from Colville's printing plant ultimately extends to the distinguished editorial post Finley held on the *New York Times* in the last decades of his life.

In the 1950s, before the banks, and the general crisis of late capitalism, undermined the economic vitality of New York City, the metropolis supported a wide range of industries and services. These in turn provided the modest employment opportunities necessary for survival of a recently married college student. (I turned down an offer of a parental allowance; we were going to show our independence!) One year I worked on Tuesdays, Thursdays, and Sundays at Streit's Matzoh Company on Rivington Street on the Lower East Side, scheduling classes on Mondays, Wednesdays, and Fridays at CCNY. Another year I worked long weekend hours at a gas station, and then later was able to find part-time social work at various agencies, such as the Police Athletic League and a nearby YM-YWHA. In summertimes I replenished our resources by working as a New York City lifeguard at Rockaway's beaches.

In the old-time college, student enterprise was considered to be a manifestation of democracy that fostered meeting and mingling of students from different social strata. Such egalitarianism persisted at least into the 1890s, when the student press boasted that—

the number of men at Knox [who] are working their own way is one of the best proofs of the spirit that prevails here. It shows that here, at least, is one college where a man's money or position makes no difference with the standing among his classmates and friends.

A decade earlier, when the Finley brothers were students at the campus, a Knox College trustee also argued that, while the "inland colleges" might not offer the intellectual treasures of the Eastern institutions, they were "permeated by the sturdy strength of the west." Students there were privileged to "breathe the spirit of the free prairies."

John Finley's social experience at Knox College bore out this interpretation. As a poor farmer's son, he seems to have enjoyed a full range of collegiate social activities, even a romance with a banker's daughter. In his freshman year, he roomed at the college dormitory and took his meals with the coeds. From another table, Mattie Boyden noticed "his nice, plain face, his tall, awkward body, with clothes rather too short in the sleeves and trousers." Before long he was eating at her

table. He claimed that he had made up his mind to marry her
fifteen minutes after coming to her table, but the young lady
was not quite so hasty. There were ups and downs in the
romance; over a half century later, Martha Finley remembered
a crisis of the freshman year.

> One afternoon he mustered courage to come to . . . see me. In those
> informal days, almost anyone answered the [dormitory] doorbell, who
> had heard it, and whoever did, came to a pipe leading to my bedroom,
> knocked on it, and said there was someone to see me in the parlor.
> Evidently I didn't hear or was not in my room. . . . He says he sat in the
> parlor twenty minutes to a half an hour, and then, when no one was
> looking beat a hasty retreat. In a few days I had an enigmatic poem from
> him, the first bit of verse he ever wrote me, suggesting that if a young
> man called on a young lady and she never appeared what was he to
> think? I had no idea what he meant, but finally we got together and it
> was all satisfactorily explained, the one to the other.

Although he took Mattie to a number of "social affairs" in the
two years they were both students at Knox College, Finley
was too busy with other activities to monopolize her time. We
may safely suspect that young John Finley felt he could not
turn his attention seriously to marriage until he was well on
the road to professional success.

> *Married at an absurdly young age, I was at college with my wife*
> *Marge. We were objects of some awe to fellow students still living at*
> *home on parental allowances. Since CCNY had no graduate programs*
> *to speak of in the early 1950s, the campus was empty of graduate*
> *students' wives, baby carriages, pregnant scholars, and other features*
> *one could find a half mile downtown on the Columbia University cam-*
> *pus, and that I would discover at Johns Hopkins later.*

The main feature of the extracurriculum in the old-time
college, before the arrival of football and fraternities, was the
literary societies. They "imparted a tremendous vitality" to
the cause of intellectual endeavor in institutions that were
devoted to piety, and rote drill in the classics.

College literary societies usually came in pairs and were
given elegant Greek names; at Knox College there were Adelphi and Gnothautii. The Finley brothers joined the former as
freshmen and made Adelphi a major focus of their strenuous
extracurricular activity. At Knox College in the 1880s, the
literary societies constituted a powerful, semiindependent
force on campus. They staged oratorical contests and sponsored lecture series for which admission prices were charged.

They brought such well-known speakers as Booker T. Washington and George F. Kennan to Galesburg; they were consulted on college policy and managed their finances with such adroitness that Gnothautii, at least once, was able to lend money to the college. Both societies raised funds for an ambitious college construction project. In addition, the college itself frequently used buildings owned by the literary societies.

Adelphi also on occasion staged shows, using student talent. In the spring of 1886, John Finley was chosen to depict *A Visit to Pluto*. Later in the year, after he had been elected president of Adelphi, John and his brother acted out act 4, scene 3 of *Macbeth*, with the two brothers as Malcolm and Macduff. In putting on such skits, the literary societies of John Finley's day seem like present-day undergraduate clubs; but this should not obscure the real power they represented on campus (in great contrast to the status of student groups before the 1960s).

> At CCNY Marge and I both threw ourselves into extracurricular life with whatever energy we had leftover from studies and part-time work. I swam and dove for the swimming team, while Marge played women's basketball. Then there was student politics; we both served on student council, and Marge was president of the student NAACP chapter one year. We both fought hard in the campaign against public disclosure of the membership of student political organizations—forcing the FBI to use informers, as I later discovered. In addition Marge worked with the anthropology club, while I sparked the organization of a philosophy club. I also became editor of the Journal of Social Studies, which I shamelessly used as a vehicle for publishing my term papers.

One index of the significance of literary societies in the life of their colleges is the extent of their libraries. Often these rivaled or surpassed the college's library. At Knox College the libraries of Adelphi and Gnothautii were swelled by books purchased with profits of the societies' many literary and oratorical events. In 1887 the two Knox literary societies had together about as many books as the college. We owe this information to the activities of John Finley as a member and, after September, 1886, president of Adelphi. While yet a sophomore, Finley proposed that a catalog of books in the Adelphi collection be prepared; and a year later he was able to gain support (in Adelphi at least) for a merger of all three libraries. This was not carried out until five years after his graduation, but the immediate fruit of Finley's efforts was a twenty-nine-page *Catalogue of Books in the College, Adelphi and Gnothautii Libraries of Knox College* (1887), carrying on its title page the notice that John H. Finley was the publisher.

The Finley brothers' student years at Knox College marked what was probably the high point of activity for the literary societies there. Ten years after their graduation, the decline of Adelphi and Gnothautii was lamented; "the brainiest men in the college," observed the student paper, "do not take an active part" any longer. The improvement of course offerings and "other attractions" were cited as responsible.

Not among these "other attractions" in the 1880s at Knox College was football, which was introduced to Galesburg in about 1891. Although he was reported active in college sports, John Finley did not play for any Knox College intercollegiate athletic team. His student days fell in that placid and innocent era before the rise of professionalized college football, when athletics meant mainly gala "field days," which were usually overshadowed by the oratorical contest later in the day. It was after his graduation from Knox, when he was attending a university far more noted for intellectual achievements than for athletic prowess, that Finley first competed in intercollegiate football—for the Johns Hopkins University team.

College journalism was another area of the extracurriculum in which John Finley distinguished himself. Knox College's student newspapers had emerged from a period of intense factional dispute in the early 1880s. Originally, the lone student paper, the *Knox Student*, had been the organ of the two literary societies, but under young S. S. McClure's guidance it became an independent journal. Resentment over McClure's control of the *Student* led in 1881 to the founding of a rival paper, the *Coup d'Etat*. But after McClure's graduation the *Knox Student* temporarily ceased to publish, and during Finley's student days "The Coop" was the sole paper. It was a sign of great sophistication to use the French pronunciation, "Coo."

Although it sported a revolutionary title and was published independently (by a "joint stock company"), the *Coup d'Etat* was anything but a voice for militant student dissent. Indeed, there was none of that. The editors followed a conservative policy. They were vigilant in safeguarding the classical curriculum and seeking to maintain the most rigid entrance requirements. In disciplinary matters, the journal called for severe punishment of student pranks and even cautioned the faculty on excessive leniency. Besides occasionally serving as the self-appointed conscience of the college, the *Coup* also printed campus news and acted as the house organ of the administration and faculty. Results of faculty and trustee meetings, baccalaureate sermons, pious exhortations, and student literary exercises filled its innocent and flowery columns.

John Finley's first appearance in the pages of the *Coup d'Etat* came in December of 1883. It was soon after he had returned as a teacher to his own Grand Ridge common school, interrupting the freshman year to replenish his finances. He had undertaken to compete in the freshman essay contest but lacked material to finish the paper on his chosen topic, "The Jew in Modern History." It happened at this time that a young Illinois lawyer, James H. Eckels, was lecturing in Grand Ridge on "The Jews." After hearing his presentation, Finley sought out the lecturer and obtained the material that enabled him to write the essay. (Later in his career, John Finley was again aided by James Eckels.) With such help he won the essay contest, the first of many honors Finley achieved during his unmatched student career at Knox College. The appearance of the essay marked not only Finley's first contribution to the *Coup d'Etat* but his initial appearance in print.

"The Jew in Modern History" was an early exercise on a theme to which Finley often returned, especially after he became president of the College of the City of New York, with its largely Jewish student body. There was a persistent ambivalence in his attitude toward Jews; and we get a hint of this in the essay of 1883. It was mostly filled with glowing accounts of the achievements of eminent Jews and a deep appreciation of the fact of Jewish survival, which was ascribed (with reference to Darwinian evolution) to some racial characteristic guaranteeing Jewish superiority in the struggle for existence. This superiority was located in the intellect. But Finley also noted the fact of Jewish alienation, rejection of Christian kindliness that proceeded from a stubborn and bitter hatred of

their fellow men chronically displayed by the "chosen
people."

> While to religious Jews I vehemently express my atheistic convictions,
> to the outside world I can hardly deny some sort of Jewish identity. But
> to me, Jewishness does not necessarily mean the ethnic sentimentality
> of kosher food rituals, automatic support of Israeli foreign policy, or the
> literary notions of marginality and alienation. To me, as to the great
> socialist historian Isaac Deutscher, Jewish identity involves the vision
> of universal social justice—socialism, in short.

Shortly after returning to Knox College from the year of
teaching in Grand Ridge, Finley joined the staff of the *Coup
d'Etat*. Earlier, his future wife, Mattie Boyden, had also been
a member of the newspaper's staff. Finley soon became assistant editor-in-chief, and his brother, Rob, was at the head of
the editorial board in their senior year. Under the editorship of
the Finleys, the *Coup* continued to be much the same sort of
journal it had been before, somewhat enlivened in 1886–87 by
Rob's cartoons.

The *Coup d'Etat* did not exhaust John Finley's journalistic
energies; during the summer of 1886 he engaged in a characteristically whimsical bit of personal journalism. Under the
name John Agricola, Finley edited and published an occasional newspaper, the *Vacationist,* editions of which were
"very small, for [they] consisted entirely of proof copies made
by hand (with block and mallet)."

The first number declared:

> This brief sheet is published in the interest of those whose nomadic life
> now separates them from the rippling cedar, the towering walls of Knox,
> and the tender associations of college days. It aims not at greatness, it
> aspires not to "pluck bright honor from her lofty perch"; but is simply
> the result of a philanthropic idea of a tyro typo, to cheer the heavy heart
> and lighten the weary way of the wanderer, is its aim; to feed the hungry
> and homeless news, and aussage [sic] the thirsty with refreshing words,
> its object. Brevity, "the soul of wit," is its most striking feature. Limited
> talent with limited means has necessitated a short and rather unartistic
> opening issue, but we hope soon to mention among our contributors
> several able writers, and to be able to present our sheet in a neater and
> more becoming form. Our friends and patrons we greet and hope to
> please and profit.

Those other "able writers" seem never to have materialized,
and "John Agricola" remained the only contributor to the
Vacationist.

Chapter 5

Oratory:

Path to Success at a Prairie College, 1886–87

Oratory has never been one of my strong points. Perhaps in Finley's day, when oratory was something of an endurance pastime and speeches sometimes lasted for hours, one of my academic lectures could have passed muster. But nowadays, especially in the political circles within which I move, short, snappy, hard-hitting speeches are what's called for. I had a vivid reminder of this during the protest against the Nixon administration's invasion of Cambodia in 1970. Invited along with others to address a lunchtime rally of government workers in New York City's Foley Square, I launched into a lengthy analysis of the historical background of the Indochina conflict; I believe I had gotten about up to World War II and the important role the Japanese played in the region when the rally's manager gently nudged me off the platform. The next speaker, the veteran activist Dave Dellinger, gave a more appropriate (and no less knowledgeable) talk, which I listened to from off the podium with admiration and envy. "Comes the Revolution" I'll have to rethink my commitment to old-fashioned, professorial ways.

College journalism in John Finley's student days (and long afterward) could be a training in maturity and a preparation for professional success. Heading up a literary society had similar possibilities, and the experience of working one's way through college could not help but be of use in the struggle for success after graduation. Even academic study might help. But for a brief period in the late nineteenth century, old-time midwestern colleges provided another, remarkably direct route to postgraduate eminence in the oratorical contests they sponsored. Since John Finley was active in oratory, as well as on all the other fronts, his own later success was clearly presaged in his college career.

Knox College was a strategic base from which to launch an effort to achieve distinction through college oratory; it was a major center of forensic activity. The "micro-coccus oratoricus," Finley once observed, flourished chiefly there. Much earlier, the *Coup d'Etat* noted in the same vein that "every college has its craze. With Columbia, judging from the *Spectator*, it is beer-drinking; with Harvard and Cornell, boating; with Wesleyan, 'college courtesy and culture;' while here [at Knox] it is contests—oratorical and otherwise." With their penchant for moralizing, the undergraduate editors concluded that "the mania is alarming." Although some might fret over the alleged waste of time, many Knox students could find in the oratorical contests a pleasant diversion. Others yet could make the preparation and delivery of an original oration the climax of their college careers.

Oratory was not limited to extracurricular efforts of the literary societies; during Finley's student days the Knox faculty included an instructor in elocution, Miss Malvina Bennett. Finley studied with her as a freshman and sophomore, perfecting his declamatory style on such orations of Wendell Phillips as "The Eulogy of Sumner." After two years of such training, Finley felt secure enough to represent the junior class in the annual junior-senior oratory contest. He won with an apologetic speech on John Brown's erratic career, which was classed as "superior" in form by a student reporter. Finley's delivery was forcible, though not impassioned, but his voice seemed to some hard and lacking in flexibility. He was to have at least two more chances to polish this oration—at the intercollegiate and interstate oratorical contests.

In 1886 the Thirteenth Annual Inter-Collegiate Oratorical Contest for seven Illinois colleges was held at Monmouth on October first. Knox students were urged to attend. They were promised, not only the innocent excitement of "crowded depots, anxious watchers, joyous telegrams, resounding bells and blazing bon-fires," but victory as well; "with John H. Finley as our champion," assured the *Coup d'Etat* (then under the editorship of his brother), "we confidently enter the lists and await the issue." Finley's greatest rival was Illinois College's crack orator, Hugh M. Wilson, whose "Federalism" was reputed to be a masterpiece. Indeed, two of the three judges "on thought and composition" rated Wilson ahead of the other

six student orators. But Finley won unanimous support from
the judges "on delivery" and edged out Wilson 529.5 to 522.

The next hurdle was the Inter-State Contest, the early prov-
ing ground for such renowned orators as Albert Beveridge,
William Jennings Bryan, Edgar A. Bancroft, and Robert LaFol-
lette. Finley was accompanied to the 1887 contest, held in
Bloomington, Illinois, by a large Knox College delegation,
confident that he "would take the prize of course." Nine
young men, each representing the winning school in his
state's local contest, sat nervously on the stage of
Bloomington's Opera House on the May evening that was so
important to all of them. Each of them, no doubt, was rehearsing to himself his set speech while waiting his turn. Among
the orations were: "Alien Landlords in America," delivered
crudely by a speaker who "was certainly a *natural* [i.e., primi-
tive] orator" a smoother and more elegant speech on Shylock's
character; and a "convincing" presentation by a Wabash College orator of "some rather radical ideas" on "Man and the
State." Most of the others also were on serious social or political themes.

> The terms radical and radicalism are among the most ambiguous in
> the American political vocabulary. (I have tried to introduce some
> clarity in my bibliographical essay on early American radicalism
> [Choice: A Publication of the Association of College and Research Li-
> braries, June, 1976].) Originating as a mathematical term meaning the
> root of a number, the most basic and fundamental way it can be ex-
> pressed, radical gradually took on political connotation, coming by
> 1887 to mean dangerous, left-wing extremism. Some of us in the twen-
> tieth century have come to accept and even exult in the term, even
> though it does not adequately distinguish anarchistic from socialistic
> radicalism.

Finley, delivering his "John Brown," spoke sixth. A
"death-like silence" pervaded the hall as he declaimed in a
quiet, conversational tone, marked by a slight Scottish inflec-
tion; he carefully avoided the florid emotionalism that some
thought synonymous with oratory. One Indiana delegate con-
temptuously remarked that "the Knox man . . . didn't orate at
all, he just *talked.*"

The oration opened with an evocation of John Brown's
notoriety and the ambiguity of his achievements; was he "the
traitor or the patriot, the murderer or the martyr"? Before

answering the question, Finley briefly recounted the essentials of Brown's biography, not sparing the Pottawatomie massacres, in which the old abolitionist dragged "from their homes five unarmed pro-slavery men and [killed] them in cold blood." The bare facts in this record seemed only to justify Brown's execution as "murderer, insurrectionist, traitor." If judged by the common standard, Brown's claim to have been seeking freedom for the black man could be discounted. "Assassins of presidents," the young orator pointed out a year after the Haymarket affair, "have pleaded the good of the country; and the anarchist, as he hurls his bomb, shouts for the liberty of the oppressed." Measured by his announced aims and public acts, by his life's "rugged exterior," John Brown was a contemptible failure. But another standard of judgment could be used. "His life was noble or base, great or insignificant, according as the motives inspiring it were noble or base, the influence exerted by it great or mean."

To justify Brown by the dual standard of motivation and influence, Finley had to employ psychology, history, and even ancestry. The "Puritan idea" of stern justice transmitted from his forebears who died in the revolutionary war existed, in Brown, alongside a deep strain of saintly tenderness. The morning after Pottawatomie, the bearded old man with blood stains on his hands asked a blessing of God. This was no hypocrisy; Brown acted always from "the solid ground of real principle: unmixed with any low motive of personal gain." History tells us that his bloody deeds arrested the tide of slavery in Kansas, just as the Harper's Ferry raid later precipitated the momentous struggle between slavery and freedom, which happily ended in victory for the latter principle. Finley concluded his oration by placing Brown among the heroes who took up arms in defense of the "higher law": Wallace, the Scottish martyr; Garibaldi; Byron; Toussaint L'Overture; and even George Washington. Was hanging the "fitting and final reward" for such as John Brown?

> The soaring shaft that stands by Potomac's stream, answers, No. The monuments, which a grateful people have erected to the memory of those who died for the slave, say, No. The gratitude of millions freed from bondage says, No. And the day will come when even the mountains of Virginia will echo back the answer, No.

*Young John Finley's evocation of John Brown's fierce radicalism in
the context of such revolutionaries as Toussaint of Haiti and Garibaldi
was not intended to ignite any fire of prairie radicalism in the 1880s.
Knox's "martyr-age" was long since past, and radical heroes were little
more than embalmed mementos of an era long gone. This embalming of
America's once-revolutionary past is a way of avoiding the revival of
radicalism in the present; it is a tendency that the scholarship I admire
and try to emulate struggles against. Radical historians can and do
discover contemporary relevance in the past without distortion and
without uncritically praising heroes and heroines as faultless totemic
ancestors. The tools of critical history can open up the possibilities in
the present and, in Paul Sweezy's indispensable phrase, help us view the
"future as history."*

After the orations were over, and while the scores were
being tabulated, the festive college crowd entertained itself
with songs. At long last the results began to be announced; the
large audience strained to hear that "the first prize had been
awarded to John H. Fi——." The Knox College delegation
burst into cheers and sang lustily ("John Brown's Body," of
course) before the other scores could be announced. Back in
Galesburg a crowd had collected around the telegraph office,
awaiting the wire, which came after midnight. Sleepy citizens
were roused out of bed by the din that resulted when the good
news arrived. The bells of the town rang out. One enthusiastic
student scaled the roof of "Old Main" to ring the college bell;
but he swung his axe so hard that the rusty old bell broke.
When Finley was formally honored by the college later in the
week, he was presented with a plush case, inside of which was
a finely polished bit of metal, bearing the inscription: "Knox
College Bell. Broken for Finley. May 5th, 1887."

The victory in the oratorical contest in May, 1887, was
clearly the climax of John Finley's college career. It percepti-
bly influenced his later life. In 1889, when he was being
considered for his first professional position—at the State
Charities Aid Association in New York City—the "John
Brown" oration helped his chances. Much of Finley's later
success as college president and journalist was also due, as we
shall see, to the rhetorical ability he acquired at Knox College.
Indeed, Finley found there a characteristically American
route to success, which reveals how extensively a poor boy
had to rely on merchandising his personality to get ahead in
the competitive world of late-nineteenth-century America.

Get ahead Finley did. His academic record—all A's save for one B—was only matched by his success in achieving distinction through the extracurriculum. After graduation his ascent would continue, even accelerate.

A fitting conclusion to his Knox College career was his selection (even before the oratorical triumph of May) as valedictorian. Finley delivered his address at the same Jubilee Commencement at which Newton Bateman preached on Matt. 12:33. Mattie Boyden came to Galesburg for the ceremonies.

Valedictorian Finley predictably chose to pay respects to Knox College's origins ("that little caravan which fifty years ago crossed the unsettled plains and laid the foundations of this institution") and to the truths for which it had stood in the succeeding half century. Knox's all-time prize pupil admitted that students—

> shall soon forget, yes, have already forgotten much that we have received [from our teachers] . . . , but we shall not forget those fundamental principles which by precept and example have been laid deep in our hearts and minds, and upon which we may safely build; truth wins, right prevails, God rules.

The valedictorian then spoke with respect of Galesburg and its citizens, and concluded by picturing the graduates in military metaphor as venturing forth "to different parts of the field" to do battle in behalf of the principles of religion and morality learned at Knox College.

The pious prairie college that nurtured John and Robert Finley in the 1880s was unmistakably an old-fashioned institution, although there were signs of modernity. The experience of studying at one of the pioneering institutions in the East would soon make the contrast clear to the two Illinois lads. Yet Knox College had evolved by Newton Bateman's day to where it could transmit the dominant American secular ideology of the day—the pursuit of success. The spiritual influence of the college was intended to help ensure that this pursuit would be along legitimate paths, and, in the case of the Finley brothers, this influence was a lasting one. Especially in the scope it allowed for extracurricular responsibility, Knox College propelled them on to active professional careers; and nothing taught there would interfere with their search for honorable success.

Book 2.
Choosing Professions

Chapter 6

More and Less than Scholarship:

Postgraduate School Life in the

Golden Age of the Johns

Hopkins University, 1887–89

When I arrived in Baltimore, awestruck at actually being in a university environment, my attitude was probably close to Finley's when he came to the same school seventy years earlier. If in my case the awe was somewhat greater, the cause may have been that Johns Hopkins was then legendary in ways it could not have been for Finley—for the very graduates who would establish the legend, such as Frederick Jackson Turner, the great historian of the American frontier, were his contemporaries. Especially for us historians, the university reverberated with its past glories. A contemporary of mine posted doggerel verse on the library stacks that reflected this: "In Baltimore did H. B. Adams/A stately seminar decree,/Whence Frederick Jackson Turner ran/Through heaver trails unknown to man/To get his Ph.D." Full of esoteric references to Professor Adams's celebrated seminar, and to the dissertation that Turner composed on the fur trade, this verse captures much of the Johns Hopkins graduate school spirit, circa 1958: there were once giants in the land, and we too could perhaps aspire to scholarly stature.

When Finley arrived at Johns Hopkins, the doctor of philosophy degree (Ph.D.) was a relatively new element in American academic life, and a university set up mainly to offer that degree was more novel still. Not simply a transplant to America of advanced German standards of scholarly/academic life, the recently founded Johns Hopkins University in Baltimore had been shaped in response to American visions and dreams. It held out promise of mature study and independent investigation; in the disciplines that soon would come to be called "social sciences," it could attract a Woodrow Wilson from Virginia, a John Dewey from Vermont, a Thorstein Veblen from Minnesota, a Frederick Jackson Turner from Wisconsin, and, scarcely less promising than the others, a John Finley from Illinois.

When he arrived in Baltimore with his brother, Rob, John found his first impressions of Johns Hopkins disappointing. The university buildings, not yet located in their present semisuburban splendor, were in the midst of the city and were far less imposing than those of Knox College; "strangers would have passed [them] by with no thought that they were the home of the first distinctive university in America," he wrote in the *New York Times* almost four decades later.

But far more discouraging was the fact that Finley did not seem to have the resources to support him while at study. During the summer he had compiled and set up in type a Galesburg directory, but the sum he collected for this was insufficient. The university had no fellowship for him, and he was advised to earn money elsewhere and postpone graduate study for a year. "In those first despairful days," he wrote later to one of his Johns Hopkins teachers, "I knew not how I was to manage to stay" at the university.

Finley's financial salvation came through his training in the Galesburg print shop. Johns Hopkins sheltered not only a dynamic intellectual enterprise but a flourishing center of scholarly publications as well. Many of the faculty in history and economics had scholarly works under way. At an interview in October, 1887, Herbert Baxter Adams, prodigiously energetic associate professor of history, "pulled an immense roll of printed sheets from a drawer in his desk" and inquired of Finley if he could read proof. The young midwesterner took the material (consisting of proof pages of the Johns Hopkins University *Studies in Historical and Political Science,* American Historical Association publications, etc.) to his lodgings, where he discovered and corrected enough errors for Adams to promise him more such work. Along with a timely loan from university president Daniel Coit Gilman, proofreading enabled Finley to earn enough money to continue his graduate study.

Seventy years later, The Johns Hopkins University Homewood campus was much more impressive, and the shape of American higher education had changed so that no poor boy was likely to arrive without some scholarship aid. In my case the National Woodrow Wilson Foundation (funded by the Ford Foundation) supplied what I thought was lavish support—nearly $2,500 a year, enough I thought to begin raising a

family. Finley, with the prudence of an earlier era, had to wait for
professional advancement before he could marry the banker's daughter
from Galesburg. But while I tarried at the university cloisters, the
pregnant wife who remained at home began to nurture resentments that
rankled for years and eventually brought the marriage to termination.
But the Baltimore-born first son, in college himself as these words are
written, was close and is close, through everything.

The academic week began with the walk from his nearby
Eutaw Street boarding house on Monday morning to attend
Herbert B. Adams's course in church history. According to the
rosters in the *Johns Hopkins University Circulars*, Finley also
studied ancient politics under Adams. Both he and his brother,
Robert, attended J. Franklin Jameson's courses in constitutional history, and John also studied modern historians with
Jameson. Together in their first year at Johns Hopkins, the
brothers enrolled in a pair of German classes, and in Associate
Professor Richard T. Ely's course on finance. In the two subsequent terms he spent at the university, John Finley took a
variety of other history courses with H. B. Adams, administration with Special Lecturer Woodrow Wilson, additional work
in political economy with Ely, social statistics with E. R. L.
Gould, a recent Johns Hopkins Ph.D. Rob Finley took a year's
course in drawing, and both brothers eventually enrolled in
the celebrated Johns Hopkins University Seminary of History
and Politics.

Just as the intellectual delicacies of the old-time college
were to be found in the senior course in moral philosophy, the
graduate study of social science at the university in Baltimore
centered in this seminary. It was far more than simply the
vehicle for "scientific history" and genteel racism that many
books and articles imply. By following Finley's education in
Baltimore, we will see that much seminary work was manifestly subscientific; and in fact, by the late eighties, Herbert
Adams's advocacy of the germ theory of American democracy,
with its strong presumption of Anglo-Saxon superiority, had
been supplanted by other interests, especially the history of
education and social reform. For the Finley brothers, however, the seminary provided an introduction to other things
than high-powered scholarship.

The seminary originated "in a small lecture room of the

Peabody Institute" in 1881 and soon moved into the university's buildings, where it began to meet regularly on Friday evenings. Adams, who dominated the seminary, defined its scope in quite unpretentious terms. "The main idea here," he announced to the seminary in 1884, "is that it is a place where the students lecture, and it is distinguished from class in that there the instructors lecture." In these student lectures, Adams admitted, "pretentions were seldom made to original investigations." Rather, students would offer judicious summaries of the "best points of view" on a subject. They would not read long essays; this "usually has a very depressing influence, but a student talking freely from a full head, and making his points clear and strong, always commands attention."

Adams did not insist that the student presentations be subject to rigid critical standards but rather proposed that they be judged leniently.

> The [seminary] instructors are young and not as well able to criticize the work as the man who wrote the paper, except as to literary form. . . . [Anyway,] Americans have better notions of refined criticism than the Germans, whose method is brutal. Criticism, not trampling, is valuable.

Under such a doctrine of "refined criticism," much of what transpired at the Johns Hopkins seminary under Adams was patently trivial. He reserved some of his harshest criticism for a hapless student, who read poorly the minutes of a previous seminary meeting. He praised effusively a paper on "Old Teutonic Life in Beowulf," because of its "flowery language," a mode that the students were urged to emulate, leaving the "terse German style" so characteristic of academic writing. A carefully wrought investigation into the history of constitutional conventions in America, the significance of which was immediately seen by J. Franklin Jameson, was welcomed as "timely" by Adams, since the hundredth anniversary of the ratification of the American constitution was approaching. (Part of the scholarly overglorification of Adams's seminary may be due to projecting backward twentieth-century critical standards on laxer nineteenth-century educational institutions; but part may be due to the fact that most writers who have touched on the Johns Hopkins seminary simply have not studied the manuscript "Seminary Records," a woefully neglected source for American educational and intellectual history. Soon, I hope to remedy this situation by preparing a scholarly edition of these Seminary Records, which will give them the exposure they have long deserved.)

Despite much triviality, the Johns Hopkins seminary was the scene of an exciting intellectual adventure in the 1880s. Scholars of the rank of Albion Small, Charles Homer Haskins, Frederick Jackson Turner, Woodrow Wilson, and Charles McLean Andrews received their graduate training in these years. It may be that these men achieved what they did despite, rather than because of, Herbert Baxter Adams. The fostering of a critical temper may have been more the work of J. Franklin Jameson and Richard T. Ely than of Adams. The influence of the students on each other must not be minimized either. Yet Adams, because of his unabashed promotional activities and his sense of scholarly community, did contribute to the sense of intellectual adventure. Student Charles Andrews, later an eminent historian of colonial America, exclaimed in November of 1887: "It is wonderful, the influence this University has upon a fellow. I can hardly explain it. It seems to develop the faintest germ of ability and to rouse any latent enthusiasm which a man may have."

In such an atmosphere the seminary could suddenly spring to life. The young men might be emboldened to attack some recognized scholarly authority, in his absence. On one such evening, Albion W. Small (soon to become a college president and university professor) demolished, to the delight of the seminary audience, Von Holst's *Constitutional History of the United States.* The American federal union was not, as the German scholar implied "born in a moment," but was rather, Small argued, the product of an evolutionary development. Adams also got in some licks that night against Von Holst, who earlier had been actively sought for the very position Adams held. The German historian seemed to Adams to have written "in the interest of Prussian imperialism," and was "culpable for his impious treatment of the [American] writers who preceded him and especially for his attack on Mr. Bancroft." Another graduate student that evening took the measure of Justin Winsor. Charles Homer Haskins (later to achieve great distinction as a mediaevalist) attacked Winsor's *Narrative and Critical History of the United States* on the grounds that it "might be narrative," but it was "certainly not critical, and *hardly* history."

John Finley did not join actively in this fun. He attended his first session on October 14, 1887, when Daniel C. Gilman addressed the group on his recent tour of California and Alaska. The president stressed the educational value of travel. Richard T. Ely reenforced this point with reminiscences of his own student travels in Germany. Herbert B. Adams then read selections from his forthcoming work, *Thomas Jefferson and the University of Virginia*. The next regular Friday evening meeting of the seminary featured students' reports on articles Adams had assigned them for review, and, in addition, Adams continued with his discussion of Jefferson. Ely commented that a good monograph could be written on Jefferson's idea that the "present lives for itself." At the third seminary session of his first term in Baltimore, Finley listened to Adams continue his talks on university education and heard, possibly for the first time, discussions of schemes for popular higher education and of the Chautauqua movement. On the same evening, Charles M. Andrews delivered a paper on "Popular Suffrage in Maryland."

Finley did not actively participate in the critical, scholarly side of seminary work. He is mentioned only twice in the "Seminary Records." In February, 1888, he read a paper by the English pioneer in settlement house work, Arnold Toynbee. Earlier that same month Finley was official scribe when graduate student E. P. Smith delivered a long, analytic paper on socialism, which concluded that "the acceptance by Christian capitalists of a thoroughly righteous plan of co-operation would bridge the yawning chasm [between social classes] and destroy the foundation on which socialism is based."

In the 1950s seminar work in history at Johns Hopkins was conducted with rigor. Graduate seminar papers were duplicated and circulated beforehand among seminar participants—both students and faculty. Naïvely I prepared my first paper on "The Sources of Violence in American Labor History" as something of a multimedia presentation, with recordings of labor ballads as accompaniment to the text. I argued that ethnic heterogeneity and the widespread use of strikebreakers and industrial police were the causes. My paper was coolly and politely received. Its conventional liberal conclusions showed among other things how far I was from socialism in 1958. Soon I would come closer.

In neither seminary appearance did Finley show promise of becoming an original scholar on the Johns Hopkins pattern (although an interest in reform and social work is indicated). One of the reasons why the records of the seminary are so silent on Finley is that he was quickly involved in a wide range of extracurricular activities. Probably the most time consuming was his collaboration with Richard T. Ely on a book on taxation.

In 1888 Ely was fresh from service with the Maryland Tax Commission, and he brought matters of taxation often to Johns Hopkins audiences. Probably a book on the subject had already been begun when Finley was engaged as research assistant. Ely entertained some definite policy notions. He argued for a form of land value taxation, different from Henry George's scheme, that would yield fair, ample revenues to local governments. States, and the federal government, in his view would have to abandon real estate taxation in favor of other taxes, such as on income.

Finley was set to work gathering historical data and excerpting reports of tax commissioners from all over the country to buttress Ely's views. The young graduate student, whose "literary efforts before that time had been in translations of Greek dramas or in more or less rhythmic or rhetorical compositions on historical or imaginative themes," claimed much later to have found "state statistics and municipal budgets as absorbing as the troubles of Prometheus or the wanderings of Ulysses. . . ." Whether or not Finley found the work on the *Taxation* volume intellectually satisfying, he certainly did grasp the opportunity for some months of paid work. This work was performed with "extraordinary diligency and a display of unusual ability." A hostile reviewer, who considered the book's policy recommendations "worthless," found much to praise in the historical and analytical chapters contributed by Finley. Ely graciously rewarded his young collaborator by adding "John H. Finley, B.A." to the title page of the published volume.

It is unlikely that compiling statistics on taxation was the only social science research Finley undertook in his year and a half at Johns Hopkins. As a member of the Seminary of History and Politics, he was in weekly attendance at what was perhaps at the time the foremost research-producing educational agency in the country. Although the records show that he brought no original research to the seminary table, two articles Finley published in the *Chautauquan* magazine in 1892 may be safely assumed to be either the result of actual work done as a graduate student at the university, or some reasonable facsimile thereof.

Finley's articles on colonial trading companies seem to have been based upon little else than their charters and such standard accounts as John Smith's *Travels*. He dismissed the Hudson's Bay Company as an irresponsible monopoly, and the Holland Company as merely a land speculation enterprise. In dealing with the Virginia Company, Finley paused to narrate John Smith's exploits and the convening at Jamestown of America's first representative assembly. But he reserved his greatest praise for the founders of the Massachusetts Bay Colony. These sturdy Puritans were only secondarily motivated by the desire for gain. What really sent them into the wilderness, Finley argued, was their determination to escape the tyranny of the Church of England. On the political side, the New England Puritans were also impelled by what Finley called "republican instincts," and the urge to practice "civil and religious liberty."

Some evidence is available on whether such scholarly work measured up to Johns Hopkins standards. In a confidential letter in 1889, President Gilman praised Finley's "good sense, vigor, devotion to a high standard of duty" and a number of other sterling personal qualities. Nothing was said about him as a scholar. A decade later Finley was appointed to a Princeton University professorship. He wrote to Baltimore informing Professor Herbert B. Adams that he would be teaching politics in Princeton. "You know, perhaps better than anyone else, how poorly equipped I am, technically, for giving instruction in this department." There is no record of a reply to this modest letter, but Adams did pass it on to Gilman, with a marginal note: "We ought to make him a Ph.D. on easy terms."

Gilman wrote back to Adams: "In regard to Finlay [*sic*], I second your motion. Can we not present some paper of his as a thesis [?]." But apparently his work was not good enough, for Finley never did earn a Ph.D., at Johns Hopkins or anywhere else (though honorary degrees came thick and fast in later years).

It is with irony and still a little bitterness that I read of these efforts to get Finley his Ph.D. "on easy terms." In my case tough terms of exceedingly dubious academic significance were offered: since the Ph.D. was awarded for completing (in addition to other requirements) a dissertation of "publishable quality," my adviser who rejected the Finley thesis told me that, if I could find a commercial publisher to issue the book, he would get me my doctor's degree. At the time I had no idea of how to deal with this offer. Later, after I gained some inside knowledge of the New York publishing world and of the wheeling and dealing that often facilitates the publication of a book, I had even less respect than before for the man who made the offer and the system that gave him power to do so. (I should add that the present publication of this book is the result of an independent, aboveboard later transaction, and has nothing to do with the deal suggested by my former graduate school adviser, since in the interim I won the doctorate with a book on another topic.)

When compared with his spectacular academic career at Knox College, John Finley's academic distinctions at Johns Hopkins University seem exceedingly modest. He was an inconspicuous spectator of the intellectual adventure of the Seminary of History and Politics. Despite previous fame as a college orator, Finley never became a member of the debating society founded by Woodrow Wilson, the "House of Commons." But Johns Hopkins was more than high-powered intellectual effort and (more-or-less) scholarly seminars; in other areas of university life, John Finley was an active participant.

Surprisingly, there was football. The interest in athletics was "unusually great" during the years Finley was at Johns Hopkins, and, although he was a graduate student, he competed in intercollegiate football against such schools as Saint Johns College, the University of Virginia, the U.S. Naval Academy, and Princeton. Finley was an energetic and athletic man all the rest of his long life, but football never became his profession. Other activities at Johns Hopkins link up more directly with his later professional interests in social work, education, and journalism.

There was a journalistic adjunct of the Seminary of History and Politics that became an obvious focus of interest for the young man from Illinois, determined on an editorial career. The seminary had access to recent newpapers, which were "cut to pieces for scientific purposes" by the students. Some of the "choicest extracts from a few leading papers," H. B. Adams wrote, "were placed on special bulletin boards." Other clippings were labeled and carefully filed away under such headings as socialism, communism, divorce, labor, journalism, railroads, strikes, unions. Seminary reports were based upon the clipping file. During 1887–89 this "Newspaper Bureau" was managed by the Finley brothers; earlier Albert Shaw had handled it. Students who do this work, Adams wrote in 1884, "are learning to be journalists and editors." Without professing to be a school of journalism, the seminary by 1899 had supplied five Johns Hopkins men "to become prominently identified with the leading monthlies." John and Robert Finley were among them.

In addition to the newspaper bureau, the university indirectly provided another journalistic opportunity for John Finley. He had proven to the faculty during his first weeks in Baltimore his ability to read proof. Two of the Johns Hopkins faculty, Richard T. Ely and Herbert B. Adams, were called to lecture at Chautauqua, New York, in the summer of 1888. A daily newspaper, the *Assembly-Herald,* was issued at Chautauqua, and Finley was brought along by Adams to read proof. "I spent a terrible summer [in 1888] at Chautauqua," Finley later remembered. There seemed to be a great deal of work and barely enough time to sleep.

But there was time for a little romantic activity. At the end of the summer Mattie Boyden was beginning a journey to Europe.

In going from Chicago to New York to take the boat [she wrote] I was to pass through Buffalo. John came to Buffalo [from] . . . Chautauqua to see me and knowing the stay was not long in Buffalo, he bought a ticket to Batavia [,] the next stop to the east. Evidently he was somewhat excited and at the gate in going to the train, he handed the gateman, instead of his ticket, a card photograph of me which he had in his pocket. The gateman jokingly handed it back saying, "The young lady might object." We had [Finley's future wife remembered] something over an hour together before the train reached Batavia and he had to leave. I think we both realized that our affection for each other was sure and steadfast, though there was no talk of an engagement.

Finley's second summer at Chautauqua, in 1889, may have been a little less hectic than the first. He must have occasionally wandered over to the great lecture tent in "the grove by the lake," especially when his former teachers were speaking. Richard T. Ely lectured on the labor problem and on social classes in the United States. Ely presented to the Chautauqua audiences an unflattering picture of class lines "becoming more inflexible and difficult to cross [and] America . . . becoming more like European countries." Furthermore Ely held that the attempt by those in the working class to rise out of that class was futile, and even a sin. Social classes in America must practice "co-existence" and cultivate harmonious relations. The obvious implication was that well-to-do people of good will should try to establish friendly relations with members of the working class and endeavor to improve the condition of the unfortunate. John Finley, as we shall see, was already involved with such schemes of social amelioration.

Chapter 7

Training in What Was Not Yet Called "Social Work"

Johns Hopkins, 1888–89

Vividly, I remember the precise moment when my own college experience coalesced into a firm career decision. CCNY Professor Aaron Noland, who taught a vibrant introductory world history course, was sitting somewhere on campus munching a sandwich. It was a year or so after I had attended his class, and he asked me what I planned to do. "What you're doing," I replied, impertinently. His eyes widened. "You mean eat a sandwich?" he replied. Of course he knew I was referring to what as a starry-eyed undergraduate I saw as the glories of the academic life. Noland encouraged this ambition and gave me a copy of his first published book with the inscription, "To the best student I ever had," on the fluleaf. It will be nice to reciprocate with an inscribed copy of this book.

If graduate school life at the pioneering Johns Hopkins University was not for everybody a preparation for heavy scholarship, it might offer to some the opportunity to express citizenly concerns and take beneficent action. In the case of young John Finley of Illinois, the Hopkins education, even short of a doctorate, could open doors to professional employment, as the next chapter will show. It was the fermenting field of charities and philanthropic reform that provided for many students at the new university in Baltimore a link between their academic studies, currents of civic action, and professionalism.

Philanthropy was becoming systematized in the late nineteenth century. Once thought of as the independent and exemplary benevolence of individuals who by their own efforts had attained opulence, and who expressed altruistic impulses by gifts of money, philanthropy was coming under public scrutiny. Andrew Carnegie, later a friend of Finley, did

59

as much as anyone to bring about the new attitude toward charitable giving. In his famous 1889 speech, "The Gospel of Wealth," Carnegie outlined the principles of rational, progressive philanthropy: charitable giving was a responsibility that devolved upon persons of great wealth, for by acquiring riches they also took on the burden of "stewards" for the general well-being of society and were therefore under the obligation to use their money wisely. This meant in such a way as not to increase misery in the long run by the scattering of alms to alleviate short-term distress. Carnegie's own meteoric rise from poor weaver's lad to industrial magnate demonstrated the dramatic social mobility possible in American society. Philanthropic aid should be dispensed, Carnegie thought, in such a way as to foster individual initiative and self-advancement; it should be done in accord with, and not opposed to, Darwinian notions of natural selection.

Carnegie was not alone in these conceptions. The development of a charitable program consistent with advanced notions of social evolution was well under way, both in England and the United States, when Carnegie announced his "Gospel of Wealth." Johns Hopkins was an active epicenter in this movement. Its first president, Daniel Coit Gilman, consecrated the school in 1876 to the task of "reaching out for a better state of society than now exists." In practice, this meant extensive involvement in the Charity Organization movement, an international movement that originated in England and was transplanted to the United States in the late 1870s. The Baltimore chapter of the Charity Organization Society was founded in 1881 by President Gilman and a group of local businessmen, and the concerns of this organization deeply penetrated the university work on social science.

As a fledgling graduate student, Finley could hardly escape these currents of concern and study. His fellow students in the Seminary of History and Politics were carrying out a comprehensive survey of contemporary philanthropic practices. Finley's own involvement in seminary work was almost exclusively confined to considerations of the social significance of various schemes of charitable reform. One winter evening he presented a paper on the famous English settlement house pioneer, Arnold Toynbee. A few weeks earlier, Finley took notes for the "Seminary Records" while another graduate student delivered a paper on socialism, which concluded that "the acceptance by Christian capitalists of a thoroughly righteous plan of co-operation would bridge the yawning chasm [between social classes] and destroy the foundation on which socialism is based." Such a philosophical attitude permeated the treatment of social questions at Johns Hopkins and carried over into the formative years of the profession of social work.

> When a college undergraduate, I took a part-time job as recreation aide at a neighborhood youth center in Westchester County. Under the impression at first that my tasks were confined to supervising Ping-Pong and knock-hockey, taking out and putting away equipment, I soon found that my supervisor, a social worker, expected a more arcane set of skills: manipulating group dynamics, aiding social adjustments, etc. Impressed with what was for me a novel approach to human interactions, I made a mental note to look some day into the origins of social work. That day came when I entered graduate school in history and began studying American social history. One of the products of that study was of course this very book.

Finley and his teacher, Richard T. Ely, carried out a survey of over twenty colleges and universities which showed how widespread in the 1880s was the Johns Hopkins commitment to education for social reform. Schools like Cornell, Michigan, Columbia, and Harvard were doing "good work" in such fields as sanitation, prevention of vice, public and private charities, the theory of property, and "higher education (as furnishing directive power of society)." The results of this survey, published in the *Christian Union* in November, 1888, revealed nothing less than a new academic field emerging—"social science." Finley and Ely defined this field as encompassing "the prevention of evil, the relief of misery and misfortune, and the uplifting of humanity."

Study and application of the principles of enlightened philanthropy were central to this conception of the new academic social science. The cities of late-nineteenth-century America, with their growing hordes of needy inhabitants, were social laboratories for scientific investigations of how to improve society. The Charity Organization movement, which President Gilman introduced to Johns Hopkins, represented itself as a key part of the larger campaign to regenerate society

and cure its ills by the application of scientific truths. The
nature of these truths, which eventually became the principles
of the new profession of social work, can be clearly gauged
from tracing Finley's own education in its principles.

Recently off the press when Finley arrived at the university
was Herbert B. Adams's "Notes on the Literature of
Charities," in the fifth series of Johns Hopkins University
Studies in Historical and Political Science. A casual biblio-
graphical survey of "some of the best and most available literature on charities," Adams's "Notes" suggested what the correct principles of charity were. Most essential was the idea
that philanthropy should *not promote* mendicancy and fraud.
Adams referred to the horrendous consequences when these
principles were violated, as when "twenty persons receiving
charity from one church in Baltimore were found by inquiry to
be all impostors." Overly liberal dispensation of material relief not only encourages fraud but leads the able-bodied poor
to pauperism. Men out of work are tempted by traditional
charitable agencies to follow the path of least resistance and
accept relief instead of seeking jobs. In order to avoid these
dangers of fraud and pauperism, relief ought to be given with
circumspection, and a variety of other means for the relief of
poverty ought to be applied. Johns Hopkins University was
active in the exploration of these questions and in the propaga-
tion of a set of answers about them that became the principles
of scientific philanthropy.

In his "Notes on the Literature of Charities" Adams referred
to "Dr. Richard T. Ely's admirable paper on the general principles of philanthropy, with respect to charities, [which]
should be read by every student." This paper, first appearing
in the Baltimore *Sun* (March 9, 1887), was read at Chautauqua
when Finley was there, and was widely reprinted. When he
began to edit a philanthropic journal himself in 1889, Finley
appreciatively quoted Ely's statement on the principles of
philanthropy in an early number.

To Ely, philanthrophy was an integral part of Christian
commitment. Piety is love of God "and the science which
deals with this part of the gospel is called theology. . . . Love
to man is philanthropy, and the science which deals with this

part of the gospel is called sociology." To act like Lady Bounti-
ful, distributing largesse to "pet paupers," is not philanthropy
but selfishness. Distributing free food and clothes is "a curse
instead of a blessing" to the poor. "Philanthropy," Ely argued,
"must be grounded in profound sociological studies. Otherwise, so complex is modern society that in our efforts to help
man, we may only injure him." Benefactions such as Enoch
Pratt's Free Library in Baltimore, or Andrew Carnegie's similar bequests, motivated by Christian stewardship, received
the seal of approved scientific philanthropy from Ely.

> The demonstration of the historical connection between the rise of
> social work and the new academic environment of late-nineteenth-
> century America remains one of my three modest contributions to
> scholarship thus far. (The other two are my documentary studies of
> Indochina and my exploration of early-nineteenth-century American
> radicalism.) Published in various journals between 1963 and 1975 (with
> one essay more on the topic yet to be completed), my essays on social
> work history have brought me inquiries from scholars in America and
> abroad, as well as invitations to lecture and teach. Why disguise the
> pleasure I take at this recognition, surely one of the more harmless ego
> satisfactions available to an academician teaching at a nonelite univer-
> sity?

The Johns Hopkins political economist's presentation of the
principles of the charities movement of the 1880s reveals how
closely was Christian motive tied to social science. A
nonegalitarian tone is also clearly evident. Ely did not advocate any redistribution of income. He accepted the stratified
society as given, and he urged that the wealthy and leisured
classes had an ethical and religious obligation to improve
(within limits) the quality of life among the poor. This meant
an elaborate program of interclass visiting, education, and
(where absolutely necessary) relief; and the universities were
assigned a major role in this movement.

At Johns Hopkins, the Seminary of History and Politics was
naturally a focus of interest in scientific philanthropy. At its
very first meeting (when it was called the History and Political
Science Club), a paper was presented on "Tramps, Their
Cause and Remedy." In the spring of 1887, a battery of graduate students explored various facets of charity. In January,
1888, settlement house work was brought to the attention of
the seminary by Stanton Coit of New York's pioneer

Neighborhood Guild. The next month, as we have seen, Finley read a paper by the English settlement house worker, Arnold Toynbee. But the settlement movement represented a different sort of philanthropic impulse than most of the other components of scientific charity. It was both more radical and less ideological than charity organization, and its relation to the development of professional social work was more indirect.

> Were I teaching in a university with a full doctoral program, I could train some advanced students in American history and set them to work on such problems as the relationship between the settlement house movement and the mainstream of Charity Organization. I have literally dozens of other such topics filed away in a folder labeled "student thesis topics." But I fear I shall never get the chance at the Polytechnic Institute where I now teach. Its doctoral programs are (thus far at least) limited to science and technology fields, and I generally teach only undergraduate students, who with occasional exceptions are not equipped or motivated to do advanced researches in American history. But I really ought not to complain, for I am at least spared the agony of training historical specialists who are sure to be unemployed after earning their degrees. Also, the Polytechnic Institute has been good to me—providing a congenial atmosphere for teaching and scholarship, an extraordinarily stimulating group of colleagues, and an environment of relative faculty autonomy and academic freedom.

At Johns Hopkins in the 1880s, the seminary was less important than the University Christian Association for the consideration of the theory and practice of scientific philanthropy. John Finley played an active role in this association, serving to set up "friendly visiting" committees under the association's auspices, which worked closely with the local COS. Saturday excursions to the leading charitable institutions in Baltimore—the almshouse, penitentiary, Little Sisters of the Poor, the COS office—were held. The "prying young [university] men," as H. B. Adams called them, also visited workingmen's clubs, primarily to deliver talks. Finley himself spoke on one occasion in early 1888 on the subject of contract labor "to an intelligent class of workingmen." The antiradical function of scientific philanthropy was barely veiled. Baltimore banker and charity organization enthusiast John Glenn wrote to President Gilman praising the philanthropic work of the Johns Hopkins "boys." By such soothing interclass communication, a healthy dose of Christian socialism is administered to the potentially unruly workers. This is, Glenn added, "the true antidote to political socialism."

> Social work, like other professional specialties, has an official, stylized history that describes the Noble Aims and Lofty Motives of the Founders. My own researches into the early history of American social work has revealed a more complex reality, including antiradicalism as a major factor, not only in the seedtime of the profession, but in later periods of the development of social work as well. In challenging the parochial orthodoxy of the Immaculate Conception of social work, I have often run afoul of social work educators who have objected to what they considered a jaundiced and hostile interpretation of the profession. In my essay "The Whig Interpretation of Social Welfare History," I fired a counterblast at orthodoxy. But I paid for this impertinence by dismissal as adjunct professor at various schools of social work, lest I corrupt the apprentices with my heterodoxy.

The university-sponsored excursions into the workingmen's districts of Baltimore were closely supervised. The students were carefully innoculated with charity organization doctrines so that sentimental or radical notions about the poor were expunged. Material relief was considered generally bad; poverty was seen as the result of individual shortcoming; the best way to rise out of poverty, therefore, was by individual self-help; that process could be accelerated by contact with the well to do. These were the orthodox principles that were to be verified by the Johns Hopkins students of philanthropy. Little contrary evidence was perceived; the "science" to which John Finley was exposed was far more deductive than inductive.

Members of the University Christian Association were especially energetic in the study and practice of scientific philanthropy in the winter of 1888. Supplementary to their excursions in Baltimore city, in which Finley participated, was a series of lectures by Amos G. Warner. Warner held a Johns Hopkins doctorate and was serving as general secretary of the Baltimore COS while he completed his graduate study. Subsequently, he held other responsible academic and philanthropic posts, and in 1894 he brought out the first edition of what became the standard exposition of the orthodox tenets of scientific philanthropy—his *American Charities*. Warner's task in 1888 was to provide a theoretical foundation for the activities of the University Christian Association. There is no record of the attendance at the lectures, but surely

Finley was among those who came to hear Warner outline the principles of scientific philanthropy. To be sure, Finley imbibed them from others too, but there is every reason to consider Warner a most potent source.

The lecture series dwelt on the reconciliation of political economy and philanthropy. Warner referred to the apparent opposition between charity, which expresses altruistic sentiments, and political economy, which stresses the legitimate primacy of self-interest. These can be reconciled, Warner argued, on firmer ground than the mere "philosophic subtlety which is supposed to prove that all human acts are necessarily inspired by self-interest." Any solid reconciliation would have to come from adoption of a common program. Such a program was available in scientific philanthropy. The practical convergence Warner championed was well described by Finley in 1889:

> The economist has come to a practical agreement with the philanthropist as to the means society should employ in lessening pauperism, though he has arrived at his conclusion from a totally different standpoint. "What is best for the individual is best for the state," the latter argues. "What is best for the state is best for the individual," the former contends.

The reconciliation was based upon joint acceptance of the doctrine that charity must be administered in accordance with the laws of social evolution.

The Spencerian notion of the struggle for survival permeated scientific philanthropy as taught at Johns Hopkins; life was seen as a basically competitive arena, although a nostalgic longing for cooperation was often heard at the university too. The role of philanthropy then, as Warner and others saw it, was to elevate the poor so that they might hold their own in the struggle of life. This was to be done first by organizing charity to eliminate indiscriminate almsgiving. The constant temptation that led to a weakening of the will to struggle among the poor would then be removed. Simultaneously, a great educational campaign should be mounted to instill in the poor the qualities necessary for survival—thrift, temperance, industry, etc. "The best charities," Warner significantly observed, "are educative charities."

Chapter 8

A First Professional Career:

Social Work, 1889–92

Social work must conjure up as many images as there are readers of these words—and more. There is the "reductionist" image, which ascribes to the social workers superhuman powers of understanding, the ability to reduce every human action to its underlying social stimulus. (Many contemporary social workers are not comfortable with this image and, despite the focus on "social" factors in their training, prefer to see themselves as psychologists or psychiatrists. But these latter professional groups generally close ranks against the upstart, low-prestige social workers.) Another image is the social worker as snooper, prying into the lives of clients while surreptitiously envying their looser, supposedly more erotic lives. (The social worker heroines in such films as Blume in Love *and* A Thousand Clowns *illustrate this.) John Finley began his professional career as a social worker before the field and its mottled reputation began to take shape. Yet, some of the outlines are dimly perceptible in the 1880s and '90s. Finley's early career therefore not only illuminates an aspect of the American professional universe in its gestation period, it also shows how a young man from the provinces "made it" in the late nineteenth century.*

By the end of the calendar year 1888, after fifteen months at the university, Finley had been fully initiated into the mysteries of scientific philanthropy. Scholarly research clearly did not interest him. He and his brother had come to the university to prepare for journalistic careers, but there seemed no such chance at the time. However, another opportunity did appear.

In December President Gilman received an inquiry from Louisa Lee Schuyler in New York City. Miss Schuyler, descendant of Alexander Hamilton, had founded and continued to be the dominant force behind the New York State Charities Aid Association, a group dedicated to the rational reform of the public charities of the Empire State.

I am trying [she wrote to Gilman] to find a very capable *gentleman Secretary* for the *State Charities Aid Association,* and I have thought you might possibly know someone who could fill the position and might like to have it.

It was not an easy job.

Good writing and good speaking are both required, as also good judgement, and real philanthropic interest in the work. . . . This winter we are especially engaged in trying to get improved Legislation for the Insane.

Miss Schuyler did not think that a job with her association need be thought of as a "step down" in the career of an ambitious young man. This might have been true "in the old dole-giving days," but with the advent of "the charities of today—the modern method," things were different. She was with the spirit of scientific philanthropy when she described the State Charities Aid Association as "more like a *Social Science Association,* which puts in practice its own opinions—be they legislative or otherwise."

In response to this request, Gilman brought Finley's name to the attention of Miss Schuyler, and on the tenth of January, 1889, Finley came to New York to meet with her, apparently at his own expense. Miss Schuyler and Mrs. William B. Rice interviewed the young man and "liked him very much." There was one difficulty: Finley had some agreement with Richard T. Ely that he stay on at Johns Hopkins until April. For his part Finley was "absolutely loyal to Professor Ely," and Ely "made . . . strong objections" to the departure of his student and research assistant. Perhaps through the intervention of Gilman, or the offering of a higher salary, Finley in February, 1889, became secretary of the New York State Charities Aid Association.

Since its founding in 1872, the association had concentrated its energies in the supervision of New York's public charities, specializing in the training of knowledgeable volunteer visitors to state and municipal institutions. In a series of State Charities Aid Association *Handbooks,* public-spirited citizens could discover what was the minimum legal temperature of a poorhouse (sixty-eight degrees), how a public institution ought to be disinfected, the correct arrangement of flues for proper hospital ventilation, and exactly whom to contact when tenement house laws were violated. As the Charity Organization Societies took upon themselves the burden of coordinating private charitable effort, this association assumed responsibility for introducing needed reforms into public charities.

In 1889 Finley became secretary of an organization supporting the full range of principles to which he had been exposed at Johns Hopkins. In arguing that "mendicancy has become a profession and the study of pauperism a science," Miss Schuyler was declaring her association's adherence to the tenets of scientific philanthropy. The long list of association publications included such classics of charity organization literature as Octavia Hill's *Homes of the London Poor*. Distinguished members of the London COS, such as Miss Hill herself, were "corresponding members" of the SCAA; and the association had a permanent representative in the New York City COS. The complementary work of the State Charities Aid Association reveals that scientific philanthropy was not quite synonymous with charity organization. Other sorts of charitable endeavor could also claim the mantle of "science."

When Finley was hired in early 1889, the association was engaged in its greatest effort to that date in molding public policy in the interests of scientific philanthropy. A crusade was under way to pass legislation guaranteeing reform in New York State's policies toward the insane, and twice before Miss Schuyler and her fellow reformers had failed to induce the New York legislature to endorse their program. In March, 1890, another attempt would be made.

The problem was one of getting the Albany politicians to adopt that form of public support of asylums that would be both humane and in accord with the latest psychiatric principles. New York state law had long before officially recognized that the insane were wards of the state. In 1836 and 1864, asylums to accommodate the growing numbers of insane were set up. By law, the counties were responsible for their own patients and were required to reimburse the state treasury for each one lodged in the state's six asylums. The insanity rate was rising rapidly all through the nineteenth century; by 1890 there were sixteen thousand so classified in New York State

alone. "Chronic" cases overflowed the crowded state hospitals
into local county poorhouses, where their plight was witnessed by trained State Charities Aid Association visitors. The
accounts and reports of these visitors were as grim as Dorothea
Dix's eloquent *Memorials* of forty years earlier on the same
subject. Writing in Albert Shaw's *Review of Reviews* in 1890,
Finley quoted a recent association report to illustrate the
sheer barbarity of the situation.

> Within a small room, in an old and dilapidated wooden building, suit-
> able only for an outbuilding, on a dark and wintry day, was found a
> demented old woman, apparently about seventy years of age. She was in
> a state of turbulent dementia, scantily clad, barefooted, exceedingly
> filthy, and unable to appreciate her condition or surroundings. She went
> about the narrow confines of her cell-like room, beating a spoon against
> the wall and uttering unintelligible cries. The furniture in the room
> consisted of a dilapidated bedstead, on which was a tick half-filled with
> wet and filthy straw, the quantity being insufficient to make a comfort-
> able bed, even if the material had been wholesome and clean. A young
> pauper girl, apparently about sixteen years of age, who brought the old
> woman food, said that the woman was left alone, there being no other
> occupant of the building except five or six filthy men patients who
> occupied the other rooms, and these without attendants either day or
> night, except a pauper who took them to a distant building to their meals.
>   In the women's ward of another [county] institution the scene pre-
> sented was that of a veritable bedlam. In this ward were found, indis-
> criminately huddled together, paupers, children, vagrants, and insane,
> all in a state of extreme disorder. One motherly-looking woman was
> discovered going about the place barefooted, with apparently nothing on
> but a skirt. . . .

The remedy for these horrible conditions was evident: "to
remove the dependent insane from the county poorhouses of
the State of New York and to place them under the medical
supervision of the State hospitals." There, the conditions for
humane treatment were present: sanitary, warm buildings,
with the different classes of patients separated from each
other, provision for rehabilitation, and constant attendance.
Here truly Finley found a worthy cause for which to battle.

> *A week or so before this chapter was drafted a powerful film about
> life in a mental hospital,* One Flew over the Cuckoo's Nest, *won a whole
> package of Academy Awards. Earlier I had read the Ken Kesey novel of
> the same title, which presents an even more compelling picture of life in
> a mental institution than the film. But even more powerful was the
> actual time spent at a state mental hospital where my wife was em-
> ployed as a social worker, and where I occasionally visited. My reaction
> to the patients was heavily conditioned by prior reading: not only the
> Kesey novel, but the psychiatric writings of Ronald Laing. In actual*

contact with mental patients, I found it difficult to accept Laing's near glorification of insanity; their pain and misery were just too palpably evident. Admittedly, these are not Deep Thoughts. There is much about the world of mental illness that I am ignorant of, and I probably will remain so.

Arrayed against the association was what the *New York Times* called the "more or less political influence at work in the counties." The position of the opponents of state care was largely reducible to the fact that it was cheaper to care for the indigent insane in a county poorhouse than to pay the state the going rate of $1.50 a week per patient.

The association's bill for compulsory state care for the insane was drafted by the most distinguished academician in the organization, Professor Theodore Dwight, dean of the Columbia University Law School. The bill aimed at abolishing the basis upon which the noxious system of county care had been erected: namely, that since a good number of patients are "chronically" insane, treatment in a state hospital would do no good. Realizing that the legal distinction between "chronic" and "acute" cases was being used as an inhumane "economy" measure, and that it had no foundation in pyschiatric practice, the State Charities Aid Association proposed to wipe it out. Then, better to facilitate the entrance of the insane into adequate institutions, New York State was divided into districts. Each state hospital was made responsible for the insane within its district. This skillfully drawn legislative proposal further authorized immediate erection of inexpensive but sturdy outbuildings on the grounds of existing state hospitals. These would accommodate the patients returned to humane and professional care from the veritable bedlams of the various county poorhouses.

In March, 1890, a delegation from the State Charities Aid Association journeyed to Albany to plead the cause of this state care bill. The exemplary lobby included a representative sampling of the sort of persons of stature and influence who had association membership. John Finley, the young secretary, was along, but it is unlikely that he was able to wield as much influence among the legislators as Miss Schuyler, or Columbia University professor Charles Chandler, who publicly testified for the measure.

*How many times now have I taken the bus to Albany to demonstrate
or lobby for this, that, or the other cause? Too many to count. Legislators seem ambivalent about our presence. Verbally they seem to be all
in favor of the exercize of such citizenly prerogatives as the right to
petition the government. But the actual presence of raucous clamoring
citizens in a legislative arena stimulates a hostile response from legislators; they would no doubt prefer to be influenced by smooth, professional lobbyists who infest the anterooms of state and national legislatures and, unlike the groups that I travel with, have expense accounts
for the "persuasion" of lawmakers.*

Precious victory was won when the bill, with bipartisan
support, passed the assembly sixty-nine to fifty and the state
senate twenty-one to six. Despite the opposition of some association members to his administration, Governor David B.
Hill signed it on April 15, and a gala celebration at New York
City's Chickering Hall marked this final triumph. Later that
year, at the American Social Science Association, President
Andrew D. White of Cornell announced that the passage of the
State Charities Aid Association's state care law was—

> a triumph of religion, morals and right reason, a blessed triumph over
> barbarism and greed, but it has been long in coming. It has been urged
> every year for nearly half a century in our state legislature. . . . Why
> this long delay? Simply because public opinion was not informed. No
> efficient body of men was [yet] trained to know the truth regarding the
> matter, therefore the people at large were completely in the dark.

In constituting just that sort of enlightened and "efficient body
of men [and women]" to awaken public opinion and precipi-
tate legislative action, the State Charities Aid Association secured a measure that "undoubtedly marked one of the great
milestones in the history of the treatment of mental illness in
the United States."

But the work of the association was not over once the legislative victory was won; it had only entered a new phase.
Continual supervision and inspection were necessary to ensure that the insane were indeed removed from the squalor of
the county poorhouses and that the cabins on the grounds of
state hospitals were adequate. In the pages of the association's
journal, Finley reminded his fellow reformers that the job of
overseeing the state's newly established system of treatment
for the insane fell legitimately to them. Government bureaucracies tend to lapse into mere routine. Official administration

of public charities must be complemented by the efforts of trained volunteers who "represent the public concern." These volunteers, said Finley, bring not only enthusiasm to their assumed tasks, but also leisurely application and "absence of perfunctory methods of observation"—qualities "essential to real reforms." Voluntary public service was to him also in accord with the American democratic spirit. In other countries (Germany, perhaps) government officials could be trusted to handle philanthropic work themselves; but here in the United States such "public affairs . . . are emphatically the business of all of us."

Finley's experience with the State Charities Aid Association strengthened his faith in the possibilities of voluntaristic reform. Over time, this faith would harden into dogma. Later, during the depression of the 1930s, the methods of voluntarism and individual treatment woven into the fabric of scientific philanthropy came under fire. Collectivist solutions were then advanced. Finley, still under the influence of doctrines he imbibed in the 1880s and '90s, would condemn the modest collectivism of the New Deal when he was editor of the *New York Times* in the 1930s. Not all social workers were flaming radicals, or remained so in the middle years of their lives.

The position that Finley took with the State Charities Aid Association brought him many duties besides lobbying for state care of the insane. He had to keep minutes of meetings, handle accounts, keep up with correspondence, make monthly reports, and organize visiting committees for "every institution of charity supported by public funds in the State of New York." To these considerable tasks Finley added his own pet project, which had its roots in his early ambitions and his Johns Hopkins experience—the establishment of a journal of scientific philanthropy.

The *State Charities Record,* although not "the first review on that subject in America", as Finley later claimed, was indeed an early effort to bring the doctrines of scientific philanthropy to bear on actual charitable practice. In the spring of 1889, Finley gained the agreement of his new endorsers that the State Charities Aid Association begin publication of a modest monthly of small circulation, originally directed mainly at "specialists" in philanthropy. It was hoped that the *State Charities Record* would increase its circulation and thereby "increase the number of 'specialists'" as well. The journal was of course intended to carry news of the association's work, but its young and ambitious editor believed that it could also serve as a vehicle for reformist notions of the new academic social science.

From the beginning, people at Johns Hopkins were involved in the enterprise. Upon conceiving his plans, Finley at once communicated them to Herbert B. Adams. The editorial venture was described, and Finley revealed that he intended something more than a house organ of the State Charities Aid Association; he wanted a review of theory and reform in philanthropy. But a limited budget was assigned to the *Record*, and Finley had to inquire of Adams whether "gratuitous contributions of papers" could be obtained from university men. A favorable reply was apparently gotten, and the first number appeared in October, 1889.

The columns of Finley's *Record* in actuality contained a dearth of material from outside contributors; only occasionally did an item from the Johns Hopkins historical seminary appear. The failure of repeated appeals to Adams in Baltimore to send articles or to get students to review books perhaps was due to the obscurity of the journal or inability of its editor to pay his contributors. Some of the Hopkins graduate students, even Rob Finley, were already placing their papers on social problems in more prominent periodicals. The opening pages of each number of the *Record* were reserved for the invited contributions on social science. But as in an earlier journalistic venture, the Knox College *Vocationist*, Finley was frequently obliged to fill out the columns of his publication with material from his own pen.

Although the participation of other Johns Hopkins men in the SCAA *Record* must have been disappointing to Finley, the doctrines he defended in the journal's pages were those very tenets of reformist social science that were transmitted to him during his university days. Charity workers, Finley wrote, may begin their investigations of social reality by ferreting out "impostors and frauds," but they are not merely detectives for the rich. They have a higher purpose as "discoverers whose object is to find the good, promote its development and make it contribute to the welfare of society." Their pursuit of the highest social aims entitles charity workers to lavish praise. They are as fully entitled to the accolade "philanthropists" as those who give their wealth to the poor. Through the joint efforts of charity workers and academic social scientists—

> there have been established certain principles which experience has proved should obtain in all giving. This knowledge thus collected, while not exact or full enough to give it the dignity of a science, is perhaps sufficient to warrant the use of the term "scientific charity. . . ."

The principles of scientific charity enabled their champions to distinguish correct from incorrect philanthropic practices; and in reviewing the periodical literature, Finley did not hesitate to attack what were considered pernicious measures or theories. When the British reformer Sidney Webb advanced the thesis (in the July, 1890, *Contemporary Review*) that relief to the poor should be given without any stigma attached to the unfortunate recipients, he was refuted. Finley, invoking orthodox tenets of scientific philanthropy, argued in the October *Record* that "this stigma, which industry attaches to indolence, is a safeguard to the public against the imposition of the idle and the vicious and a stimulus to exertion and thrift."

> *The conservatism of these early social workers, and of reformers generally who wish to bring about a kind of social peace and harmony, is extremely important (yet difficult) to grasp. Americans seem addicted to what I call the "incremental illusion"—the notion that reform piled upon reform will someday add up to some fundamental social change in the direction of justice and equality. This is, I am convinced, an illusion. Reforms can sometimes strengthen entrenched ruling classes who see the need for minimal concessions in the interests of social harmony and the stability of their own rule. Despite this sober outlook, the necessity for popular struggle on behalf of reform cannot be denied without slipping into arid political sectarianism, and the left in America has too long been plagued by this self-inflicted disease of sectarianism.*

The principles of scientific philanthropy included large doses of middle-class morality, which were hard to square with the scientific pretensions of the movement. On certain issues charity workers would demand that punishment and treatment be clearly distinguished: that the insane, for example, be not punished as the criminal; that various forms of criminality be not lumped together; that dependent children, whatever the cause of their dependency, receive separate treatment from adults. One of the key principles of scientific philanthropy (and one particularly stressed by the State Charities Aid Association) was, as Finley put it: "Classification, all down the line." But a judicious blurring of the line between poverty and crime, alien in spirit to the scientific concept of classification, was considered wholesome. Finley himself argued that the poor should not be made to feel quite like criminals, yet he insisted that some stigma of moral inferiority be maintained. Clearly this ambiguity is the expression of a profession in transition between its role as protector of the rich and the long-deferred discovery of its own professional goal.

Despite uncertainty in its sense of direction, the developing profession of social work continued in the 1890s to produce fresh journalistic projects. Perhaps the most significant of these was the appearance in 1891 of the *Charities Review,* which styled itself "A Journal of Practical Sociology." The *Charities Review* was the official organ of the New York City Charity Organization Society, an organization that was housed in the same "stately residence" as the State Charities Aid Association. Patrician COS president Robert W. DeForest, after observing John Finley's "journalistic predilections" asked the editor of the *State Charities Record* to handle the new monthly as well.

Backed by DeForest's ample funds, Finley realized many of his editorial objectives in the new publication. He was able to obtain contributions from outside experts on reformist social science and was not obliged to fill the *Review* with products of his own pen. Its first number opened with a general definition of charity organization by DeForest. Restating the standard notions of scientific philanthropy, the *Review*'s patron concluded that it was both love and science. There were also excerpts from a Johns Hopkins study on Arnold Toynbee, forwarded to Finley by Herbert Adams. Albert Shaw, an energetic Johns Hopkins graduate, contributed an article on municipal lodging houses to the initial issue of the *Charities Review.*

Subsequent numbers also included articles by academic

spokesmen for the doctrines of scientific philanthropy, or allied notions. Finley's old teacher, Jeremiah Jenks, was represented in December by "A Word to Trades-Unions." (The word was a warning to avoid radicalism and strikes and rather to strive to increase efficiency of work.) Amos Warner wrote on "Free Education and Free Food," arguing that the former is praiseworthy while the latter is debilitating and dangerous to its recipients. Besides Warner, many others exposed to the unique combination of academic interest and philanthropic motive in Baltimore during the 1880s and '90s contributed to the *Charities Review* under Finley's editorship. Among the other Johns Hopkins contributors were Herbert Adams, John Rogers Commons, William Henry Welch (of the medical school), and Jefferey R. Brackett.

As editor of pioneering philanthropic journals, Finley had notable success. Editing both the *Charities Review* and the *State Charities Record* during 1891–92 was an immense accomplishment. It is likely that reports of his huge energies in behalf of scientific philanthropy explain the repeated offers of an academic chair at Stanford University. Finley rejected these offers finally when, in the spring of 1892, as we shall see, he was called to the presidency of Knox College. This new position of course obliged him to sever ties with the State Charities Aid Association and drop the editorship of the *Record*. But he continued to edit the *Charities Review* from Galesburg, Illinois, until 1897.

Finley brought his interest in scientific philanthropy back to Galesburg with him. In June of 1890 he delivered the Master's Oration at Knox College. The text of this oration apparently has not survived, but the college newspaper, *Coup d'Etat* (which Finley edited a half decade earlier), summed up Galesburg opinion on this promising recent graduate.

> It was with considerable interest that the audience awaited [*sic*] to see what the East had done for John Finley. The oration was in the line of his professional work, and was an exposition of the great laws that underlie the great science of sociology, and was spoken in a manner so direct and unaffected as to lead the audience to forget it was oratory, and listen as though to an accomplished conversationalist. The general verdict was that the speaker had found the secret of real oratory, and that he had indeed reduced his life work to a science.

And after 1892, when he was selected as president of the

college, Finley continued to advance the science of charity in a series of articles written in Galesburg and printed in prominent national periodicals.

But as time passed there, and his presidential duties mounted, Finley's interest in scientific philanthropy seemed to wane. This may also have been due to the lack of recognition accorded him for having guided the *Charities Review* through its infancy. Finley's editorship was rarely acknowledged publicly. His name did not appear on the masthead until March, 1896. At any moment Robert DeForest might decide to abandon support of the *Review*. Any one of these reasons might be sufficient to explain why, in 1897, Finley ceased his connection with the *Charities Review*.

This brought to an end a phase in John Finley's career. With the exception of one more journalistic adventure (to be narrated in a subsequent chapter), his professional efforts were for the next quarter of a century to be manifested in the field of education. Only much later, in 1921, did he return to journalism, as editor of the *New York Times*.

The impact of graduate training at Johns Hopkins and the beginnings of a professional career in social work were not obliterated by Finley's educational cares. Indeed, in an age of transition when clergymen were no longer suited to monopolize the office of college president in the United States, such experience as Finley had might be thought appropriate for that position. The training in social science was, as we have seen, practically an initiation into the social gospel. His work in the broad area of scientific philanthropy provided an exercise in responsible administration. By the last decade of the nineteenth century, then, John Finley was ready to continue to ascend the ladder of respectable professional success.

Book 3.
Return to the Prairie

Chapter 9

A Young Man's Mission:

Assuming the Presidency of Knox College,

1892–93

This episode in Finley's life, symbolized by Plate 4 (Newton Bate-man solemnly handing on the Knox tradition to his former student and successor), is a case study in discipleship and continuity. How different in my case. As an undergraduate radical at CCNY, I was persona non grata to the conservative professors and administrators, and when I returned there to teach two years after graduation (thanks to the invitation of maverick senior faculty), I was marked for careful surveillance, and eventual dismissal.

In 1889 John Finley left Johns Hopkins University to accept a position with the State Charities Aid Association of New York. Martha Boyden at that time was spending "a wonderful year in Europe." When she returned to the United States in the fall, Finley met her ship at its New York pier, and they spent a few hours together before the train took her to Chicago. Martha saw him again when in June, 1890, he delivered the Master's Oration at the Knox College commencement exercises. At that time he visited with the Boyden family in Sheffield, Illinois, and the two young people probably became engaged.

The Boydens were a well-to-do and closely knit family. There were four brothers, an ailing mother, and a prosperous banker father. Martha's father, a hard-headed, practical businessman, professed to be a little amused by what he saw as John Finley's idealism, "but they respected and liked each other." The Boyden household, into which he was warmly accepted, substituted for the family ties that Finley lacked. The ailing Mrs. Boyden in particular was his "devoted admirer," and Martha's brothers would become close friends. As

time passed, Grand Ridge, "a pretty sad and hard-worked
place for him after his mother's death," receded in importance. John Finley continued to be extraordinarily close to his
brother until Rob's death in 1897. He remained also the admired brother and confidant of his sisters, but he hardly ever
"spoke of his father, who," in the words of a grandson, "may
have gone somewhat downhill with his second marriage."

John Finley's own marriage to Martha Boyden was delayed
because of the illness of Mrs. Boyden. But in the spring of
1892 Finley was called to the presidency of his alma mater,
Knox College; and with Sheffield and Galesburg so close together, Martha could marry and still be close to her family.
The ceremony took place at the home of the bride on June 29,
1892. Of Finley's family, only his father and one of his sisters
attended. With a $1,000 check from the banker father-in-law,
the young couple left for the West. Finley had been appointed
delegate to the National Conference of Charities and Correction, representing the New York State Charities Aid Association. The conference was held that year in Denver, a city that
briefly served also as the newlyweds' honeymoon site. Returning soon to Illinois, Martha remained with her family while
her husband, engaged with college work in Galesburg, came
up to Sheffield on the weekends.

Knox College constituted a formidable challenge to the
twenty-eight-year-old newly married president. He did not
seek the position, and he later claimed to have accepted this
diversion from his journalistic ambition only out of a sense of
obligation to his alma mater. In addition to this lack of original
interest in an academic career, Finley had the further disabil-
ity of his youth, which made it unlikely that he could preside
over Knox College in the manner of an old-time college president. Yet the trustees who "caught him young" hoped for
"blessed results" from his administration. They were "simply
charmed with Mr. Finley's manly bearing and eloquence."
Soon afterward he was authoritatively described as "a thinker,
a worker, an orator, a man of good personal appearance, and
yet modest withal." Professor George Churchill, well into his
fifth decade of teaching in Galesburg, expressed belief "that in

five years . . . [Finley] will stand in such a position that any
college in the land would be proud to have him as president."

The young man's attractiveness as a presidential candidate
can be partly explained by what the trustees considered his
manifest success in the East. Galesburg folk were much impressed with Herbert Baxter Adams's appraisal. "[Finley] is
too valuable a man to be shut up within college walls. His
place," declared the Johns Hopkins professor, "is in a large
city where the people can get the full benefit of his administrative ability." Despite his youth, he already seemed "possessed of those principles and ideas which insure success"
and thus in his own person demonstrated the validity of Knox
College's educational goals.

Success was not an abstract goal; it was a specific achievement. Knox College hoped to prosper from the particular form
John Finley's success took. Student journalists in Galesburg
were frank:

> The election of Mr. Finley . . . will be favorable to the best interests of
> the school. Mr. Finley has a wide acquaintance with moneyed men, the
> class of men who have means and are willing to use them in a good
> cause. His official position [with the State Charities Aid Association] has
> brought him personally in contact with such. No one can deny that what
> Knox needs most is money and a good deal of it too.

George Churchill also noted Finley's promising acquaintance
with "many of New York City's best and wealthiest men."

If Finley's success and his contacts formed one reason for
calling him to Galesburg, there was another, less clearly ar-
ticulated one. American education, in response to changes in
the society, was undergoing a transformation in the late
nineteenth century. Universities had appeared, in fact as well
as in name, and their appearance was accompanied by a quick-
ening of intellectual life that may have amounted to a second
American Enlightenment. Widespread dissatisfaction with the
old-time college was evident, even in Galesburg. In September, 1891, a faculty committee had urged extensive change
in the college. New laboratories for physics and chemistry
were called for, along with a new fireproof library, an endowed chair of modern languages, and "an increase in the

general funds" to be used for higher salaries. A report to the
trustees, also in the year before Finley assumed the presidency, pointed out "the necessity of the election of a Professor
of Political and Social Science." The students too realized that
Knox College must change.

> We must be able to say to the student who desires a year's work in
> Sociology or Political Economy: "You can find it here. . . ." To the
> student who desires to take a Scientific Course: "Here are all the neces-
> sary appliances, laboratories, microscopes, etc., which are necessary to
> . . . a thorough course."

Thus, John Finley, recently in touch with the most advanced reaches of American higher education at Johns Hopkins, and in contact with potential college benefactors, was
welcomed back to Galesburg. A representative of "the progressive spirit of the age," Finley was evidently thought capable of translating the inchoate, uncoordinated desires for
change into specific educational objectives and policies. But
neither was anyone wanted for the presidency who would
lead any rebellion against Knox College tradition. It was a
matter of satisfaction that a recent alumnus "thoroughly in
sympathy with the existing order of things" was chosen. It was
believed that Finley would maintain the principles for which
Newton Bateman had labored. "These same principles," said
the *Coup d'Etat*, "thoroughly inculcated . . . in the person of
one of the most promising of his students may abide with us
for many years to come."

> *The return of a "favorite son" to the place of his early nurture and
> success is a ritual of modern life that demands the skill of a novelist to
> delineate. In Finley's case it was a triumphal reappearance, but often
> the ritual displays ambiguous elements. Teachers who were enthusias-
> tic about aiding the early unfolding of some budding talent or ability
> may be unable to deal with the competition of a returning "favorite
> son." What was once a relation of master to apprentice sometimes sours
> when it is threatened by the specter of equality. In an academic envi-
> ronment, as I learned bitterly, returning as a colleague among one's
> former teachers can be a disappointing and frustrating experience. If it
> happens to be a "favorite daughter" who participates in the ritual of
> return, there is even more opportunity for bitterness and disillusion-
> ment.*

John Finley's formal election to the presidency of Knox
College, with a substantial salary of $3,000 a year, came about
by action of the board of trustees on March 22, 1892. This

action was not primarily prompted by any burning interest of Galesburg in the schemes of university training being worked out by Daniel C. Gilman in Baltimore, or Charles W. Eliot in Cambridge. It is true that there was a prevailing opinion that the time for modernizing Knox College had come. Newton Bateman, seventy years old, could not do it; his twenty-eight-year-old, university-educated successor might. It is significant to note that Finley's training in social science was thought an appropriate preparation for the post of college president, which was once in America almost the exclusive domain of clergymen. It has already been suggested that science, even as fostered at Johns Hopkins University, was not very far removed from Christian commitment. Whatever changes were to be introduced at Knox College, it was clear that the traditional dedication to Christian piety must not be disturbed. Finley's own piety allowed no doubts on his sympathy with the religious tradition of the college. His intellect and energy had been but recently recognized in Galesburg, and verified in the East. His involvement with philanthropists might help Knox College carry the financial burdens resulting from any enlargement of its educational program.

During his first presidential year (1892–93), Finley was technically on leave to raise money for the college. He did not get the opportunity to deliver an inaugural address until commencement time in 1893. In June of that year, to "a large and enthusiastic audience" in the college auditorium, he made a speech that was shrewdly balanced in its emphasis on continuity with Knox's past as well as on the need for modernization. He began in ornate oratorical style that was a departure from the style that had won him forensic distinction in his college days.

With his former teachers and some of the very founders of the college on the stage with him, Finley opened his inaugural address with a reference to the religious origins of Knox College. He hoped that his name would be "not unworthily associated" with those of his pious predecessors. He solemnly pledged "here in the presence of her trustees, her teachers, her sons and daughters, her friends" his "constant devotion" to his alma mater.

To her I give as hostage with my pledge, that confidence shown by the
Trustees in calling me to this work, and I shall strive as earnestly to keep
it as would a father to save the life of his child, given as surety for his
promise. To assist the Trustees in performing the duties of high trust
committed to them, to be a helpful associate to the teachers who share
with me this duty, to seek with the students, like knights of old, the Holy
Grail, not o'er mere and mountain, but by pure and noble lives in yonder
[college] walls; this shall be my constant effort.

After offering rhetorically what sounded like an undated
letter of resignation to the trustees, Finley moved into the
substance of his talk. Having made it clear that Knox would
continue to be a Christian college, he nevertheless suggested
that the social problems of the day demanded fresh educational approaches. The generation then being trained in the
colleges would have to handle "the chronic evils of old and
crowded countries . . . , [which, Finley predicted] will be felt
in this Nation within thirty years." Only that much time left to
educate a generation to proper ideals before the "vessel of
State" is swamped by "ignorant charity, ignorant zeal and
ignorant theology."

> Here is one of the few moments in Finley's life when he voiced the
> xenophobic nativism that was current in his social stratum in the era of
> mass immigration. To WASP Americans in the 1890s, and for decades
> afterward, the appearance on these shores of Catholic, Jewish, and
> other polyglot groups seemed to threaten the hegemony of formerly
> dominant classes. Later in his educational career, Finley would partici-
> pate in Americanization efforts aimed at supplanting "ignorance" with
> acceptance of a homogeneous American creed.

What were these ideals, and how could Knox College best
promote them? Finley did not believe that mere "technical
knowledge of trade and profession" was adequate. In order to
master the problems of the new age, the college graduate must
be "possessed of a heart that loves the right, and equipped
with a mind trained to apprehend the truth." Truth and righteousness; it was not considered necessary to define more
precisely these educational ideals. How best to pursue them
was a matter that had to be explored.

Such problems as immigration, sanitation, industrial consolidation, pauperism, charity, and street lighting put a great
strain on the old-time college. Finley observed that its traditional curriculum would have to be augmented by more
substantial work in natural and especially social science. But

he did not propose to plant a university in Galesburg. Colleges have a function all their own, he said: to foster "*manhood*—a word that suggests symmetry of development, nobility of purpose, [and] purity of character." Universities foster "*scholarship*—the application of manhood's powers to the getting and giving of truth." In so distinguishing between the complementary functions of college and university, Finley was voicing conventional notions. But when he talked about specific desirable changes, he could not maintain the nice distinction between college and university work.

How was a college to develop "manhood" without giving at least a preliminary test of the powers "to get and give" truth? Finley did not say. Instead he called for a large dose of university-type training at Knox College. Departing in his inaugural from the old-fashioned "faculty psychology" of Newton Bateman (who was sitting nearby on the platform), Finley spoke in favor of specialized study. "Mastery of one subject," he argued, "should be the chief object of a college curriculum;" such study would not only be applicable "to discover[y of] truth in other fields," it would also help mold character.

Finley concluded with a plea for cooperation between college and university, for extension lectures to the Galesburg public, for better facilities and more teachers at Knox College. And he ended on a characteristic inspirational note, accepting the office vacated by Newton Bateman, and discerning a "brighter light" in the distance: a light that represented to Finley "God's promise" for him and for the college he served as president.

Chapter 10

Problems of a Prairie College
in the 1890s:

Depression Times and
Academic Showmanship

The conjunction of educational effort with economic dislocation, characteristic of the 1890s, is also a pervasive phenomenon in contemporary America. Bright young men and women, who would a few years ago have held academic and professional posts, are now experiencing downward social mobility, while their early educational and intellectual interests atrophy. Learned young men and women now drive taxicabs in New York City.

According to Harold Stoke's standard work, *The American College President* (1959), the task of this chief academic official is to discover the inner purpose of his institution and to state the common cause so convincingly that all concerned will endorse it and enlist their energies in its behalf. This is what Finley tried to do in his inaugural address and often thereafter during the 1890s. The purpose to which he dedicated Knox College was that of bringing the institution abreast of the modern age without abandoning the core of pious commitment of the past.

To realize these goals, money was necessary, and fund raising was Finley's most serious problem during the eight years he held the presidency of Knox College. Part of the financial challenge he had to face was posed by a highly conditional bequest. In 1889 Daniel K. Pearsons, a Chicago physician, real estate operator, and philanthropist, communicated to the Knox trustees his intention to make a bequest to the college. Fifty thousand dollars worth of Chicago property was promised for a "Professorship of Latin, or some other [language?]," and a loan fund for "poor and worthy students at the rate of one hundred

89

dollars a year during the regular classical course of four years at three per cent interest annually." There were some initial conditions: two-thirds of the board of trustees were required to "be members of some Evangelical church or churches," and the largest single denomination represented on the board was to be the Presbyterian Church of the United States of America.

Pearsons publicly made his proposal at the Knox College Alumni Reunion ceremonies in 1892. At that time the crusty benefactor proffered the $50,000 if Knox could match it with another $200,000 within two years, and if the college "behave[d] herself" during the interim. Pearsons's motivations in making such bequests were clear. "I long ago made up my mind that I could not carry a cent out of this world with me," he said. Therefore he "determined to see for myself where the money was going. I believe in a man's being his own executor." In colleges of proven piety, his fortune could be considered safe ("no court can take [it] away from me") and wisely invested: "[I] have seen a great deal of fruit from it already and expect to see a great deal more during my life, and am sure it will go on bearing fruit for ages to come." Pearsons could have said of Knox, as he said of another target of his generosity, Beloit College:

> I give . . . because its past history indicates that the institution is to be perpetual. The college has always taught a pure faith and never diluted it with higher or lower criticism. I give . . . because [the college also] believes in poor boys, who are going to make the great men of the future.

Pearsons's self-proclaimed aim was not to work off some anxiety or guilt with his bequests, but to perpetuate piety and subsidize social mobility. Knox College under John Finley was a good choice for a donor so motivated.

The new president's training in social science at Johns Hopkins did not enable him to foresee the depression that would arrive soon after he returned to Galesburg. General economic conditions made it difficult, not only to raise money under the conditions set by donor Pearsons, but even to meet the running expenses of the college. During the decade Finley labored at Knox College, income declined as expenses and student enrollment increased. The result was a perennial deficit that began to reach alarming proportions by 1898. Table 2, drawn from the Knox College treasurer's journal, reveals the extent of the financial crisis.

One of the first casualties of the mounting economic crisis was Finley's grandiose plan for a foreign tour. A Galesburg newspaper reported that he had planned to travel abroad to "study university methods and probably take a degree in some great European university." But under a sixteen-thousand-dollar deficit, Knox College needed to keep its president at home. After a year of work, Finley was trying unsuccessfully to meet the conditions of Pearsons's bequest. "The times are rather unpropitious," he explained to the trustees in June of 1893. Foreign degrees were out of the question, and Finley had to settle for native products. His first, an honorary LL.D. , was awarded by Park College, Parkville, Missouri, in 1897. He would accumulate no less than thirty-one more honorary degrees in the course of his long lifetime.

After two years of strenuous but disappointing soliciting, it was clear that nothing like the necessary $200,000 could be raised. Pearsons then agreed to split his bequest: to give $25,000 in cash on July 1, 1895, if the first $100,000 was raised by then, and the second $25,000 a year later, if the second $100,000 had been obtained. The benefactor was, happily, inclined to be flexible on these deadlines, for a couple of weeks after the first one had passed, Finley was able to report that he had obtained pledges amounting to $100,000, so that the donor's revised conditions were "certain to be met." Although the actual amount of cash needed was not in fact raised in the required time, the president nevertheless enjoyed the trustees' commendation "for his splendid and successful efforts."

As the financial situation worsened, Finley's efforts to raise money increased. An opportunity presented itself in 1894. Therese Bentzon, a French writer studying the problems of women in America, had come to Galesburg to study Knox College's coeducational system at first hand. In the *Revue des Deux Mondes*, she wrote warmly of the college and its gentle influences upon the manners of the town. Mme. Bentzon marveled over the success "of the very young president of Knox" and expressed Gallic surprise that "love does not distract [the students] from school work." The very highest authority, President John Finley and his young wife, stamped coeducation with their official approval; "we . . . can say no harm of it," admitted Martha Finley, "since we met and loved at [Knox] College."

A substantial portion of this laudatory article in translation appeared in the soon-to-become-famous *Magazine* of trustee S. S. McClure. McClure offered to furnish copies of the article to serve as a fund-raising brochure. Finley prepared a covering letter, which glowingly described the advantages of Knox College.

> It has a good equipment for academic work, a strong corps of teachers and a large body of earnest students. The moral atmosphere of the college is wholesome, the association of teacher with student close, the standard of morals high, the discipline conducive to the development of self control in the students.

The income of the college the next year rose slightly, perhaps because of funds brought in by this brochure. But despite a severe cut in building and maintenance expenditures, the deficit continued to rise. By the end of the 1896 academic year, the situation had deteriorated even further, instructors were let go, and the budget was cut. The board of trustees regretted this action, also recognizing that only in part had it "relieved the situation, and that heroic measures must still be taken to relieve the College from its financial paralysis." A 10 percent faculty salary reduction was planned, but the trustees rejected the suggestion that it be voluntary. Some months later the trustees themselves, on S. S. McClure's suggestion, contributed to a five-thousand-dollar "safety fund" to help ensure the solvency of Knox College. At the same time it was "deemed inadvisable" to raise tuition charges.

It was in the midst of this financial turmoil that the promised transfer of property under Daniel Pearsons's bequest was made. Interest income amounted to about three thousand dollars each year for 1896 and 1897. But in 1898 the situation continued to worsen, and it became necessary to dip into the capital of the Pearsons Fund to meet current college expenses. Interest payments from this source consequently dropped to seventeen-hundred-dollars in 1899. Income from farm property owned by the college in Iowa and Kansas also showed a marked decline during the decade, and some of this land was sold. Property in the town of Galesburg owned by Knox was leased under a restrictive clause from the early pious days: no liquor could be sold there. But when storekeepers who held such leases demanded permission to sell drink, the trustees relented, even though Knox College participated officially in local temperance activity.

John Finley was an active and energetic president of Knox College, but part of the hope cherished for his presidency—great addition to the endowment—was not realized. Conditions improved somewhat near the end of the decade, and in 1898 Finley hoped to raise fifty thousand dollars. But much of this money was apparently earmarked to make up depletions of the capital fund. Although "cultivating the stony endowment field" (as one trustee put it) had become a bit easier, the young president nevertheless left Knox College in a financial situation worse than the one he found upon entering the duties of president in 1892. A lingering sense of guilt over this was perhaps what drove Finley to fund raising in behalf of his alma mater long after he had left Galesburg.

In light of the financial problems that beset Knox College in the 1890s, it is surprising that its young president, John Finley, accomplished so much. One reason was his cultivation of academic pomp and pageantry, which could bring a college glory and fame with relatively little expense. In fact, what meager reputation Finley has in the annals of American higher education is—as Frederick Rudolph put it in his standard history, *The American College and University* (1962)—as "one of the greatest showmen in the . . . academic world."

There seems to have been little practice of academic ceremony under Finley's predecessors as president of Knox College. It may have been under Daniel Coit Gilman at Johns Hopkins that Finley first grasped the possibilities implicit in academic celebrations. He no doubt attended the impressive Commemoration Day ceremony staged by president Gilman in February, 1888; solemn processions and dignified addresses on the noble pursuit of knowledge were featured. "Such entertainments," Gilman observed in his 1906 *Sheaf of*

Remembrances, "produce a strong impression. . . , for in a very striking manner these gatherings show the brotherhood of man and the cooperation of scholars in the advancement of knowledge." These "entertainments" also fitted into Gilman's program of building favorable community relations in Baltimore. Finley may not have wanted primarily to demonstrate advancement of knowledge in Galesburg, although he certainly did grasp the public relations function of academic ceremonies. And he also saw their usefulness in serving his other purposes as president of Knox College.

What gives an academic institution distinction? From his Johns Hopkins experience Finley learned what was necessary to make a *university* great: highly motivated students gathered around distinguished scholars. Within the limitations imposed by the financial situation and Knox's pious orientation, Finley in his recruitment policy did try to build a strong faculty, as we shall see. But these limitations, and others, stood in the way of creating a major center of learning in provincial Galesburg. To raise up a *college* to distinction called for different things, such as outpourings of sentiment and tradition; Finley saw that these could be supplied by frequent and appropriate ceremonies.

The first and most significant application of this insight came in 1894, when Knox College marked the anniversary of its founding over a half century before. The new president somehow discovered that February 15 was the date in 1837 when the Illinois legislature (which then included Abraham Lincoln) issued a charter to a delegation of Galesburg worthies who had come to Vandalia to incorporate the coeducational manual labor college. Knox College had not taken official notice of this event until Finley, with the hearty approval of the many surviving Galesburg patriarchs and matriarchs, sponsored a birthday celebration of the founding "here on the prairie of a Christian institution of learning . . . [around which] the town was planted."

College classes were suspended on the day of the ceremonies. In the morning at the Old First (Congregationalist) Church, historical orations were presented, most of which honored in a pious spirit what Finley called the "good old days."

The Church [a local newspaper reported] was packed. The students were there with their old gold and royal purple [Knox] colors prominently displayed. Old gray-headed graduates were there with their hearts filled with the enthusiasm of other days. Boys and girls were there with their mind's eye on the Knox College diploma as the pinnacle of earthly ambition. The faculty was there and the speakers were all there, each loaded to the muzzle with a speech.

Old grads, descendants of the original founders, and aged faculty reverently vied in reviewing the familiar chronicle of the settlement of town and college. Other speakers insisted in an often-repeated note that Knox College maintain its original fidelity to *Christo et Ecclesiae,* even if Harvard and Yale had abandoned the struggle. A Johns Hopkins classmate of Finley, Professor Albion W. Small, was invited to come down from "the great university [of Chicago] on the lake shore" to assure the audience that (in Finley's words) "the lean and hungry universities" did not intend to devour the fat and innocent colleges.

The afternoon was given over to a musicale, rich in hymns, under the auspices of the Knox College Conservatory of Music. And in the evening at the Presbyterian Church, the audience gathered again to hear the formal address that climaxed the entire commemoration. Introduced by eminent alumnus Clark E. Carr, Col. George R. Peck delivered an appropriately inspirational culminating speech, "The Kingdom of Light." Peck was described to the Galesburg folk as a paragon who had "refused a United States senatorship and flung away political ambition in order to be nearer the people." He enjoyed the precious proximity to the "people" from the position of general solicitor to the Santa Fe railroad, a job which presumably offered other benefits as well.

Peck's speech itself, including the same sort of themes that John Finley often aired, was a good example of the way in which even the small radical potential in higher learning was effectively blunted. He opened with a ritual denunciation of "commercialism," a vice that somehow flourished more or less independently of American business civilization. Peck urged Knox College students to consecrate themselves to some higher function than worldly success. "The Kingdom of Light" was that Platonic vision by which higher education was, in Peck's view, to redeem a society otherwise given over to a carnival of commercialism. Needless to say, no immediate reform was contemplated; just let the scholars work on while the men of affairs enjoy their "dream of domination." Later on, in "the nineteenth century, or the next one," the sheer presence of college-trained devotees of "Light" would tip the scales in the direction of reform, which would cleanse society of the taint of commercialism. This pleasing inevitability would be but an illustration, Peck declared, of "the law of the universe that all things must serve the silent but imperious power of thought."

> The invocation of "the silent but imperious power of thought" by a railroad lawyer in 1894 is example of how the materialist apologists for capitalism make sophisticated use of philosophically idealist notions to mystify and confuse their radical opponents. Sadly, I must conclude that these mystifying efforts have had great success in hindering the development of a mature left in America. It is unfortunately easier to envisage a transformation of consciousness as preceding a beneficent change in society than it is to contemplate a lengthy, complex struggle toward such an end. Too many leftists have pursued the chimera of consciousness transforming, forgetting the sensible admonition of Marx: "Life is not determined by consciousness, but consciousness by life."

Thus the audience at the Knox College Founders' Day Commemoration was assured that, although conditions were far from perfect, regeneration was bound to come; and happily it was to come through such institutions as that very college. Messages such as these reflected a favorable image of Knox College, and of the young president who staged such academic ceremonies.

Besides the initiation of a Founders' Day, John Finley seized other opportunities to demonstrate his academic showmanship. The centennial of the birth of William Cullen Bryant in 1894 was another such occasion. Finley planned to celebrate the event "with appropriate exercises." The student paper commended the president "to whom all the credit for this excellent program is due." Finley had "spent no little time and labor in making . . . [the] celebration a success and a red-letter day in the history of Knox." In far-off New York, pleasant surprise greeted the news that the poet's birthday would be celebrated in such a place as Galesburg, Illinois.

The event was held in Old First Church on a "bright and

crisp" morning in November. Although John Finley initiated
the celebration, Newton Bateman served as chairman. Appropriate musical numbers, addresses, and poetry readings entertained the large crowd. John Howard Bryant pronounced a
"monody" of his own in tribute to his brother. Professor
William E. Simonds of the Knox faculty placed William Cullen
Bryant's poetry in the context of the spread of New England
culture. Other speakers made mention of Bryant's abolitionism, and the fittingness that the centennial be celebrated
in what was once a center of abolitionist fervor in Illinois.

Two years later Finley again launched Knox College into
brief national prominence by arranging the celebration of the
most memorable event in Knox's past. On an "arctic" October
day in 1858, Stephen Douglas and Abraham Lincoln had held
the seventh of their celebrated senatorial debates on the college's campus in Galesburg. To commemorate the thirty-
eighth anniversary of this event, Finley gathered a choice
group of notables at Knox College.

The weather in 1896 was much more fitting for an outdoor
gathering than it had been in 1858. Huge crowds thronged the
college grounds as President Finley opened the exercises.
"These prairies," he observed, "have not been the scene of
bloody carnage. No Lexington, no Gettysburg claim this [cam-
pus] as its historic battle ground. But the principles that were
back of Lexington, that struggled again for victory at Gettysburg, we do claim, met here." An alumnus who had served the
Lincoln and other Republican administrations offered his reminiscences of the Galesburg debate of 1858, which he had
personally witnessed. Chauncey Depew, celebrated Republican orator and railroad president, held forth on the theme of
national unity. Robert Todd Lincoln, standing where his
father had stood thirty-eight years before, made one of his rare
public appearances. U. S. Senator John M. Palmer of Illinois
was the lone Democratic speaker; he unveiled an elaborate
bronze tablet commemorating the debate of 1858. The tablet
was made after John Finley's design, and smaller bronze rep-
licas were distributed to subscribers of the memorial fund.
After the speeches the guests (including Gov. John Peter
Altgeld and Andrew S. Draper, president of the University of

Illinois) and the students mingled over cocoa in the parlors of the girls' dormitory. Knox College and her young president basked in the success of the occasion.

But the triumphal staging of Lincoln-Douglas Day in 1896 was surpassed three years later, when John Finley managed the notable feat of bringing the president of the United States and his cabinet to Knox College. An admiring observer testified that Finley knew how to "word an invitation so that it would be accepted." Preparations for the gala event, including invitations, were under way long before October 7, 1899. For when the presidential train pulled into Galesburg that morning, Finley had already left the presidency of Knox College to take up editorial work in New York. But he came back to Galesburg for this occasion and welcomed President McKinley and the other cabinet officials in behalf of Knox College. A battery of distinguished orators (including Secretary of State John Hay) delivered addresses vindicating Lincoln's position in the debates of 1858 and celebrating his martyrdom.

Although it was hoped that the presidential party might stay for the afternoon football game with the University of Illinois, the distinguished guests (among them now, John Finley) took the train back to Chicago. Thousands had gathered on the Knox College campus for the event, many paying one dollar admission. The student newspaper summed up the impressions of the day:

> The historic event, the memorable place and time, the illustrious debaters [of 1858], the momentous question discussed by them, the honored guests and speakers, the similitude between the positions of President Lincoln during the Civil War and President McKinley at present, the eloquent passages of the orators, all combined to make it an historic day for the college, city and state.

In addition to keeping a fairly steady stream of eminent politicians (mostly Republican) flowing into Galesburg, Finley arranged to bring many other notables to the college. A visit of the popular Scottish poet Ian MacLaren in 1896, and of the Norwegian explorer Fridtjof Nansen two years later brought to Knox College the spirit of heroism and adventure. Jacob Riis sounded the message of social reform in "a lecture which will not be forgotten in Galesburg." These eminent guests not only presented Knox audiences with the living representatives of the high ideals of the day, but made the public aware of the college. An advertising man credited Finley with "genius for the restrained but effective publicity of associating" the college with the "well known names" of the guests he had lured to Galesburg.

Chapter 11

Continuity and Innovation at Knox
College, 1894–99

*A former teacher of mine, the historian of education Wilson Smith,
once warned that the great danger in writing about a college's past is
that the narrative will be swallowed up by filiopietistic sentimentality.
Chronicles of college life written in this genre become uncritical celebrations of local figures of parochial significance. In the past three decades educational historians have virtually jettisoned this older approach, and have written about patterns of change and survival of
collegiate tradition that link academic developments to the broader
trends in society, as I try to do here.*

Feats of academic showmanship were central, and not
peripheral, to Finley's educational task at Knox College.
Through them he allowed the community that supported the
college to express its loftiest sentiments. But Knox was
founded and maintained not solely to cherish certain ideals;
the college also had certain more conventional academic
functions to fulfill. Among them was the generally felt
need—which in part explains John Finley's arrival as president in 1892—to bring its educational offerings into line with
modern trends. Curriculum reform was a means to this end,
and the 1890s witnessed considerable curricular change.

At the beginning of his presidency, Finley found the
courses of study at Knox College basically unchanged from his
own student days in 1882–87. The first two years of the classical program still required heavy doses of standard ancient
authors, "natural philosophy" taught from a new edition of
the same textbook, and mathematics. Sophomores and
upperclassmen were offered a narrow range of "electives" in
modern languages, mathematics, and Latin. New items ap-

peared in 1893–94—for example, courses on the history of the
Middle Ages and English constitutional history. For the next
academic year, Anglo-Saxon and the history of political institutions were added. Fresh courses continued to appear, so that,
by the time Finley left Knox College, the curriculum included
such items as the history of ancient Israel, comparative
physiology of nervous organs, organic chemistry, meteorology,
and the history of art.

The educational changes that transformed Knox College
under Finley's presidency in the 1890s did not simply amount
to accretions to the curriculum. The deliberations of a series of
crucial faculty meetings during the latter part of the decade
accomplished much more. We shall see that the inner structure of the curriculum was redesigned, the faculty was reor-
ganized, and a far-reaching change in the conception of the
entire educational process was effected.

When Finley graduated from Knox College in 1887, he had
completed with great distinction the classical curriculum. A
scientific course was available as an alternative, which his
brother Rob chose. There was also a diluted literary course for
young ladies, which was not described in the *Catalogue*. By
1893–94 the literary course was listed in the *Catalogue* beside
the classical and scientific. Those enrolled in this course
studied no Greek and were offered an easier text in natural
philosophy. Apart from a botany course, and the absence of
Greek, the scientific course did not in 1893–94 essentially
differ from the classical. Thus, as Finley assumed the presidency of Knox College, the curriculum was fairly homogeneous and basically traditional.

By the end of the decade, a sweeping transformation of the
curriculum had been instituted. Alongside Knox College's
dedication to "mental discipline and broad culture" there
appeared the explicit intention "to meet the varied needs of
those who desire thorough preparation for the leading technical and professional schools." Varied indeed. The *Catalogue*
for 1899–1900 lists seven possible courses of study or
"groups." Each of these (except the classical course, "still
recognized . . . as the standard of excellence in collegiate
work") was closely tied to a career objective. "Group III., for

example *Greek-Philosophical* . . . is planned especially for any who expect to study theology." "Group V., *Mathematical-Physical*, lays especial stress upon physics and mathematics and is particularly adapted to the wants of those who expect to study civil, mechanical or mining engineering." "Group VI., *Chemical-Biological*, . . . furnishes a thorough preparation for the study of medicine," etc.

Increasing amounts of the students' time in these varied programs was allotted for "free electives." But extension of the elective principle alone was not the major feature of the educational modernization of Knox College. Of greater significance was the open appeal to the worldly ambition and career aims of the students. We have seen that, even before the modernization under Finley, Knox stimulated the desire for success. But then it was done mainly through the extracurriculum and other indirect means. By the last years of the nineteenth century, the secular success ideology had triumphed in the area of the formal educational program at Knox College as well.

A necessary condition for these changes in the direction of careerism and specialization was an expansion and transformation of the Knox College faculty. Finley was an appropriate man to preside over active faculty recruitment; his own graduate training at Johns Hopkins had thrown him into contact with advanced university circles. When he arrived at the college, the faculty comprised mostly homegrown, venerated professors with little training in their subject matter "specialty." After only a few years the faculty roster sparkled with newly hired university-trained specialists. Scholars with advanced degrees were appearing with increasing regularity: a biology professor with a Harvard Ph.D., a physicist with a Bonn doctorate, a Yale-trained mathematician, a Johns Hopkins chemist. Such men certainly distinguished Knox College—as well as straining its budget.

By 1896 the faculty thought so highly of itself that it requested President Finley to seek a listing for Knox College in the international roster of learned institutions, *Minerva*. Finley did attempt to gain such recognition for his school, and success crowned these efforts in 1900, when Knox College first took its place beside Harvard, Princeton, Columbia, and others in the pages of *Minerva*.

By the end of Finley's presidency, the modernization and rationalization of Knox College had been virtually achieved. A standardized credit system was established, substituting 180 units of admission credit for the lengthy list of books and studies required when Finley began college. A similar credit system was applied to the curriculum itself. A unit of college credit consisted of "one fifty-five minute recitation for one semester," and 120 were needed for graduation. By 1899 Knox had departed so far from the traditional education of the old-time college that a student could earn a B.A. with only ten credits (two one-semester courses) of Latin and no Greek, or a B.S. without studying either of the learned tongues.

Finley himself had been a distinguished student of classical languages in the old-time Knox curriculum. He often wished "that every man might have put into the background of his life what Greek put into mine." He knew that, with the passing of the primacy of classical study, much had been lost. Finley wistfully noted that once the B.A. was the symbol of the "completion of a synchronous curriculum, of the attainment of fairly identical content of knowledge by fairly homogeneous bodies of classified young men. . . . Now it connotes the collection of varying totals of credits or units from a widely elective list of knowledges by widely heterogeneous bodies of undenominated classes." In making such a comparison between the old-time college curriculum and modern courses of study, Finley was measuring the change that had been accomplished under his presidency.

> As Thorstein Veblen pointed out in his classic Higher Learning in America (1918), the very vocabulary of the new education–the measurement of education in such pecuniary terms as "credits"–signals the domination of learning by commercial values. As with most General Trends in American society, this one was blithely endorsed by Finley with only a touch of rhetorical nostalgia. His strength was in near-complete identification with the dominant forces, and it is no use posthumously quarreling with Finley's conventionality–even for a biographer who occasionally finds it maddening.

A college such as Knox exists on many levels. The curriculum and staff changes indicate that a sweeping transformation was achieved in the 1890s. Yet there were important but subtle areas of continuity that are not evident merely from an inspection of the college's formal records. Religion was one of these areas.

The desire to ensure evangelical piety was one of the major motives for the founding of Knox College, and the cultivation of religious sentiments among the students was a continuing aim there. Fewer graduates were choosing the ministry as a profession, but a pious posture remained a strong feature of the college's promotional literature—its "image." Finley himself, nurtured in Galesburg, was a young man of proven piety who could be counted on to continue the religious emphasis. His first year as president was marked by a full-scale, old-fashioned revival in the town and college. The students suspected that the revival was instituted from above by college and municipal authorities in order to counteract influences emanating from the world's fair in nearby Chicago. But revivalism was a fading feature of college life in the late nineteenth century: the revival of 1893 was apparently the last at Knox College. Other means would have to be found to sustain piety.

The presence of the venerable ex-president Newton Bateman as professor of mental and moral philosophy made the task easier. Bateman would handle "evidences of Christianity" and the other courses by which piety was inculcated into the students. Beginning in 1896 Finley planned to invite "some of the leading ministers of the West" for a few days at a time. These divines of different denominations would meet with students informally, deliver chapel talks, and conduct services.

Far more important than these visits of eminent clergymen for the preservation of piety at Knox College was the personal influence exerted by its young president. John Finley's own frequent chapel talks and addresses to the students were poetic sermons, rich in imagery, always pointing up vividly expressed, if commonplace, morals. He could convincingly liken the college to a swiftly flowing river, in which the faculty acted as banks directing the torrent toward properly exalted destinations. Another chapel talk was built around the idea of "inflected" speech of the Aryan peoples, showing in its many tenses, persons, and voices the vigorous, active lives of Anglo-Saxon people. Education was conceived of as a training for such a many-leveled life, in which the student would display "obedience to the God above us, love to those about us, help to those beneath."

One of Finley's last chapel talks at Knox College began with a discussion of the American Indian ritual of the "busk," at which worn-out possessions of the previous year were cast into a common fire. Finley advocated revival of the custom. Collect the rubbish, he urged, "the impure things, the worn-out theories, the vulgar habits, the narrow, unkind dogmas, the selfish, the dishonest practices. Burn these. Have a 'busk'." The students were advised then to rekindle a new spiritual flame, but in doing so to avoid "the lower and common sources of stimulus, . . . the lives of ordinary men, successful perhaps in the world about you." Instead they were referred to "that life which, focusing the divine nature in a human body, became the Light of Men, the True Light which lighteth every man that cometh into the world."

Finley was a gentle and persistent transmitter of Christian faith in an environment in which that message was certain to be gratefully welcomed. Piety was an unquestioned part of Knox tradition, infusing itself so gently through the college that its particular presence is hard to document. But comparison with the self-conscious, often frantic search for religion in present-day American colleges makes clear how pervasive was the religious atmosphere at Knox under Finley. For all of the conventional moralizing, it was a modern religion that Finley helped inculcate, one that sought accommodation with modern science and industrialism. This was probably the best tactic to steer students past the dangers of scientific skepticism. No doubt many of them could have admitted to Finley, as one did in 1900, that it was under him at Knox College "that my mind was wakened to the claims and promises of the Redeemer."

I approach the subject of religion in this book well aware that many, if not most, readers will be more sympathetic with Finley's unobtrusive, conventional, masculine–thoroughly American–piety than with this

*author's combative and aggressive atheism. Most of my experience with
religion has been garnered where religion appears perhaps in its very
best garb: in struggles waged by the left against war, imperialism, and
oppression, and for social justice. Well aware, therefore, of these occasionally progressive aspects of religion, I am still constrained to judge
the whole enterprise, and its philosophical underpinnings, as a mass of
obscurantism and in the last analysis a barrier to social progress.*

In the midst of this complex pattern of educational innovation and religious continuity, there appeared a novel element
in the life of Knox College—intercollegiate football. Until the
early 1890s oratorical contests formed the center of extracurricular life, and athletic events were more like all-college
free-for-alls, with "everybody" participating. Meanwhile formal intercollegiate football had arisen in the East, and some
voices at Knox began as early as 1889 to express "admiration
and envy" for the "great [athletic] tournaments of the Eastern
colleges." Two years later a Knox football team for the first
time took the field against other midwestern teams, and enthusiasm for the sport rose rapidly after that.

The introduction of football came about through student-
alumni initiative, aided by the influence of some of the faculty
who had been active in college athletics in their student days.
The Athletic Association formed to organize and administer
the games soon became an independent power on campus, to
whose deliberations even the faculty sent representatives. Faculty interest was especially aroused when football, ostensibly
introduced for the highest purposes—health, morality, and
innocent gratification—raised certain moral issues. Was the
recruitment of professional athletes to play on the college
team a stain on Knox's honor? Apparently the faculty in 1895
thought so, for it empowered President Finley to express dis-
approval of such practices. But it was a mild censure, for the
faculty at the same time excused students who wished to
attend a football game in nearby Carlinville. A full professor in
the college lead the delegation.

Although John Finley had himself played college football,
he seemed a reluctant enthusiast for the sport as president of
Knox College. Opening the new college term in September,
1895, with an inspirational talk on the solemn theme of the
duties of a Christian scholar, he ranked the ability to "kick

football (all well enough in its way)" low among the responsibilities the students ought to assume. Despite this pious
admonition, football became even more popular. The signs are
unmistakable. A new constitution for the Athletic Association
ensured that no more "errors or abuses will creep in." A. G.
Spaulding & Bros., athletic outfitters of New York, Chicago,
and Philadelphia, began to advertise regularly in Knox College publications beginning in 1896. In October of that year,
the cover page of the *Knox Student* for the first time carried
news about the football team. And the trustees appropriated
$500 in June, 1896, for the use of the Athletic Association.

During the decade of the nineties, intercollegiate athletics
became firmly fixed in Galesburg, raising a host of problems
for Knox College officials. Professionalism and the academic
standing of athletes were recurring issues. The faculty dealt
with them by assuming ever stricter control over the athletic
program. This trend culminated in the decision of 1899 that
the college should bear the expense of the entire athletic
program, as well as exercise control over it. Charges of professionalism continued to be directed at Knox College, and even
some of those most proud of the college's exploits on the
gridiron occasionally wished that the football craze might disappear.

There is no evidence of firm direction given to the evolution
of athletics by John Finley in his capacity as president of Knox
College. But this does not indicate any special administrative
ineptitude on his part; passive acquiescence in the triumph of
football was the general response among college presidents in
America. But Finley's attitude toward certain other events and
movements impinging on the college from the world outside Galesburg does demand special treatment. These are
militarism, the Spanish-American War, and Knox College's
reaction to them.

A cadet corps had been part of the college since 1884, and
Finley himself, as a student, doubtless enjoyed the smart grey
uniforms, the sabre practice, the artillery exercises and drill.
He may have taken part in mock cavalry charges, like the one
that went up Galesburg's Prairie Street one afternoon in 1894

and reminded an old Union cavalryman in town of his Civil War exploits.

In the course of about fifteen years, five Army officers successively filled a professorship of military science and tactics at Knox College. These soldiers reported to Washington that the students were enthusiastic, while they themselves were fully integrated into the faculty, receiving advanced degrees and occasionally teaching German, French, natural philosophy, or trigonometry. Beginning as a voluntary program for upperclassmen, the cadet corps increased in scope so that just before the Spanish-American War it had become compulsory for almost all the boys at the college. But despite the program in military training, there seems to have been little martial spirit at Knox College. An Army inspector reported his displeasure at finding no books on "military subjects" in the college library. And when the crisis of 1898 came, a pacific atmosphere predominated in Galesburg. The students were commended for their resistance to the clamor for war. It was considered foolish to go to battle simply because of the journalistic cry "Remember the Maine."

Antijingoism apparently was the dominant attitude at Knox College. A military dispatch to Washington after hostilities in Cuba had ended noted drily that only "eleven students or ex-students who have received military instruction at this college have joined the U.S. Army since the commencement of hostilities with Spain." After the war the cadet program was quickly disbanded at Knox College, probably due to the manifest lack of enthusiasm for the allied causes of Cuban freedom and U.S. expansion.

As president of the college that displayed such indifference to the "splendid little war," Finley did not publicly dissent from the prevailing attitude. This is noteworthy in light of his later attitudes. Soon after he left the Galesburg campus, he would speak and write in behalf of American imperialism. And in his later educational philosophy, an element of rhetorical militarism would become increasingly prominent. Finley's silence in 1898 may have been mainly prompted by prudence in the face of the prevailing antiimperialism at Knox College.

It is in the area of imperialism and Finley's defense of U.S. expansionism (to be discussed more fully in Chapter 14 of this book) that I feel most estranged from the man whose biography I have written. To some extent this estrangement is the product of a generational gap. By the time I began to write, speak, and demonstrate against the war in Vietnam, a much more lethal side of U.S. imperialism had been revealed than in Finley's era. Yet I have more than a hunch that, had he lived on a quarter century longer, Finley would have identified more with a William Westmoreland or a W. W. Rostow (to name two prominent American "hawks") than with a Dave Dellinger, a Tom Hayden, or a Staughton Lynd—all notable American antiwar activists.

As an embodiment of the ideals of modern piety, scholarship, and honorable success that he consistently placed before Knox College audiences, Finley himself was attracting attention during the 1890s. He organized and presided over a session of the International Congress of Charities, Correction and Philanthropy held at the World's Columbian Exposition in Chicago; later, he edited a volume of the conference papers. In 1896 he was active in behalf of sound money and McKinley in Illinois, and Eastern Republican leaders knew of his work. And in 1898 the prestigious Union League Club of Chicago chose Finley to address its important George Washington's Birthday celebration.

In his speech on that occasion, the young college president sketched in broad strokes the evolution of America from the era of the Revolution, when honored figures were brave soldiers like George Washington, to the age of peace in which the major figure is the student.

> The soldier pushed to the wild frontier to protect our borders against the intemperate aborigine, or civilized in some college detail, or enervated in the social duties of an urban fort, is making way for his sturdier successor, the student.

Finley perceived fierce enemies to contend with in humanity's great battles of the future.

> [Some men are trying to] pierce the joints between our states.... There are enemies in [the immigrant] ships at our ports whose hungry faces and pestilential thoughts menace our workmen; there are red men, more dangerous than savages, red men of anarchy, in our major centers of life; there are [also] aldermanic [Benedict] Arnolds who, for personal gain, would sell for gold and offices the very streets of their city. . . .

Soldiers in the army that will take the field against these evils must be ready, as George Washington was, "to sacrifice their

personal fortune[s] on the altar of the public good." This new
army, "whose battles are to be waged in the upper air, whose
sieges are to be fought out with batteries of logic behind
redoubts of principle," will be made up of "gunless, swordless
students of truth and lovers of men." American youth, boys
and girls like those at Knox College, will be "trained in letters,
in the language of the world's commerce, in honor, in honesty,
in purity and obedience." Truly, they will constitute "the best
standing army in the world."

> No doubt because he was anticipating the reaction of his conservative
> audience, Finley appears at his most bellicose and reactionary in this
> speech. Yet these nativist and antiradical sentiments cannot have been
> far from his true convictions. It is hardly conceivable that even the most
> charitable biographer, especially one whose ancestors came on the very
> immigrant ships Finley was referring to, and to whom the color red
> denotes not a danger of anarchism but the hope of socialism, will be
> comfortable with such attitudes as those expressed in Finley's Union
> League Club speech.

Before the distinguished Union League Club audience of
businessmen and politicians, Finley struck just the right tone.
A mixture of conservative and democratic notions was coupled
with the proper reverence for higher learning. The address
earned Finley the attention of influential people. An ex-
president of the United States wrote him a few months afterward and "very well remember[ed] meeting" the young college president and hearing him speak at the Union League
Club. "[I] have often referred with delight to your address on
that occasion," added Benjamin Harrison.

In the 1890s, under John Finley, Knox College had
achieved a kind of dynamic equilibrium. Within the limits
imposed by the financial crisis of the decade, considerable
change took place, but this was balanced by a continuity with
traditional piety and a generally wholesome collegiate way of
life. Social and political forces from the world outside of
Galesburg impinged on the college, but they did not unduly
disturb the placidity of campus life. The young president
could by 1898 look back upon almost a decade of work in
Galesburg with considerable satisfaction. Finley's major
achievement was to make of his administration "a golden
period of youth and drama" for the college, "a time when high
adventure waited just around the corner."

Book 4.
Career in Transition

Chapter 12

Career Promises, Hopes, and Disappointments, 1899–1900

In an earlier time Finley got on, and got on well, in the academic world without a Ph.D. By the seventh decade of the new century, a Ph.D. was the precondition for retaining a job, and when my dissertation was rejected I faced what I thought was the grim necessity to switch jobs. (Dogged persistence, however, eventually impelled me to do my second thesis, for which I did finally win the Ph.D.) With family responsibilities, the loss of professional mooring and livelihood was frightening, and in Finley's surviving letters of his trying period, narrated in this chapter, there is an unaccustomed undercurrent of fear.

John Finley's prairie-born ambition to become a journalist was not extinguished during the decade he spent as president of Knox College. His younger brother, Rob, was working in New York City with a new monthly journal, the *Review of Reviews*, edited by the Finleys' Johns Hopkins classmate, Albert Shaw. Separated during the 1890s by half a continent, John and Rob continued to plan and dream of new editorial ventures similar to those they had envisioned in Grand Ridge decades before. But Rob Finley died suddenly in 1897, and the work they hoped to do together John would have to attempt himself as soon as he could lay down Knox College duties.

The occasion came late in the year after Rob's death. An attractive offer from the enterprising journalist and Knox College graduate S. S. McClure ultimately proved irresistible, although it caused some initial "mental torture" due to John Finley's deep sense of responsibility toward the prairie college he loved and served. He could no longer consult his brother, for death had taken this closest adviser. Finley then

turned to his former Johns Hopkins teacher, Herbert Baxter
Adams. He indicated to Adams that the management of a new
monthly magazine was offered him; also that he was being
sought as president of the State University of Iowa. Soon
Finley would have to decide "whether I shall go on in this
[academic] work or descend into that place for which I seem to
some of my friends at least better fitted." Adams replied
swiftly with what may have been the decisive advice in this
situation.

> It seems to me [counseled the older man] that you ought to stop worrying
> yourself about presidential possibility and return to your own ideals.
> You will not enjoy the presidency of a State University in Iowa or in any
> other western commonwealth. Your natural vocation is that of an editor,
> and the sooner you go to New York the better.

Although local sentiment in Galesburg insisted that he remain, Finley wrote to Adams: "Your judgement has always
outweighed the advice I have had from others. I am confident
that I have decided for the best."

The offer that S. S. McClure made to Finley in late 1898
concerned vast journalistic enterprises the outlines of which
were magnificently unclear. An alliance would be cemented
between the publishing houses of Harper and McClure. Each
of the periodicals put out by these firms—*Harper's Monthly,
McClure's Magazine, Harper's Weekly*—would remain intact
after the merger. Somehow "a great Encyclopedia and a popular Review" would also emerge. John Finley was slated to edit
the review.

Finley spread the word: "We've got some big enterprises
underway and in prospect." He chose an imposing tentative
name for the new forthcoming periodical: *The Harper-
McClure Review: An Illustrated Record of the World's Work.*
It was to be a monthly, selling at ten cents an issue. It would
not duplicate any existing review. All the others were presumed to have some other purpose (whether low, commercial,
or purely literary), while Finley's new periodical would
amount to "a great educational agency and thus [would be] in
line with . . . [its editor's] former work." It was an infinitely
attractive prospect, a return to his earliest and deepest ambition, subsuming his educational interests as well.

Provincial Galesburg had nothing comparable to keep Finley there. He accepted McClure's offer "several weeks" before the official announcement of his resignation from Knox College on March 25, 1899. The Chicago *Times-Herald* carried Finley's statement, in which he revealed that joining McClure's enterprises "has been my plan for several years past." Although he had intended to remain at Knox College until the fall "so that the interest of the institution shall not suffer by an interregnum," Finley brought his family (including two young children) to New York in midsummer. While waiting for the new enterprises to materialize, Finley set to work in the Harper offices helping edit the *Weekly*.

This was immensely pleasing work for a man who had been restive for a decade in college affairs. "I've reached the place to which I 'have been divinely called,' " Finley wrote ecstatically from his new office. Friends shared the elation. Albert Shaw, editor of a review that would compete with the one Finley was preparing to issue, was reported to have "only good expectations regarding your new enterprise." A former teacher, Woodrow Wilson, wrote from abroad that, just as Finley had been "the right man in the right vocation at Knox," so would he prove "an even better man in a better place now." And back in Galesburg, the big-city success of Knox alumni was a marvel and a spur to local ambition.

But despite hopeful prognoses, the momentous editorial scheme was heading toward disaster. For one thing, McClure himself had only a hazy idea of the financial plight of the house of Harper when he planned the merger. Deeply involved in the machinations of the J. P. Morgan and Carnegie financial interests, the venerable publishing firm was in trouble. When Finley heard the details, he described Harper as slowly sinking into a "quagmire."

Another possible factor in the failure of the enterprise was McClure's absence during the critical weeks. In letters from various European cities, McClure did little more than issue vague assurances to his "dear Finlay [*sic*]" that the plans were sound. In August he expressed confidence in his young associate, Finley, and conviction that the new magazine would soon blossom. A month later McClure wrote from London voicing his "hope that you are getting on well with that new Review." Apparently replying to some of Finley's editorial plans, the future muckraking publisher agreed that the trusts would make a grand theme for some early number. But he didn't think the first issue could appear before December.

By the fall of 1899 it became clear that the plans for merging the two publishing enterprises had been highly conditional. McClure withdrew from the venture in mid-November, and Finley saw his rosy plans come tumbling down around him. He explained the consequent mood of depression to an academic acquaintance, President Nicholas Murray Butler of Columbia University.

> I have been so distraught with the changing and unguessable conditions which the[se] days have been bringing forth—so busy in the almost daily effort of readjustment that I have had no time to see my friends, no time to write them even; nor have I, frankly, been in the mood.

Finley might have stayed on at *Harper's Weekly*, but the shaky financial structure of its venerable publishing house was probably as little attractive to him as to McClure. He went instead to *McClure's Magazine*, in a distinctly lower editorial capacity than the one that had been promised him on the new magazine, and that had enticed him and his family to come to New York from Galesburg. He might still have a chance to succeed in journalism, he felt at the time, but there was "no sure guarantee" of this.

Eventually there did emerge, within a year of the wreck of the Harper-McClure venture, a new publishing house that issued a journal close to Finley's specifications. In fact he was involved in the planning of this enterprise and gave the journal its name—*World's Work*. But by that time Finley was again about to retire to the comparative serenity of academic life, this time at Princeton. To Herbert Baxter Adams at Johns Hopkins (who had urged him to leave Knox College for the journalistic opportunity in the first place) Finley wrote that editorial ventures had brought him mostly disappointment, and he feared that more of it was in store for him if he stayed on in New York.

> *Business or professional failure, or the prospect of such failure, triggers off tremendous anxiety for a man in American society, above and beyond all realistic concern of livelihood and standard of living. De-*

fined and defining themselves as "breadwinners," men deal with these problems in strange ways. It was always a mystery to me why my father found it necessary to scatter his family when he lost his pharmacy in the early 1940s. When I talked to him about this on his deathbed in 1969, I got only vague references to the supposed need for a lone, valiant struggle to put his affairs in order before sending for us. It is as if the myth of the noble knight in shining armor doing heroic single combat lived on in somewhat debased form as a bourgeois rite of manhood.

Finley did not abandon journalism in 1900. As we shall soon see, he began at that time to produce what would soon amount to a vast corpus of magazine writing, in both prose and verse. Twenty years later another, more sound journalistic offer would come to Finley; and in 1921 he would join the editorial staff of the *New York Times*. But in 1900 he withdrew just far enough outside of the fourth estate to miss participating directly in the journalistic renaissance of muckraking that opened the twentieth century.

Just as his fortunes were at their lowest ebb, when he and his family were virtually stranded in New York with their hopes and plans dashed, there came to Finley the irresistible offer of a Princeton professorship. This opportunity did not quite fall from "out of the skies," as he claimed. Woodrow Wilson, who had taught Finley at Johns Hopkins in 1888, had since joined the Princeton faculty. On a journalistic errand to the New Jersey campus in 1899, Finley met his former teacher, who raised the possibility that Finley himself might come to Princeton to teach. By the spring of the next year, the university trustees were on the verge of filling a newly endowed chair of politics; and Finley, sponsored by Woodrow Wilson, was actively being considered. From the perspective of dangerous and risky journalistic ventures, a return to the higher learning was equivalent to slipping into a safe and pleasant haven.

By June the formalities were completed, and Finley was duly elected to the endowed chair. The endowment amounted to $100,000, invested at 4 percent, and thus yielded an income of $4,000 a year. Finley gently protested the inadequacy of this salary to support his growing family. He had no independent income. But Princeton president Francis L. Patton turned aside the objection by noting that Finley himself had "been the president of a college" and could therefore appreciate the university's inability to pay more. Besides, few chairs were so well endowed, said Patton, and $4,000 "is as much as any other professor in Princeton is receiving." Finley was also promised ample time for literary work, which had already brought him "reputation and rising fame."

Plate 1. Page of John H. Finley's Translation of
"Prometheus Bound" (1887)
Credit: Finley Collection, Manuscript and Archives Division,
New York Public Libary

Plate 2.   Robert and John Finley, about 1887
            Credit: Knox College Archives

Plate 3. The Seminary Room, Seminary of History and Politics, The Johns Hopkins University, about 1886
Credit: Johns Hopkins University Archives

Plate 4. Newton Bateman and John H. Finley, about 1892
          Credit: Knox College Archives

Plate 5. Martha and Baby Ellen Finley, about 1894
Credit: Knox College Archives

Plate 6. Original Building of City College of New York at 23rd Street
Credit: City College of New York Public Relations Office

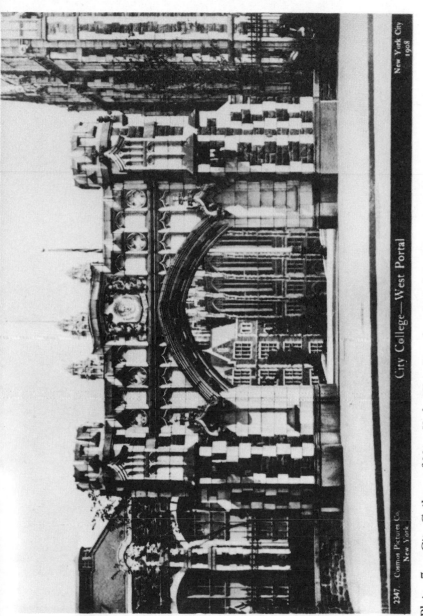

2347. Cosmos Pictures Co.
New York

City College—West Portal

New York City
1908

Plate 7.   City College of New York: West Portal and Mail Building,
about 1908
Credit: City College of New York Public Relations Office

Plate 8.   John Finley as President of City College
Credit: New York Public Library

Plate 9.   New York State Education Building
Credit: New York State Education Department

Plate 10.   *New York Times* Building, 43rd Street
Credit: William E. Sauro/NYT Pictures

He HAS walked around the world to his office. Dr. John Huston Finley, lecturer, writer, past-president of three colleges, and an editor of the *New York Times*, is probably the world's leading walker. On his seventieth birthday recently he walked a mile for each year —and did it in twenty-one hours. Never wears an overcoat, rain or shine, but always carries a stick and a pedometer. Born in Grand Ridge, Ill., he started gathering his 21 degrees soon after graduating from Knox College. Has been decorated by Japan, France, Italy, Finland, Norway. His favorite sport is to clock his own mileage day after day on his route to and from the office—as if he were striding out for far horizons.

Plate 11.   Finley at 70
              Credit: Knox College Archives

Chapter 13

Princeton University at the Opening of
the Twentieth Century, 1900–1903

There is now a precisely delineated structure to American academic life, with an elaborate ritual for obtaining and retaining university positions. This system was just taking shape in Finley's day, when the academic world was more homogeneous and simple than it was to become. In a later day a publicly committed Jewish radical from New York could expect only a very limited range of job offers, especially if he had in his credentials file such letters of "recommendation" as I had. One job that presented itself in the early seventies was at a midwestern university that was nearly disgraced when Richard Nixon arrived to deliver an address and there were no demonstrators to greet him. The school needed a house radical and contacted me. I declined the dubious honor.

The question of why Finley was chosen for the Princeton faculty is one that does not admit of sure answer. The letterbooks of President Patton, who hired him, provide no clue, nor are there relevant documents among the papers of Woodrow Wilson, who promoted his candidacy, or those of Finley himself. The answer must be inferred from the development of the university.

The presidency of Francis L. Patton was a transition between two momentous eras in Princeton's history. Patton succeeded James McCosh and was succeeded in his turn by Woodrow Wilson. Under McCosh the College of New Jersey was rescued from its Civil War decline, given stability and a distinctive tone. As Thomas Jefferson Wertenbaker shows in his bicentennial history of Princeton, Patton merely laid the foundation for a genuine university, which Woodrow Wilson and others later carried to completion.

President Patton's apparent strategy of faculty recruitment was to add "scholarly young men to the teaching force" at Princeton. Rather than researchers of high caliber, he sought promising men "full of pride at their scholarship and achievement in letters." It was also not thought necessary that the literary and publishing activity of prospective professors be in any narrow scholarly groove. Princeton's faculty was studded with nonspecialized literary lights. Walter A. Wykoff, author of travelogues and stories about tramping, was professor of history. Henry Van Dyke, formerly minister at the Brick Presbyterian Church in New York City, writer of romances, storybooks, and sermons, came to Princeton as Murray Professor of English Literature a year before Finley arrived. There were a number of other such literary gentlemen. In favoring this type of man on the faculty, President Patton was abandoning the idea of a faculty made up of local figures, concerned parochially with the Princeton community but enjoying no wider reputation. But he was not yet prepared to recruit a body of specialized scholars. Hence the Princeton faculty was clearly in transition at the turn of the century. Finley, who was beginning to contribute articles and verses to prominent national magazines, was a likely recruit. Despite his lack of classroom experience, and without any substantial scholarly work to his credit, he fit nicely into the slowly changing Princeton milieu.

The chair to which he was appointed in 1900 was reputed to be the first professorship of politics in America. Before Finley came to Princeton, the work offered in social science, to judge by the course descriptions in the college catalogs, was thoroughly traditional. If it was at all challenging to students, the reason probably was that most of the teaching was done by Woodrow Wilson. Finley proposed to enliven the curriculum by offering such courses as contemporary politics, comparative state legislation, municipal government, and the expansion of Europe. President Patton professed to be "happy in the thought that our curriculum is to be enriched" by these innovations.

It was claimed that Finley was "a new kind of political science professor—informal, hardly ever using written lectures or even notes." Apparently he did not adopt the traditional practice of requiring recitations from some textbook. Instead, mock legislative assemblies were instituted, so that by their own active participation students could gain under-standing of the political life of such countries as France or England. Finley also set the undergraduates who enrolled in his courses to work at independent research. They might be asked to report on such topics as "Suits Against a State." One student admitted that Finley was able to "get work out of boys who hardly knew what work was."

> *At Finley's Princeton it may have been a matter of stirring under-graduates otherwise perfectly content with a leisurely "Gentleman's C," but at Polytechnic Institute where I have been teaching mainly lower-middle-class students for over a decade, the problem is different. My students (bless them!) have been arduously trained to accept even the most absurd tasks assigned by those in authority, and "getting work out of them" is rarely an issue. But I resist the notion that college life is merely a training in work habits to fit students for their destined niches (an idea that, drenched as they are in the petty-bourgeois work ethic, they hardly ever question). Historical thinking is critical thinking: an exercise of situating the historical individual among the social forces that buffet him or her about, thus bringing the personal and the politi-cal together. Insofar as it also connects with or draws upon the stu-dent's own experiences and insights, it transcends the subject matter, considered as an entity apart from the student, the teacher, and their most intimate and private concerns. It is here that the most puzzling pedagogical problems arise, for no teacher ought to abuse power to reach into the jealously guarded private lives of students, yet no teacher (of history at least) can be counted successful unless he or she does connect the objective data taught in the classroom with this private domain.*

To inject an added note of realism into his classes, Finley on occasion invited active political figures to Princeton. Jacob Riis thought that there was nothing much more to the "science of politics" than "'shoving' Tammany and Croker" when he could, yet he came to the university to address Finley's stu-dents.

Another friend, Booth Tarkington, could not come because of his work as a member of the Indiana legislature (his literary career was some years in the future). "What a bully notion that is," Tarkington exclaimed, "studying state legislation—much more cheering than studying state legislatures." Wistfully, he expressed the wish that Finley's students had studied the subject with him in Indianapolis. He could have used their votes! And what lessons the innocent Princeton undergradu-ates would have learned there!

"How to keep other people from stealing what you want yourself."
"How to undermine an opponent by rumor." "Passing bills for the good
of the State to make a good job for your brother who pays you half."
"How to steal a legislature if you are governor." "How to form a corporation and pass bills that require the State to contract with that corporation
at $300,000 a year." "Etc. etc. etc."

But Tarkington did not want Finley to preach cynicism to his
students. He admitted that the life of a reform-minded state
legislator was often a trying one. "It takes one's nerve to retain
respect for laws when one sees *how* they are made." It was
probably not necessary for him to add, in his letter to Finley,
that he hoped the Princeton professor was preaching "Git into
Politics" to his students. "I don't see how a man with *any*
patriotism reconciles himself to staying out." And for a final bit
of advice on what Finley should convey to the Princeton boys,
Tarkington urged, "Teach 'em to be bill-*killers*."

Finley needed no prompting from anyone to preach the
gospel of reform, rectitude, public service, and opposition
to bad laws. It was his own characteristic message. One of his
students acknowledged Finley's inspiration in leading him
into a wholesome political career. "A man [like you] who has
attained success without having cut himself off from things
which inspire the masses . . . gives a stronger impression than
those whose library is their world." The man who wrote these
lines, Hubert Fisher, became a political figure of note in Tennessee and a U.S. congressman despite "disgraceful factional
turmoil in state politics and . . . flunkeyism to corporate wealth
and special privilege. . . ." Fortified by such influences as
Woodrow Wilson and John Finley, a man could go forth from
Princeton and, even in the morass of Tennessee politics, become "a forerunner of the newer ideals of democracy and
social service."

Finley's entire training and background, even his ancestry,
inclined him to favor and transmit these ideals. After he left
Princeton for the College of the City of New York, he would
have greater occasion to demand of the young men who came
to him that they dedicate themselves to the public good.

The teaching of contemporary politics did not lead Finley to
complete any serious and mature work of scholarship. He did
agree in his last months at Princeton to undertake a study of

the executive branches of federal and state governments for The American State Series, being edited by Johns Hopkins professor W. W. Willoughby. The book was scheduled to appear in the spring of 1905. Not only did Finley miss that deadline, he almost failed to do the book altogether. A collaborator was finally obtained (probably through the publisher, the Century Company), and *The American Executive and Executive Methods* was published in late 1908.

When the volume appeared, Finley was president of the College of the City of New York, and predictably the undergraduate weekly there printed a glowing review—possibly the only favorable notice. Elsewhere the reviewers were almost unanimous that it was a wretched book. They charged it with excessive literalness and formality in its treatment of the executive power; Finley stressed the static, administrative side rather than the dynamic, political aspect of the subject. It was pointed out that the book's structure was unimaginative and that the text often degenerated into a mass of undigested legal citations. The author himself admitted that it was "a very prosaic book, whose composition was very much like the building of a stone wall." Finley's *American Executive* was also deficient in the graceful literary style that lent distinction to his later books.

> When *The* American Executive *appeared, Finley was already in a position that shielded him from the unfavorable critical responses, unlike those of us who are hypersensitive and combative in response to hostile reviews. In the case of my more politically oriented books on Indochina and contemporary American politics, the ideological motivation of the unfavorable notices (as for example the review of my* Vietnam *by R. F. Turner in the conservative quarterly the* Intercollegiate Review*) was easy to spot and irked me less than the more subtly hostile attacks on my book on antebellum American radicalism (such as the review by D. C. Skaggs in the February, 1975,* American Historical Review*). My tendency is to rush into print with a defense (as in the December, 1975,* American Historical Review*), exhibiting I suppose the insecurities and status anxieties of my position in the academic class structure. A Finley would have let these attacks roll off his back.*

In his middle thirties during the years he spent at Princeton University, John Finley was coming of age. His genial and benign philosophy was taking on what would be its final form; he occupied an enviable academic post; his voice could be heard on matters of national policy; some sort of reputation as a poet or versifier was growing; and he had found the Princeton social environment thoroughly congenial to his tastes.

He came to Princeton in the summer of 1900 armed with a letter of introduction to Princeton's most distinguished citizen, Grover Cleveland. The Democratic ex-president in the twilight of his career had taken up residence in the town and become trustee of the university. The letter of introduction came from James H. Eckels, who almost twenty years earlier had helped Finley win the Knox College freshman essay prize. Eckels had meanwhile served under Grover Cleveland as comptroller of the U.S. currency, and soon afterward he received an honorary degree and other marks of distinction from Knox College. He urged Finley to present himself to the retired president. "You will find him a great help in aiding you to reach right conclusions in important public questions."

Finley may have gotten to know Cleveland without the letter of introduction, and the help he received from the ex-president went far beyond political instruction. In her manuscript "Memories" of her married life, Mrs. Finley set down her recollections of how the lasting friendship began over the matter of where the young professor, his wife, and three children would live.

> Princeton was then . . . a much smaller college and village than now, and there were few houses to rent. In fact there were only two which could be considered and one so far from the University and schools it was out of the question. A small house on Bayard Lane, belonging to a General Woodhull we decided upon, although we knew we should have to move the next spring as General Woodhull was retiring from the Army then. The house was in the block below the Cleveland home, and our children soon became acquainted with the Cleveland children, as Ellen was in school with them. In the fall, probably in October [of 1900], we were invited to dine with the Clevelands. . . . It was quite a dinner party, probably about a dozen people, and in a pause of the conversation, Mr. Cleveland said [,] "What are you going to do, Mr. Finley, when General Woodhull comes back in the spring?" To which John replied, "That is just what is worrying us, Mr. President. It looks as if we would have to build a house for ourselves, which we do not want to do, or be on the street." Mr. Cleveland continued, "I've always said that if I could find anyone I liked well enough, I would build him a house in my apple orchard." It happened that in the large plot of ground which the Clevelands had, there was an old apple orchard, on Bayard Lane, some distance from the house. On leaving the dinner party, we exclaimed almost simultaneously, "Do you suppose he meant it?" and I determined to

make my party call as soon as proper and ask Mrs. Cleveland. This I did
and she told me that she had heard her husband speak of building a
house in the apple orchard, and suggested that Mr. Finley call on Mr.
Cleveland and talk it over. And to bring the story to a very pleasant
ending, this was done. Mr. Cleveland suggested that Mrs. Cleveland and
I consult a young architect they knew and find what sort of house could
be built for the rent we cared to pay. This was done, plans were soon
drawn, the house was begun in the early spring, and we went into it in
the following fall.

Built to Finley's specifications, the new house on Bayard
Lane included a spacious third-floor study for the professorial
occupant. A desk extended the entire length of the room,
under a set of windows that opened on a vista of distant
wooded hills. A perfect place for scholarly work. Downstairs
there were often guests, including the Clevelands and the
Reverend Henry Van Dyke, who had recently left a pulpit in
Manhattan to become Murray Professor of English Literature
in the university. The ex-president "was greatly interested" in
Finley's teaching, and they often discussed political questions
together. Their allegiance to different political parties did not
prevent the relationship from becoming close and deep.

The Finley and Cleveland children played together often
on the Princeton lawns. The ex-president's daughter and the
youngest Finley girl both came down with diphtheria in 1902,
and while the Cleveland child recovered, Finley's daughter
died. The grieved father wrote, "With all the universe of lights
about/How strange that one—one little light gone out/Should
leave the earth so dark, so drear!" This tragedy drew the two
families even closer together. Summers they spent on adjoin-
ing estates in Tamworth, New Hampshire. Even after the
ex-president's death in 1908, the remaining members of the
two families would continue the earlier intimacy.

To the folk back in Galesburg who witnessed Finley's early
ascent, Princeton, with all its associations, "seemed . . . so great a
thing" they could imagine nothing better for him. A Knox alumnus
on the Illinois prairie supposed that Finley's academic atmosphere
in New Jersey "must be surcharged with literary and educational
ozone and stimulus." It was indeed intellectually enjoyable and a
socially congenial place for him. He became something of a booster
of Princeton. When Daniel C. Gilman was considering retirement
from the Johns Hopkins presidency in 1901, Finley wrote:

This place is in many respects the most nearly ideal environment that I have found and if you are wishing to spend the rest of your days in academic shades and yet within easy reach of New York, you certainly cannot find a better place than Princeton.

Finley himself, teaching in the university while maintaining journalistic contacts, admitted that he found the "semi-academic, semi-editorial life a happy one." Finley spent three years in this congenial Princeton environment, during which time he gathered his forces for the next stage in his professional career—the presidency of the College of the City of New York.

Chapter 14

Princeton:

A Forum for Teaching and Writing in

Behalf of Imperialism, 1900–1903

Traveling in the Caribbean a half century after Finley's visits to Puerto Rico and Cuba, I was caught up in the excitement of revolutionary change. Coming to Cuba in the summer of 1960 as a skeptical observer, I was "turned around" not so much by the showcase atmosphere of a revolution a year and a half old, but by the less spectacular aspects of nueva Cuba. The very chaos and disorderliness of the revolutionary transformation—as when former peasants debate for the first times in their lives the conditions that will govern their lives—were the most impressive features of life in Cuba to me. Something of an anarchist then, I had less sympathy with the emerging socialist order in Cuba. But in time I came to see the need for order and discipline in a socialist society, while remaining horrified by the kind of "order" Stalin imposed on Russia. I also came to believe that the main task of a North American socialist is not to pass retroactive judgments on how others create or try to create socialism, but to struggle for the realization of a humane socialist society here. . . . Nothing in Finley's life prepared him to appreciate thoughts or commitments such as these: he was a defender rather than a critic of the status quo.

If Finley's labors at Princeton teaching American domestic politics brought forth nothing better than one inconsequential book, the course in colonial expansion had more significant issue. His teaching covered "the phenomenon of the spilling over of Europe into the other continents, the processes under which the expatriates have conquered and occupied new lands and erected new States and the relations of the new to one another and to the old." Finley described these courses to his friend, Albert Shaw, who replied that they "strike quite at the heart of situations that are today most interesting." To what extent Finley was able to achieve in his Princeton teaching systematic analysis of imperialism cannot be gauged. He

left no lecture notes, and student reminiscences proved un-
available despite systematic searching.

The adoption of Finley's course on the expansion of Europe
at Princeton coincided not unsurprisingly with America's own
"emergence as a great power." In his teaching therefore he
hoped to come "to our own expansion problems," as well as
those of the European powers. Finley had the opportunity to
make his own on-the-spot investigations in the American
Caribbean colonies during the years he taught at Princeton.
He could therefore bring to his classroom firsthand knowledge, as well as voice his views nationally during the debate
on imperialism carried out in the United States after what
historian Philip S. Foner reminds us should be called the
Spanish-American-Cuban War.

The summer before he came to Princeton, Finley visited the
newly acquired island of Puerto Rico, traveling there on a U.S.
Army transport ship. He perceived healthy "political beginnings" and wrote sympathetically of the work of the American
commissioners. One of these men, Jacob Hollander, the Johns
Hopkins economist, was putting the taxes of the island in
order. Another American commissioner gave "his days and
nights to reconciling a system of law that holds a man guilty
until proved innocent with one that presumed his innocence
until the guilt is established." Obstacles to the establishment
of a stable political order, on the Yankee model, Finley located
in the tradition and temperament of the natives. A hot-
blooded, proud race, the Puerto Ricans were natural obstruc-
tionists. When their politicians could not get their way in some
matter, they resigned from office—so unlike the sensible and
"pragmatic Americans."

Finley's acquaintance with the mores of the natives was
gained on a two hundred-mile walking tour of the island. He
had already demonstrated his love of hiking, and upon reading
Finley's piece on Puerto Rico, one old Galesburg friend
"thought it was very much like the boy . . . who made a forced
march one afternoon and evening through the wet snow from
Monmouth to Galesburg." Since he did not read or speak
Spanish, Finley's information was gained by wandering about

the island, observing the peons in their huts and villages, and questioning the North American commissioners. These sources brought him to the realization that he had witnessed a great experiment. Puerto Rico, he wrote in the November, 1900, *Review of Reviews,* was like a great anvil "on which two civilizations, two people, with diverse traditions, are being welded."

There was a certain asymmetry in Finley's view of the cultural merger; the balance clearly favored the Yankee side. "The Latin traditions," Finley observed, must with whatever difficulty necessary become subordinated to "the saxon point of view." The racial pride through which Finley viewed Puerto Rican society was revealed in his discussion of the devastating hurricane of August, 1899. The great suffering and poverty that followed this hurricane were witnessed by the touring professor. In his article of November, 1900, Finley asserted that "an equal number of Yankees with characteristic energy and ingenuity and industry, would have effaced all marks of the ruin of the previous year." In his analysis of the failure of the Puerto Ricans themselves to handle such a natural disaster with Yankee zeal, Finley blamed excessive U.S. relief funds, which only confirmed the natives in their climate-bred lethargy. Here he made use of some notions from "scientific philanthropy" about the vicious effects of material relief; and these doctrines became part of the fabric of Finley's justification of imperialism.

Finley contrasted the lethargic Puerto Ricans, who he believed could not adequately provide for their own welfare, with the enterprising Yankees whom he saw busy on the island building schools, draining swamps, collecting taxes, dispensing equal justice, and seeking railroad franchises. Even the last-mentioned characteristic of "our civilization" could not help but bring good to Puerto Rico. Thus, Finley's first public pronouncement on America's newly found colonial "responsibility" bubbled over with enthusiasm for what Anglo-Saxon civilization was accomplishing in the island.

The article was greeted with waves of gratitude from the people so praised, and with great interest by others. Jacob

Hollander, one of the praiseworthy Yankees (although no Anglo-Saxon), wrote of Finley's piece in the *Review of Reviews:*

> It seemed to me easily the best word that has yet been written about Porto Rico, and I am sure both my collegues [sic] and myself appreciate the thoughtful and kindly tone in which you have spoken of us.

William H. Hunt, secretary (and later governor) of the island, ruefully noted that "with the exception of yourself. . . , writers and newspapermen generally write hopelessly and with the darker side as the more attractive."

> If our friends in the North will be a little patient [Hunt added a few months later], and remember the size of the undertaking, it will help us along too. You have done your full share in telling them of the difficulties which beset us, and it is a pleasure to know we have your sympathy and good wishes.

Jacob Riis, from a different perspective, wrote upon reading "Political Beginnings in Porto Rico"—the first prose piece of Finley's he had seen—"it is fine."

> *The enticement is strong to write in behalf of powerful established regimes, especially when personal contacts, affinities in philosophy, and ethnocentrism reinforce this tendency. But even these regimes lack power to coerce all opinion, as we discovered during the antiimperialist movement of the 1960s, when our government-subsidized education gave us the tools to criticize and attack government policy. To be sure, some charged us with ingratitude, biting the hand that fed us. But this was an indefensible position, which would reduce citizenship to abject obedience. As the Indochina conflict spread, our own understanding deepened to include realization of the internal contradictions of imperialism. Finley, writing during the virtual dawn of that imperial system, displayed no interest in the antiimperialists of his own day, who were beginning to explore these contradictions.*

While Finley and other writers were busily showering praise on the efficient Anglo-Saxon reconstruction of social reality in Puerto Rico, a grim reality was being created there. Lacking any tradition of colonial responsibility, the United States allowed its control of Puerto Rico to degenerate into what Gordon Lewis in his *Puerto Rico: Freedom and Power in the Caribbean* (1968) called "imperialism of neglect." Despite the official intent to create a Jeffersonian democracy of small landholders, the lack of systematic attempt to carry out this declared United States policy resulted in just the opposite development. Within one generation, Puerto Rico became economically transformed into an island of large sugar and coffee plantations. Absentee owners drew off much of the profits, impoverishing the Puerto Ricans themselves, particularly the agricultural workers. The rich island's deformed economy soon exhibited the characteristic marks of imperialist penetration.

Finley had no perception of this. In the very month that his article appeared in the *Review of Reviews,* the state of New Jersey incorporated the South Porto Rican Sugar Company, one of the "big four" firms that would soon dominate the island's economy. Flouting laws passed by the U.S. Congress just weeks before Finley's trip there, the North American firms for almost a half century could hold a *hundred* times the amount of land legally permitted them. Independent Puerto Rican sugar producers, the *colonos,* were forced into a semiservile status, corrosive to their culture. As Luis Muñoz Marin, later governor of the island, put it—

> The American flag found Porto Rico penniless and content. It now flies over a prosperous factory worked by slaves who have lost their lands and may soon lose their guitars and their songs.

Into this system of colonial exploitation, which was being constructed behind the facade of administrative efficiency that caught Finley's eye, there soon intruded some typical attitudinal by-products. Contempt for the "natives" was growing. One San Juan correspondent admitted to Finley, "we learn very little of the people or the language, as we have little or nothing to do with the Porto Ricans, or 'spiketies' as everyone calls them." Another letter from a Yankee businessman reveals that colonial "responsibilities" quickly gave birth to a "colonial mentality," which was not quite synonymous with the spirit of brusque activism and altruistic efficiency. Finley was invited by this businessman to come to Puerto Rico, "become one of us, perhaps buying a coffee plantation and wearing a Panama hat, white duck clothes, an air of *far niento* for the rest of your days." The ambience of *far niento,* the attitude of languid luxury among despised natives, was easy for even the hard-driving, egalitarian Yankee to slip into. Characteristically for him, Finley did not choose to comment on or, what is more likely, did not perceive this ominous side of the "merger of cultures" in Puerto Rico.

Two years after his visit to Puerto Rico, Finley accepted the invitation of *Harper's Weekly* to go to Cuba just as the American military government was handing the symbols of sovereignty to a native government. The accounts of this visit he wrote in 1902 and 1903 expressed far more explicitly Finley's frank justification of U.S. policy in the Caribbean. He used his firsthand observations to buttress some of the contemporary argument for active U.S. expansion on the basis of alleged Anglo-Saxon superiority. And in these Princeton years, the professor of politics began to apply some more-or-less-sophisticated geopolitical insights to the question of America's new role as a world power.

On May 20, 1902, Finley was an eyewitness of the transfer of sovereignty to the Cuban Republic, almost four years after control over the island was granted to the United States by Spain. His article "Our Last Day in Cuba" (*Harper's Weekly,* June 7, 1902) was a cautious apology for Governor-General Leonard Wood's administration. He admitted that Wood had played the dictator, but it was "the dictatorship of a kindly, knowing surgeon, rather than that of a soldier;" and furthermore, Wood tempered the exercise of his power by continually consulting with "the best men of Cuba." Finley also conceded that the "collective motive" behind the U.S. adventure in Cuba "was not without some alloy of selfishness." But even if the Yankee achievement did not quite measure up to its announced aims," we had at any rate resisted the temptation which has come to every people in power, and this day [by hauling down the U.S. flag over Havana, we gave] evidence of the strength and sincerity of our purpose." What about the Cubans themselves? Did they resent the residual sovereignty the United States retained under the Platt Amendment? Finley quickly disposed of this question by observing that he perceived no resentment among the "jubilant" Habañeros who celebrated their formal independence with gay festivities.

The motives behind the U.S. military occupation of Cuba, Finley claimed, were only touched lightly with selfishness and presumably were altruistic for the most part. But the execution of policy was even more praiseworthy, and had he appreciated the achievement of Maj. Walter Reed at the time, Finley would have doubtless credited the United States exclusively with the successful crusade against yellow fever. He admitted that the Yankee administration was not completely free from mistakes, but these arose through excusable errors of judgment "and not from any want of desire to do the right and best thing for Cuba." The crackdown on those Cubans who treated the streets of Havana as sewers, and the sanitation drive in the city were justified, even if funds were thereby diverted from needed rural projects. In his article, "Our Account with Cuba" (*Harper's Weekly*, July 5, 1902) Finley professed to be—

> sure the people of the island cannot begrudge what has been invested in giving those shut up within their capital city access to a sweeter air, in providing a purer water to drink, and in lengthening and making more efficient the economic life of those upon whom the prosperity of the country must depend.

If Governor-General Wood's sanitation policy was essentially correct, so in Finley's eyes was the rest of the military wardship in Cuba. Thousands of the dollars that Wood was charged with squandering had gone for agricultural implements for the peasants. Charity organization methods had diminished the public relief rolls spectacularly; another year more of scientific philanthropy, Finley mused, and "it would have been possible to eliminate able-bodied beggary." Finley as educator emphatically—and predictably—agreed with Wood's pronouncement that "the future success or failure of the republic depends upon the schools." The heavy expenditures on education were therefore especially praiseworthy. Other social services, orphanages, asylums, were likewise justified. "I am confident," Finley concluded, "that nothing has consciously been spent for the exploitation of Cuba and to her own injury for the benefit of our own country or for the personal gain of those in authority." In summing up "Our Account with Cuba," Finley declared that the occupation was an act of statesmanship on a par with the formation of the United States. It was "as brave and creditable a chapter as has been written [in the annals of American history] since the days of the Civil War."

> *Finley's laudatory gloss on American imperialism in the Caribbean was a precursor of the attitudes of the academic and administrative mandarins who blithely closed their eyes to the data that were becoming overwhelming by the mid-1960s, and defended U.S. policy in Indochina. Elsewhere I have written extensively on this subject, and I have learned much from such books as Daniel Ellsberg's* Papers on the War *(1974) and Noam Chomsky's* American Power and the New Mandarins *(1969), as well as from the* Pentagon Papers *themselves. We need to know more about the social and psychological forces that shape such a bland and terrifying conformisn. This study of John Finley might help a bit.*

In addition to writing a badly needed defense of Wood's administration, Finley journeyed to La Isla de Pinos off Cuba's southwestern coast "to see this bit of earth which may some day become ours." This pleasing possibility was due to a clause in the Platt Amendment. It singled out the little Isle of Pines (the original Treasure Island) as territory omitted from "the proposed constitutional boundaries of Cuba, the title thereto being left to future adjustment by treaty." No sooner had the Spanish war ended than enterprising North Americans had flocked to this pleasant island-plateau whose pine-covered hills ensured that it would be habitable for what Finley called "temperate man."

Finley's visit formed the basis for a February 1903 article in *Scribner's*. He began it with a bit of annexationist sentiment, and the entire argument of it leans in that direction. This may have been due to his editor's suggestion that, by an allusion to possible U.S. acquisition of the Isle of Pines, "the attention of the reader would immediately be attracted." But the Platt Amendment itself, Finley's own developing ideas on U.S. expansion, and the sentiments of settlers with whom he spoke were ample cause to advance the idea of annexation. Finley had already written in behalf of the North Americans in Puerto Rico and supporting Gen. Leonard Wood's interest in Yankee tutelage on the mainland of Cuba. In his article on the Isle of Pines, Finley in the same way consciously became the spokesman for annexation-minded U.S. settlers there, who had quickly made themselves at home.

They have already pre-empted a good portion of the forest land and productive plain and have begun the planting of oranges, bananas and pineapples [he reported], in anticipation of the day when their lumber and fruit may be shipped without duty to our own ports. They urge that it is the only tropical territory within the American system not only climatically adapted but unreservedly open to American colonization, the native population bearing so trifling a proportion to the sustaining capacity of the island, and that the moral effect of an Anglo-Saxon colony in the midst of the West Indies would be thoroughly wholesome.

Finley also cited arguments that stressed the strategic value of the Isle of Pines for the impending North American control of the Caribbean.

Finley admitted that the native Pineros (who had sunk into a characteristic "dreamy sleep," he was told, until "busy, bright" Yankees began to awaken them) would not like being "hitched to our enterprise." But being polite, they were sure to make no protest. Civilization was clamoring to be let in and had already established some outposts on the Isle of Pines. Finley visited with one North American who, with a Danish cook, an ice plant, and a swimming pool "was moving the boundaries of civilized and temperate happiness nearer the equator." With such hopeful preliminary footholds as ice plants and pools already established, schools and magistrates could not be far behind. But Finley offered the whimsical hope that the "esthetic and romantic" qualities of the island could survive "the exploitation of its material resources. Here is an ideal home for a philosopher and artist."

The Yankee residents on the island found an able spokesman in John Finley. His article was read there with interest and eagerness. The Isle of Pines never became a center of art and philosophy, as Finley had hoped, but his prediction of rapid North American economic penetration was more nearly realized.

It may be safely assumed that the imperialistic sentiments of his articles on Puerto Rico and Cuba also animated his teaching of international politics at Princeton. An undated speech of his in the Finley Papers, New York Public Library, probably delivered in 1903, goes far beyond the discussion of particular localities to apprehend the larger significance and deeper meaning of United States expansion in the Caribbean. We may take this utterance as Finley's mature analysis of the subject, and the essence of his Princeton message.

Finley discerned geopolitical imperatives that demanded further expansion. In the nineteenth century, he pointed out, the white man mainly followed the lines of latitude in his search for colonies. Thus the Anglo-American pushed horizontally across North America in his conquest of that continent. But Finley perceived that the opportunities for horizontal expansion were drawing to an end; the closing of the frontier and the likelihood of "soil exhaustion" in the western states suggested expansion in another direction—southward to the tropical lands.

At the opening of the twentieth century, the course of empire seemed to Finley to be turning toward the equator. The Cape to Cairo railroad, the development of roads along the axis of South America, the expansion of Russia to the Persian Gulf, the linking of the Baltic and Black seas through canals, were indications of this new direction of Western imperialism. On the basis of these examples, Finley advanced the hypothesis of a geopolitical "Pythagorean proposition" in "the field of politics." At right angles to a traditional horizontal base, the European was extending his civilization to "the tropics and subtropics." In a characteristically whimsical pun, Finley added that this southward shift in the direction of the white man's "conquest" was "chiefly [done] to season and sweeten the food which he has earned in the sweat of his face, and to give the spice of variety to his temperate life."

John Finley was probably the most lighthearted geopolitician ever to offer a justification of imperialism. But the style of Realpolitik was alien to him, and it is hard to believe he was really serious in offering such ideas. Two other arguments were thoroughly natural to his temperament and training. The first, as has already been indicated, involved the set of notions Finley imbibed in his graduate school days, which went by the name scientific philanthropy. Just as social workers have license to inculcate such beneficent virtues as thrift, frugality, temperance, and self-reliance in the poor, so Anglo-Saxon nations have the right to bring similar values to "those helpless people" in tropical lands. They have unfortunately "remained in the race's first homestead" and so lack the hardy virtues generated naturally in temperate zones. The folk in the tropics are like the degraded paupers of the northern cities; they display certain "moral weaknesses," which are the responsibility of the Anglo-Saxon to remove. Imperialism must be practiced with the spirit of enlightened charity, Finley preached, "not the charity of the almoner giving indiscriminately and without thought, but that of the modern humanitarian who approaches as a friend and helps to self-help."

Making it difficult if not impossible to approach the benighted natives of the tropics in friendship, as Finley proposed, was the attitude of Anglo-Saxon superiority that he entertained. This was the second source of his justification of imperialism. The naiveté with which Finley urged the adoption of the white man's burden stirs reactions in the mid-twentieth century that would never have occurred to ordinary Americans at the century's outset. Assumptions of racial and ethnic superiority were commonplace in Finley's milieu. He himself did not shrink from suggesting that Anglo-Saxon practices could legitimately be introduced among the colonial peoples, if need be, on the points of bayonets.

> We may disagree [Finley said] as to the political relationship which should exist between us and peoples of the tropics, between the white and the black or the yellow, but if we believe in our own civilization, we must agree that there are some peoples on the face of the earth good enough to compel others, whether they will or not, to give their children a chance to live a better life.

"The Western Civilization Trust," as Finley called it, which "controls practically the entire output of dress, morals and politics as well as the industry of the temperate zones," seemed about to extend its control to the rest of the world. Finley could not help but applaud what the future held in store.

> *It is a simple point, yet widely disregarded: that benevolent aims, whether genuine or only ostensible, do not guarantee benevolent results. This is most evident in the field of philanthropic programs, of which I have made several careful studies (see chapters 6 and 7 in this book). Acclaimed schemes of benevolence and amelioration frequently mask a more systematic and mystified oppression. So Finley weaves here the benevolent doctrines of early social work into a defense of imperialism. It ought to give pause for a healthy skepticism to reassert*

itself when we hear of Some Great Scheme to Do Good for People, especially if that scheme does not arise from the people actually concerned, but is imposed from above.

He was thus able to weave his defense of American imperialism from diverse strands, but only after the policy itself had been initiated. This simple sequence—first the policy and then Finley's justification—suggests the major reason for his advocating the pursuit of Manifest Yankee Destiny in the tropics. Finley was the sort of man who, when a movement had been set afoot by men whom he respected, felt an irresistible obligation to support it. So, when a group of genteel activists, such as Theodore Roosevelt and Leonard Wood, began to act upon the conviction of a need for American expansion, Finley was swept along. The new consciousness of United States "responsibilities" in the world was indeed the product of an intellectual formulation by some pioneering American thinkers in the late nineteenth century, as Walter La Feber shows in his *New Empire* (1963). But once the ideological consensus had been forged, and action initiated, then there was the need for the lesser talents of the justifiers of what had been done. During his years as a professor at Princeton, Finley managed to perform this service of swelling the chorus of justification for America's new imperialist policy.

Chapter 15

Verse and Philosophy:

A Trial Balance on the Man and His Ideals
at the Beginning of the Twentieth Century

This chapter makes me a bit uncomfortable. In the unlikely event that some biographer ever traces my footsteps, as I have Finley's, what sorts of "trial balances" and "final balances" will be struck? The terrifying question of what one has done with one's life is raised: whether ideals have been abandoned, opportunities missed. Can anyone give unambiguously positive answers to these questions? I can't.

In addition to achieving eminent academic position and making his voice heard on major national policy, Finley at the turn of the century was on his way to a modest reputation as a minor versifier. As a young father, while still at Knox College, Finley had begun to compose rhymes to entertain his daughter Ellen and her friends. In 1897 he gathered this material into a book, *Ellen, Her Book: Being a Collection of Rhymes about Ellen Boyden Finley and Some of Her Childhood Friends, by Her Father,* which was printed in Galesburg. In these little lyrics he celebrated the appearance of a first tooth as an event as noteworthy as Columbus's discovery of America. He whimsically described the antics of some Galesburg citizen of two or three years of age. Or he sang of the poverty of a college president-writer:

> The cupboard's bare, my child; oh bye,
> > Bye low;
> I hear the wolfie's hungry cry—
> > Bye low.
> > So go to sleep, my pretty one,
> > While father takes his inky gun
> > And hunts a little bunny-bun
> For baby's breakfast. Bye low, bye,
> > Bye low.

. . . .

A generation later (for youngsters who called him Bompa), Finley would write verse in the same vein to the delight of Ellen's children, nieces, and nephews.

> *In time I was to meet these children and some of the grandchildren of Finley, many of whom will no doubt wish that I had not cluttered up the biography of their eminent ancestor with my own autobiographical musings. My children, to whom John Finley has been almost as palpable a reality as if he were some distant uncle, would probably be more interested in the author than the subject of this book. There is some crossover between the two groups of children, as when a Finley off-spring comes to New York for a weekend and calls on the telephone. A Gettleman child gets the call and wide-eyed runs to tell her daddy that "Finley is on the phone."*

In the years he was professor at Princeton, Finley began composing verse, more serious in subject if not in manner of treatment, for prominent national periodicals. In March of 1901, Richard Watson Gilder's genteel monthly, the *Century*, carried one of Finley's offerings. He wrote a fanciful ode "To a Bookworm," envying the little invertebrate's course "[be]-tween the vellum walls of some sweet classic tome." How happy is the worm's destiny, denied to mortals, To "lay the sapient bones [!] in such sarcophagus/And is forever buried in a book." In April, 1901, Finley's "The Death of Earth" appeared in *The Chautauquan*. Appropriately somber tones were used to invoke the image of death. But death gives rise to hope; "from the fresh-made, furrowed grave will spring/A new earth. . . ." In the same year he brought out a verse on the Russian samovar, whose "pan-slavic brew/. . . stirs all the na-tion's tongues to gossiping." *Scribner's Monthly* in November, 1902, printed one of Finley's most widely noted poems, "Ploughing Time." It was a celebration of the birth of honor-able ambition on the Illinois prairie and has already been cited.

Of his early poetry, "Life Is a Lamp" (which appeared in May, 1903) exploits that metaphor that best sums up Finley's outlook on life and his philosophy of education. An examina-tion of this poem is equivalent to striking a trial balance on the man and his ideals.

> A Lamp, of gentle, thoughtful fashioning,
> As God-designed to carry flame, to bear
> Through Earth's brief dark some share of that true Light
> Which lighteth every man his hither way.
> . . . .

[into the Lamp's bowl]
On some solitary plain or starless sea
In some black cellar of a city's shame
Or in some sleepless, wide-horizoned tower,
Is poured the oil—the fuel of the past,
Of those long yesterdays which feed to-day,
Refined from out the race's age of stone
. . . And now decanted in these fragrant bowls.

Yet vain the oil, the Wick—the lamp itself,—
If there be lacking fire to light it with;

Some spark of flint of hard experience,
Some burning lens's kindling from the skies,
Some coals from off a neighbor's friendly hearth,
Some lingering embers of that natal fire;

But touched of these, the oil is quick transmute;
In Earth's free air the buried past flames forth;
The unbreathed thought is translate into speech—
The speech of eye and hand and tongue; the truth
Is luminant in poem, picture, deed,
In glance, in shining countenance, that makes
A brightness for a little space about
And transfigures all where its radiance falls.

"One must hesitate," as a reviewer of Finley's *Poems* did,
"to call these verses 'poems.'" Their shortcomings as poetry
are painfully evident: the archaic mannerisms, the often la
bored puns, the weakness of the imagery, the blurred messages. Although the stanzas of "Life Is a Lamp" will not
support weighty exegesis, they do reveal the author's conception of life and, more specifically, of education.

The metaphor of the lamp clearly stands for the school. Its
function is to provide a consecrated place where the beneficent presence of the devoted teacher is made manifest. But
the teacher is no spokesman for any individualistic outlook,
but rather the transmitter of the accumulated wisdom of "the
buried past." Ultimately this wisdom is God's. His "natal fire"
can be passed on in a variety of ways; elaborate academic
establishments are not necessary. The spark of religious reverence can even in the most humble pedagogical circumstances light up the past and, as a lamp, cast its precious
radiance on the surrounding students.

Finley's description of the educational process in the verses
of "Life Is a Lamp" was in partial accord with his practice as
professor and college president. There is some evidence that,
in his Princeton teaching, the power of his own personal

presence was foremost: that he tried to light a lamp for his students. But this interpretation of the teacher's role suffers from the implication that the student is a passive receptacle of transmitted truth. Finley himself seemed to demand active participation of the students such as few Princeton professors did at that time.

> As a teacher I often experience a tension between two pedagogical styles: the Socratic probing that elicits student response, and the polished lecture that, when it "works," prompts the students' admiration for clarity of thought and presentation. But the lecture has the drawback of confirming student passivity, while the discussion format can degenerate to a mere sharing of more or less uninformed impressions. The two styles can, however, be mixed and reconciled on the basis of critical exploration of the interplay between an investigator's standpoint and the objective reality he or she seeks to understand. This book, too, aims at being something of an exercise in such interplay.

But in his capacity as college president, Finley more nearly corresponded to the metaphor of the lamp. As we have seen, during his Knox College presidency he was the agent of the Galesburg community's purpose in maintaining a collegiate institution. Finley was amazingly inventive and ingenious in devising means to carry out this purpose of modernizing the school while keeping the core of pious commitment intact. He was himself fully in accord with the purpose, but policy was not initiated by him. On the level of policy making, John Finley as Knox College president was the transmitter of "natal fire" kindled by others. We shall soon see how he accomplished equivalent tasks as educational administrator in New York City and State.

If it can provide perspective on his educational outlook, Finley's verse also reveals his general conception of life. To him, poetry's function was to justify the ways of God to man. And he had little doubt of the beneficence of the Creator's plan. His God was like a kindly teacher. Just as the teacher's presence brings about education, so the divine Presence makes bearable worldly care, even death. This last grim inevitability is transformed in Finley's verse into a sleep, a "vigil for a resurrection day," even an awakening. The function of his poetry was to cloak the gritty texture of everyday existence in a shimmering haze of sentiment. Verse, Finley claimed, should provide "color and sweetness and fragrance and solace out of the most trying conditions of life."

In his little verse-sermons, Finley offered the message of comfort and hope. These buoyant little rhymes clearly reveal his Pollyanna temperament. For example, he wrote in 1913 in Scottish dialect on the misfortunes of life.

> When failures becloud the blue of your sky
> And troubles begin in torrents to pour,
> Just think of the floods that others have whelmed
> And say to yourself, "It micht ha' been waur,"
> —You're drenched but no droon'd; it micht ha' been waur!
>
> When out on life's sea your vessel is wrecked,
> Beyond the relief of a humanly shore,
> Cling fast to the spar God's put in your hand
> And say to yourself, "It micht ha' been waur,"
> —Some haven't a spar, it micht ha' been waur!
>
> When Death, blanching Death, stalks into your street
> And knocks with appalling hand at your door;
> Hold fast to the hope God's put in your heart
> And say to yourself, "It micht ha' been waur,"
> —What if you'd nae hope! It micht ha' been waur!
>
> . . . .
> And when you shall stand before the Great Judge,
> Who'll open the Book and scan your life o'er,
> May He in His live forgive where you've tried,
> And say to your soul, "It micht ha' been waur,"
> "Gang ye wi' the sheep, it micht ha' been waur!"

Occasionally his verse touched on social themes, revealing the limitations of his poetic vision, as well as the shortcomings of his social outlook. Just after war had broken out in 1914, Finley addressed a poem "To A Peace Advocate."

> Your work will not be in vain; for out of War
> Will come the proofs, the ghastly hideous proofs
> Gathered from fortress, trench and corpse-strewn field,
> Witnessed by myriad wounds and broken hearts,
> Inscribed, in time, on sorrowing shafts and tombs,
> And writ at last on history's calm page,—
> Proofs of the truths you've made the whole world hear,
> Proofs of the truth the whole world yet will heed.
>
> . . . .
> When the red strife is but a memory
> On new foundation will the nations build,
> And they will take for its chief corner-stone
> This stone [of peace] rejected by the purblind kings.

In this verse the "peace advocate" is condemned merely to the futility of gesturing at the battlefield, in the hope that "the nations" will one day heed him. Finley's heart was not really in these pacifist utterances; even before the United States became involved in the First World War, Finley became an ardent supporter, not of peace, but of preparedness.

Into his verse Finley poured a mixture of whimsy and tender sentimentalism. He wrote to demonstrate the essential fitness of things, to preach accommodation to this best of all possible earthly existences, and to urge preparation for an afterlife presided over by a compassionate Diety, much in the same way a kindly college president presides over an undergraduate institution. Finley's rhymes were thus the vehicles for the commonplace tenets of "practical idealism," a creed that flowed naturally from the upbringing and training that has been chronicled in this study.

Furthermore, such notions were functional for the life and career Finley had chosen. It is abundantly clear that the academic man in America, whether professor or college president, was not in his day expected to stand for eccentric, radical, or avant garde notions. John Finley, whose verse mirrored his own temperament, remained throughout the early decades of the twentieth century a champion of traditional, and comfortable, nineteenth-century verities.

Book 5.
Big City Education

Chapter 16

Return to New York City:

The Inducements of CCNY, 1903

It is in these CCNY chapters that I am most engaged with the world that Finley lived in and bequeathed. My involvement with City College, like his, began with a ritual return to the Big City–in my case after marriage and a year or so in Southern California. As Marge and I in 1953 drove east in our battered '41 Plymouth sedan, the city and its legendary school—nurturer of seedy geniuses and playground athletes— beckoned us invitingly.

It would be hard to conceive of an academic environment further from Finley's comfortable position at leisurely, aristocratic Princeton than the one at the City College of New York. Housed in a modest building on Manhattan's East Twenty-third Street, CCNY had been founded in 1847 as the Free Academy of New York and for nearly a half century had been headed by West Point graduates including the venerable Gen. Alexander Steward Webb, who in 1863 had led the troops that repulsed Pickett's charge on the Union lines at the Battle of Gettysburg. By the end of the nineteenth century, CCNY attracted mostly sons of recent immigrants. Upton Sinclair, who enrolled at CCNY in 1892, stood out as an exalted "Anglo-Saxon," despite his shabby-genteel background and drunkard father. Sinclair was asked once to join a fraternity by a "haughty upperclassman" who explained, We "want to keep ourselves apart from the kikes and wops who make up the greater part of our student body." But the young future novelist and socialist resisted these ethnic blandishments to reach out for friends among the students from backgrounds so markedly different from his own. Under Webb and his predecessor (Dr. Horace Webster), CCNY managed to combine military discipline with classical training. Rather than any center of great scholarship or famous teaching, CCNY in the late nineteenth century, and long afterward, was chiefly significant as it provided opportunities for social mobility. In the realm of higher education, New York's free college represented to the children of recent immigrants an America that could be hospitable to them and possibly fulfill their ambitions.

CCNY numbered among its student body mostly fiercely ambitious sons of the city's lower middle class. To the elderly, bewhiskered gentlemen of the faculty, the boys under their care often seemed like a horde of unwashed barbarians. Many of the students themselves were painfully aware of their own lack of social grace. The future philosopher Morris R. Cohen, who entered CCNY two years after Upton Sinclair, described the often painful process of adjustment that City College boys of humble origin had to endure before they could be at ease with people of a more refined and cultivated background. Before he could come to CCNY, Finley himself would have to recognize that, socially at least, he would be stepping downward from his Princeton professorship.

At least one of Finley's friends, the editor Albert Shaw, had the prescience to predict that Finley would not, upon coming to Princeton, settle into the "ruts of a retired and sheltered professorial life." Soon after he began his third year of teaching politics, Finley's name was being mentioned among the trustees of CCNY as a possible successor to General Webb. Many years later Columbia University president Nicholas Murray Butler would claim to have had an early perception of Finley as a "young man . . . in possession of those qualities and characteristics which give life its charm, its usefulness and its distinction," and therefore brought him to the attention of the men who would choose a new president for CCNY. But Finley's name was already before the trustees when Edward Morse Shepard sought Butler's opinion on the candidates. The most energetic of the CCNY trustees, Shepard was a New York lawyer and politician, both a "gold Democrat" and a power in Tammany Hall. He was close to Grover Cleveland, and Finley's Princeton neighbor, the ex-president, may have had something to do with drawing attention to Finley. From what-ever source, Shepard was impressed with what he heard about the man and only playfully wondered if it would be suitable to select "a man who does not conceal the fact that he is a 'Professor of Politics.' Perhaps it will be said," Shepard hoped, in a note to a fellow trustee, that Finley "does not practice what he preaches."

> *This remark of Shepard raises in its early twentieth-century context one of the most puzzling problems of American academic life—what shall a professor profess? Merely the "discipline" in which he or she was trained? Finley, whose postgraduate training came before the emergence of separate academic "disciplines" (some of them quite "un-disciplined" in any critical thinking), had no hesitation in "professing" the activist ideal of public service. Why should a socialist academic nowadays (apart from the prudent concern for keeping his or her job) not clearly take a position on the need to replace capitalism with a humane collective-egalitarian society?*

In December, 1902, after having spoken with some of the trustees, Finley apologized for having taken their time "un-necessarily." He confessed that it was "unlikely" that he would accept the CCNY presidency "even if it were unani-mously offered. This I must say . . . in spite of the fact that such a work appeals to me mightily." But he did not flatly refuse, and this was taken to be a hopeful sign by some of the trustees. After the new year, Shepard literally began a barrage of letters, asking Finley to pardon him for being such a "persistent beggar." Finley's determination to remain at Princeton began to melt by the spring, by which time he had met most of the trustees; and he began to cast about for advice.

Ira Remsen, the chemist who succeeded Daniel Coit Gil-man in the presidency of Johns Hopkins, offered Finley the testimony of a CCNY alumnus. Remsen was there "between the ages of fourteen and seventeen."

> That was a good many years ago. I fancy things have changed somewhat since then [Remsen added], but I don't know. It is, of course, quite different from the colleges you know about in every respect, and I doubt whether you would feel comfortable there. But I know too little about it to justify me in saying much about it. Looking at the matter from the point of view of the college, I hope you may see your way clear to accepting.

Frederick B. Pratt (of Pratt Institute in Brooklyn, New York) also professed to be largely ignorant of the work done at CCNY, but he was more candid in his impressions about the place.

> The college has been considered as doing High School work simply, and there have been objections to it on the part of High School principals and also University men, who feel that there is no reason for its existence in a city supplied with schools of a high school grade and with plenty of opportunities along university lines. On the other hand [Pratt observed], the College is reaching a class of poorer students than can be reached through private institutions and has proved its possibilities of service by turning out a number of graduates who have developed into strong men.
>
> I think a large percentage of the students are of foreign parentage and that a great many of them are Hebrews. . . . [But] the College offers an opportunity to a man who could develop it. . . . he would find a strong support in the pride of the middle-classes in New York in their City College.
>
> It would [Pratt concluded], of course, be a very different kind of position from the one you are holding at present, and, with all its chances for work and development, would not in any way take the place of the life you lead at Princeton.

As an attractive candidate who was sought for the CCNY presidency, rather than himself seeking it, Finley indulged his own misgivings about any move to New York. As the trustees waited for his decision, they made explicit the sort of offer they were prepared to make. "The invitation will go out to you without embarrassments or entanglements," Edward M. Shepard promised, "leaving you to deal according to your best judgement with an interesting and very promising situation." Three vacant professorships would remain unfilled until Finley's voice could be heard. His salary was set at $8,250, a handsome sum in those days. Moreover, since CCNY was a municipally supported institution, "without the technical schools of a university," Finley would be free from the ordeal of fund raising that so plagued him in the nineties at Knox College.

> [The new president, wrote Shepard] will have considerable opportunity for such independent work as he shall deem it proper to do. The trustees would not only be content but glad, to have you continue such literary work as you should deem it proper. We should rather hope that you would find it convenient to deliver . . . lectures . . . to the senior class; but that would be left entirely to your own decision.

Lest Finley worry about the modesty of the present quarters of the college, he was assured that the municipal government, after a long struggle, had authorized the construction of a new $2-million campus. Shepard, who had been active in obtaining this authorization, boasted: "We have just begun the erection of what will probably be the finest college buildings in New York (not even Columbia excepted). They are to be placed upon a magnificent and commodious site" in upper Manhattan. Shepard admitted that these inducements "on the grosser and material side" might not touch Finley's "most serious problem"—whether he would want to give up his Princeton life to preside over such an institution as City College no matter how well endowed it was. Perhaps because it was such a challenge, because it would bring him back to the big city (which had already demonstrated its pull on the farm-bred Finley), because he welcomed the chance to preside over CCNY's ethnic diversity, or for some combination of reasons, Finley, in April, accepted. Even before his formal consent was received in New York, the press had "got on" to the matter. When Shepard received Finley's official acceptance on April 20, 1903, climaxing the trustees' long campaign to get the Princeton professor, he wrote, "You may be sure that I was glad enough to get it."

Chapter 17

The Main Business of a CCNY President:

Embracing Ethnic Diversity

The only college president with whom I ever had—I cannot say "enjoyed"—personal contact was Buell Gallagher, a former minister who came to CCNY in 1952, the year before I enrolled as a student. An extreme anti-Communist, Gallagher left CCNY briefly in the early 1960s to head the California State College System, but he soon returned, his anti-Communist zeal apparently found wanting by more exacting California standards. As a student radical, and as a young instructor at CCNY, my relationships with Gallagher varied from icy formality to petty harrassment (from his side). For example, when I once spoke off campus on the topic of revolutionary Cuba, the leaflet announcing my talk labeled me as "CCNY Professor" when I was only a "lecturer." Evidently monitoring the political activity of at least part of his CCNY faculty, Gallagher got hold of the leaflet and warned me against misrepresenting my connection with the college. I was clearly slated for dismissal, which came a year or so later.

In trying to induce Finley to take the CCNY position, Nicholas Murray Butler had written from Columbia University's Morningside Heights campus that you "would be heartily welcomed here by all of us who are already in the harness. . . ."And after Finley had joined CCNY, another university president accepted him into the ranks of what was already becoming something of a fraternity, with a common set of cares and preoccupations. "I have always believed," said William Rainey Harper of the University of Chicago, "that you had very large executive ability and that you were 'hiding yourself under a bushel' when you accepted the [Princeton] professorship and tried to limit yourself to that field of work. There are plenty of men to be professors; there are only a few to be presidents of colleges and universities. The profession

will, I am sure, welcome you." Finley quickly stepped into his
new role. He thanked Butler for the cordial welcome; expressed to Charles F. Thwing of Western Reserve University,
dean of American college presidents, his happiness "to come
back to any company of which you are a member"; arranged
for a successor at Princeton; and began preparation for his
formal inaugural.

Knowing well the value of academic ceremony, Finley bent
his resources to making the occasion worthy of note. Distinguished speakers were needed, and he aimed for the president of the United States. Although Theodore Roosevelt declined to attend, he did send his greetings to CCNY and its
new president. Other dignitaries did gather at Carnegie Hall
on September 29, 1903, including a panoply of university
presidents—Remsen of Johns Hopkins, Butler of Columbia,
Hadley of Yale. Chauncey Depew, the railroad magnate, represented business, and Grover Cleveland, personal friend of
the Finley family, represented politics. The students of
CCNY, the faculty, trustees, alumni, the city of New York (in
the person of Mayor Seth Low), the state of New York (in the
person of Gov. Benjamin B. Odell), and other secular interests
represented;   clergymen—Catholic,   Protestant,   Jewish—
spoke for the spirit.

Finley began his inaugural address in a characteristically
self-deprecating tone. CCNY is a living institution he said,
with its own rhythms and purposes.

> The coming or going of one man is but a minor incident in the existence
> of this corporation; for it is not subject to the threats and mutations of
> mortality; . . . it is vulnerable only in its faithlessness to its ideals;
> mortal only in the indifference of the greater body of which it is a living
> member.

Faced with the presidency of an immortal institution, Finley
was reduced (rhetorically, at least) to administrative helpless-
ness. "I cannot here publish or defend," he admitted to his
audience, "the particular purposes or policies I cherish for this
College." He would not be specific on the issue of the curriculum; he refused to support any of the standard alternatives
of the day—the classics, modern languages, or science. That
curriculum is best "which gives those who walk in it the
companionship of the best men and the best scholars [of the

ages]." The "extent" of any study at CCNY would be determined by the resources of the school and the capacities of the
students; the "content" of the curriculum, said Finley, would
depend upon adaptation to the times.

> Perhaps the most dramatic examples I know of an educator bowing to
> community pressure (or, worse still, completely and uncritically iden-
> tifying himself with unenlightened popular attitudes) was the cold war
> Buell Gallagher waged against the U.S. Communist party and its stu-
> dent affiliates at CCNY. This reached a crescendo in Gallagher's speech
> of 1960 on "The Not-So-Silent Generation." In that talk he lamented the
> entry during the 1930s of "a new and sinister element . . . into cam-
> pus life," the Communists who wore "the same bright face of idealism"
> as earlier crusaders, but whose basic motivation was, not concern for
> ethical questions of social justice," but an impulse "to seize power for
> themselves." So ran the anti-Communist liturgy of the cold war era that
> I became increasingly disenchanted with. Not that the CP/USA is or
> should be beyond criticism; but one of its errors was surely not any
> precipitate tendency to "seize power," as Gallagher and other cold war
> liberals believed.

Finley well knew that City College would have to change
under his administration, but wisely at the outset he declined
to lay out any preconceived program. That was not his way;
John Finley would discover his mission by more subtle
methods. The collegiate development that he determined to
foster at CCNY would depend upon his progressive discern-
ment of the larger community's purpose in sustaining the
institution. In what he considered this basic task of an educational
administrator, Finley would display in New York, much as he had
done in Galesburg, Illinois, considerable ingenuity and imagination.

Despite reluctance to discuss any specific educational practices he would endorse, Finley did in his inaugural address
identify a historical trend toward urban democracy, to which
CCNY would have to respond. While he would not endorse
without qualification the notion "that the inevitable is always
the best," he nevertheless maintained that, for all ordinary
purposes (among them education), "it is a good earthly philosophy to make the best of what inevitably" will be. And he did
embrace democracy as his ideal for City College, while recognizing that this ideal would have to work itself out in an urban
environment. Committing CCNY to democracy, Finley also
warned that the college ought not to follow slavishly the "de-

mos of the day." The function of the higher learning was to
check the dangers of democracy by enhancing the more en-
during interests of the people, rather than their temporary
passions. Education was, to Finley, the "ballast" of democracy.

> Coming back to CCNY as a young instructor in the early 1960s, I soon
> became aware how CCNY officials of a half century later sought to
> check the alleged dangers of democracy: repression, in a word. Early in
> the fall of 1961, the presidents of all New York City's municipal col-
> leges, including CCNY, issued a policy ukase barring Communist
> speakers from the campuses. It was absurd, we thought, for a school
> that produced Nobel Prize winners to engage in such petty repression; it
> would not be long before the senior faculty (former teachers of those of
> us in junior positions) would put a stop to this. Days went by, and when
> no such action was taken, a group of young, non-Communist instructors
> began to circulate a petition and agitate against the noxious speaker
> ban. We created such a furor that the ban was soon lifted, but within
> two or three years all of the protesting instructors, including me, had
> been let go from the faculty.

In the preface to his history of the college presidency in
America, George P. Schmidt has wittily described the half-
mythical modern college president in whose existence the
student believes but whom, like Santa Claus, he never expects
to see in the flesh. Finley was more like the old-time college
president. He reached out generously to the students and,
with an extraordinary display of personal warmth and human
sympathy, almost literally embraced the entire City College
student population.

Students were encouraged to visit at the Finley home. One
of a trio of boys from the class of 1907 remembered the Friday
night gatherings over the distance of a half century. The college president discussed "current events" with the youngsters, who experienced exquisite delight at the treatment accorded them by so august a host and hostess as President and
Mrs. John H. Finley.

The City College boys were rarely polished gentlemen, but
Finley graciously discounted their occasional gaucheries. One
student, who became a lawyer after leaving CCNY, remembered sitting beside him at a formal dinner.

> Somehow I clumsily dug into my poorly cut grapefruit and juice squirted
> into Dr. Finley's face and eyes. I was most uneasy and ashamed, and my
> face felt quite hot. However, Dr. Finley, without any interruption, con-

tinued his remarks, partook of his food, and most tactfully and unobtrusively dabbed away the facial superfluities. I was put at ease. No one nearby was aware of what took place.

This incident of gentlemanly conduct has lived with me these past thirty-five years in loving remembrance of a good and kindly soul [this CCNY alumnus told me three decades later].

Finley often met students about the city. Invariably he chatted with them, and the boys eagerly listening to his words were heartened by little homilies. Finley's favorite was "Make a friend, read a book, take a walk." Reinforced by his personal presence, such advice could actually make disciples. One graduate of the college testified to this force of presence. He fell into stride beside Finley one day and, during a three-mile stroll, was "exhilarated" by the way the good doctor "in his simple and straightforward manner . . . could penetrate your innermost thoughts." (He also became exhausted by Finley's vigorous pace.) Somehow the younger man on this walk was induced to abandon accountancy for the law, although before meeting Finley that day he had "no more thought of being a lawyer than being at the North Pole."

In those halcyon days before offices of undergraduate guidance and departments of student life, it frequently fell to the college president to counsel students. Finley often gave advice on career objectives and, what is more, aided these careers on numerous occasions with a letter of recommendation, or a word to some acquaintance who could help out a promising CCNY boy.

In later years these student life offices, such as the one at CCNY, began to discharge other tasks beside the benign ones of campus adjustment and career guidance. They began surveillance of radical students, and probably faculty. I have no direct evidence of the latter, not yet having gotten around to requesting my file from the FBI, but I do remember a minor but poignant episode from the early 1960s. I had come back to CCNY to teach, and gradually the students began to be aware that I was one of the radicals on campus. While such a reputation brought me mostly hassles, denials of promotion, and eventually dismissal, occasionally something good would come my way. Once a radical student organization needed a faculty chaperone for some weekend outing, and I was asked to go. I did, and had a good time. Weeks later one of the unaffiliated students, a black undergraduate, came up to me on campus and in an anguished way told me that his name had been given to the FBI by the dean of students. A FBI agent called on him to offer a salary if he would join and supply information on the radical student organization that had invited him on the weekend picnic. To the student's credit, he declined.

Finley evidently felt that his duty as president also obliged him to visit students who were ill, but it was certainly a rare and tender man who would sense such duty. One graduate of the class of 1914, who would end his career in the New York City educational system as a school principal, wrote of one such event:

> In my sophomore year, I was accidentally injured. One hot Sunday afternoon, while I was recuperating in our East Side flat, my brother came to my bed to announce that I had a visitor. Imagine my surprise, when I looked up, to hear President Finley greeting me in his sonorous and cheerful voice. He told me not to worry about the term finals because arrangements would be made for me to make them up before the start of the fall semester. He said also that a certain instructor, who shall be nameless, would visit me later, since he did not come that day. That instructor never did come.

Another student who had planned to become a social worker wrote to Finley from a convalescent home in 1909: "The memory of the visit you paid me when I was ill in bed stands out in bold relief in my mind, and I shall ever look upon that night as the happiest of my life."

Some years after the new college buildings were erected on Saint Nicholas Heights, a boy drowned in the pool. Finley personally brought the news to the mother on Avenue C. A Russian Jew, she was "unable to understand a word of English." In his diary Finley wrote of the "awful experience" of walking with her on the streets of Manhattan's Lower East Side to find an English-speaking relative who could translate the grim message. A year earlier, he went to court to attend the sentencing of a CCNY student and two days later visited the parents in Brooklyn to urge "them to think of what could be done for [the] Boy on release." Evidently the right thing was done, for the young convict eventually graduated and became a pharmacist.

It would take little effort to muster vast quantities of additional evidence about this especially attractive aspect of John Finley's presidential career at City College. It was not just that he was a kindly man, but that his expressions of kindliness took so personal a form. He displayed the fatherly manner that Newton Bateman once had shown, the style of an old-time college president as usually seen at denominational colleges on the prairie, or in Eastern institutions rich in history and tradition. But CCNY was unique. It was of course in the midst of the city; it lacked "collegiate" atmosphere and tradition; its student population was far different from those of the institutions (Knox College, Johns Hopkins, Princeton) where Finley had his previous experience. Relatively innocent of systematic educational theory, Finley made his administration the almost direct emanation of his vigorous personal presence; and this presence included the overwhelming impression of physical vitality.

Upon coming to CCNY, at its old downtown campus, Finley felt the need for systematic physical exercise. He undertook training under a teacher from a nearby high school. Finley found this training so satisfactory that he felt guilty, for City College students had no such opportunities. "[They] needed the training more than I did," he remembered. The president soon secured the use of the 69th Regiment Armory, near the college, and there CCNY students for the first time were offered physical training. Apparently Finley bore the financial burden of such instruction himself until the trustees authorized the employment of a teacher.

When the college moved to its new Saint Nicholas Heights location in 1908, full gymnasium facilities were available. Finley set the students an example in the use of these facilities. They often peered into the handball courts and were delighted to see their president and some instructor in manly competition. Many of these boys lived in crowded tenements where people slept on the roofs in summertime. Finley acknowledged that he too slept outdoors on especially warm nights, on the roof of the main college building.

Clearly the aspect of Finley's great physical exuberance with which the CCNY student could identify most was his pedestrian feats. Early in life he had learned to walk long distances on the Illinois prairie, and he continued this practice at Knox College, at Princeton, and on his journey to Puerto Rico. But after he came to City College, Finley reached new heights (or lengths) in his peregrinations. He often walked to Princeton, New Jersey, and made it something of a ritual to circle Manhattan on foot on his birthday.

Eager students at CCNY sought to emulate him and established a Finley Walking Club, with the college president as an honorary officer. Under his inspiration, they might take such routes on their Sunday afternoon strolls as that from "the sensible end of the Williamsburg Bridge to Coney Island." His simple, homely exhortation, "Read a book, take a walk, make a friend," when backed up by his own impressive example, was full of meaning. When Finley left City College to become state educational commissioner, three undergraduates paid him a fitting tribute by marching from New York City to Albany to attend his inaugural ceremonies.

> *Except for some light journalism on the joys of pedestrianship, Finley left no record of what athletic experience meant to him. One can assume, however, that athletics had meaning as part of a well-rounded life. A classic scholar like Finley would be ready with the phrase from Juvenal, mens sana in corpore sano. But for some of us, there was a cultural disjunction between mental and physical activity; they did not naturally mesh: one was either a "brain" or a "jock." Those who attempted to maneuver in both realms had the sense of being bold pioneers, and it added exhilaration to life. One young historian, now a professor at a distinguished West Coast university, worked with me as a lifeguard on the New York beaches in the 1950s. We ostentatiously carried erudite volumes of abstruse philosophy and French poetry up to our wooden towers and felt we were bridging two cultures farther apart than the tendencies that C. P. Snow would soon isolate.*

When Finley arrived, there were about two thousand boys seeking education at City College, about half in the three-year secondary course. Until the 1880s the students were drawn from the "older" population strains and included many Anglo-Saxons, such as Upton Sinclair. By the turn of the century Jews were in the majority in every graduating class. Sons of tradesmen and professionals predominated; not until the "open admissions" era in the 1960s was CCNY anything like a proletarian college. The Jewish boys were studious, generally serious, and prudently displayed an attitude of tolerance. Of mainly German origin, the Jewish students seemed politically conservative. A perceptive faculty member reported, "More of them were Republicans than Democrats, none was a Socialist, and probably nobody among them even knew what a Communist was."

In due time socialism and communism would appear at the college, and student radicalism would provide problems for a succession of later CCNY deans and presidents. But during the ten relatively innocent years he presided over the college, Finley never had to deal with problems of this sort. The students in his time were as eager to become assimilated to America as Finley was to have them Americanized. A man who served under him on the City College faculty perceived that Finley "was a man of such broad and tolerant views, and was so deeply interested in helping students make a happy orientation into American life that he was a powerful influence in a true Americanization program."

The later appearance of radicalism at CCNY reflects the less "happy" aspects of American life, especially the great depression crisis of the thirties, which filled CCNY with a profusion of student and faculty radicals. Despite the later claims of anti-Communists that the Communists were negligible in the struggles of this period, my researches show that Communists were the key group. By the end of the thirties, various attempts were taking shape to rout the Communists (or at least open Communist activity) from campus. Defections from party ranks during the period of the Nazi-Soviet pact created a body of informers willing to testify about Communists on the faculty and staff. A New York State legislative investigation under the co-chairmanship of Assemblyman Herbert A. Rapp and State Senator Frederic R. Coudert, Jr., probed Communist activity at the college and turned its data over to the Board of Higher Education, the "secular arm," which dismissed over thirty staff members at CCNY and the other municipal colleges. I am now engaged in the research for a book I hope one day to publish on the Rapp-Coudert inquiry, which I see as something of a "rehearsal for McCarthyism."

Chapter 18

Showmanship and Image Building:

CCNY, 1908–13

If Finley was striving in the early twentieth century to build an image for CCNY–in ways I will try to illuminate in this chapter–by the mid-1950s an image was already available. It was the concept of the Little Red Schoolhouse, the radical college, not quite the image that Finley would have found congenial–and one that drove Buell Gallagher into near frenzy. I had my first vivid experience of the reality that lay behind this image when I eavesdropped during my first semester at CCNY on an election debate for officers of the college's Gilbert & Sullivan Society, which turned on whether the Soviet Union was a deformed workers' state or an example of state capitalism. This highly politicized atmosphere–in which Communists, Trotskuists, anarchists and other radicals argued, battled, and polemicized with the apathetic, careerist majority–gave CCNY much of the excitement I experienced there. There were some challenging teachers, but the faculty were a tame lot; faculty radicalism had been dealt a major blow in the anti-Communist Rapp-Coudert investigation of over a decade earlier.

CCNY's new uptown Manhattan campus gave Finley enhanced opportunity to practice on a more lavish scale the arts of academic showmanship that had distinguished his presidency at Knox College in the 1890s. The neo-Gothic buildings of the college included a Great Hall of vast dimensions, which the president was quick to exploit. The dedication on May 14, 1908, was a model of the sort of ceremony that flourished under Finley's auspices. Distinguished personages gathered, including Lord James Bryce, who preached the legitimacy of the desire for success. "We cannot blame ambition," the British ambassador told a sympathetic audience of CCNY boys; "ambition is one of those spurs to action that human nature cannot dispense with."

Among the other guests that day were Oscar Straus, secretary of commerce and labor, New York mayor George B. McClellan, Charles W. Eliot, and Mark Twain. An impressive moment came when Finley introduced Mrs. Grover Cleveland, who came in the place of the ailing ex-president. She would speak, Finley announced, not in her own voice "but in the voice of that Bell which rings out our hopes and aspirations for this College." The bell then rang for the first time, formally dedicating the new buildings.

President Finley indicated what the college's hopes and aspirations might be in his own address on this occasion. But since the next chapter is an extended study of Finley's academic rhetoric, it is only significant in this context to note his underscoring of Lord Bryce's point. Finley offered himself as "hostage for these eager, noisy, ambitious young men and boys" of CCNY, and thus cast the aura of his own personal presence over their feverish desire to rise out of marginal status. This status generated among the ethnically heterogeneous student body a certain "inferiority complex" that Finley perceived and tried to diminish. Academic ceremonies were one important means to this end.

Finley did not wait for the erection of a new campus in 1908 to practice his skills of academic showmanship. Before then he made do with the meager resources of the old Twenty-Third Street building. In 1905, for example, he initiated Charter Day at CCNY. This was similar to his introduction of Founder's Day at Knox College over a decade earlier. At the first of these CCNY events, Finley opened the proceedings by admitting that, unlike his prairie alma mater, City College had no identifiable patriarchs. Therefore the celebration was dedicated to a "richer and more generous benefactor"—the city of New York. The ceremonies in 1905 included, not only inspirational speeches, but a student debate on trusts, and a baseball game that the faculty lost to the students thirteen to seven.

A later Charter Day celebration in 1912 was held just after the college had gotten a new tract of land. Finley chose to mark this event in the manner of his own Scots ancestors, who periodically "beat the bounds" to mark the extent of their territory. He led the students and faculty in ceremonial march around the newly enlarged CCNY perimeter. College janitor

Michael Bonney was in a prominent place in the procession, which also included a band of Scots bagpipers.

Although few celebrations were quite so whimsical as Charter Day, 1912, the Finley years at CCNY were rich in ceremonial occasion. Each of them was designed to bring to the undergraduates (and to the youngsters of the preparatory department) a sense of pride in their institution. City College students were often given a prominent place in the ceremonies staged by President Finley. When a France Day was held in 1909, an eager boy was given the opportunity to declaim before Ambassador Jules Jusserand in the guest's native language. Two years earlier the college participated in the commemoration of the sailing of the *Half Moon* into the Hudson River. A patriotic pageant was staged at which students, faculty, and guests walked to nearby Riverside Drive to "discover" the Hudson. One of the undergraduates impersonated the patriot Nathan Hale, and Henry Van Dyke read a poem composed for the event. The students were also delighted that on other occasions President Finley was able to bring such eminent notables as Henri Bergson, Helen Keller, William Howard Taft, Woodrow Wilson, Andrew Carnegie, Rabindranath Tagore, and a host of famous explorers, distinguished authors, Nobel laureates, and visiting diplomats to the City College campus.

> *Whatever its obscure psychic roots, my hostility to ceremony was reinforced by reading Daniel Boorstin's* The Image *(1961), written by a historian I do not admire but a shrewd study of the corruption inherent in the creation and manipulation of pseudoreality. Richard Nixon's scramble into the White House was, as Joe McGinniss shows in* The Selling of the President 1968 *[1970] a vulgar application of the image-creating techniques Borstin so mercilessly exposes in* The Image. *My own repugnance toward ceremony can easily lead me to denigrate that large part of Finley's academic career devoted to display and pageantry, and I have tried to correct for this bias in this area.*

Finley's academic showmanship was intended to inject that intangible collegiate quality *spirit* into the CCNY environment. Although he had pursued a similar policy at Knox College a decade earlier, the need was far greater at City College. It is hardly an exaggeration to say that the institution in New York suffered from something of a chronic inferiority complex.

This unfortunate sentiment was doubtless due to a combination of factors: the ethnic marginality of the largely Jewish student body, the college's status as a municipal institution, the parochialism and inbreeding in the faculty. All these operated to fix a lowly repute on CCNY and to hinder the development there of a proud school spirit.

The situation was recognized and lamented. An alumnus who went on to advanced study at Cornell wrote back to the college's student paper, *Campus*, in April, 1909, commending the traditions and customs of the nation's more prestigious institutions of higher learning, which "touch the heartstrings of the students and bind them to their Alma Mater." CCNY was urged to do likewise. Finley too often mentioned the lack of "college spirit" among the hardworking and serious ("perhaps too serious") students at New York's "streetcar" college.

The proximate example of Columbia College (two stops away on the subway) drove home to many sensitive City College boys their own lowly status. The campus newspaper commented editorially on this in 1910, observing that two sorts of college students came uptown on the Broadway subway. One group was healthy looking, clean-cut, and self-possessed. Their books remained closed on the train while they read newspapers, and their talk about college matters literally "sparkle[d] with true collegiate life." These were the Columbia men. The CCNY students made a sorry contrast. They looked "dull and spiritless" with their textbooks rather than newspapers open before them, grimly studying for the day's inevitable recitation. The humiliating comparison was daily reinforced for the hundreds of students who came to CCNY by subway.

Finley did what he could to remedy the psychological and social disabilities of the students through his personal warmth and the academic ceremonies he staged. These efforts were intended to stimulate a sense of pride in the college and its achievements. In many other ways Finley attempted to accomplish these ends. He got plaques installed at the 137th Street station of the Broadway subway marking it as the City College stop. Continually he reminded the students that the municipal connections of their school ought not to breed feelings of inferiority. "You are not," he said to them, "charity wards of the city. . . . You are . . . sons of her free spirit." And just as Knox College had received, due to Finley's efforts, international scholastic recognition in the roster of learned institutions, *Minerva*, so CCNY was accorded its first such notice under his presidency. In dozens of little ways, Finley labored to raise the prestige of the college.

> *When a new president took over the school at which I now teach, I took the opportunity to send him one of my articles on Finley that described how he obtained the subway plaque for CCNY. I urged that signs be installed marking the Jay Street/Boro Hall subway station in Brooklyn as the stop for the Polytechnic Institute of New York. Previous administrations had rejected the idea, but President George Bugliarello accepted it, and I have the satisfaction of seeing the Polytechnic plaques every day I come to school.*

When the school's reputation was threatened, he spoke out publicly. One such occasion came in 1907. An official of the New York State Civil Service Board had rejected a graduate's application for a position as librarian and statistician. The grounds were lack of evidence that the applicant had "the education required for the position. The College of the City of New York," the rejection notice went on, "is not of collegiate grade, according to the standards of the best colleges." Finley, along with trustee Edward Morse Shepard, directed a barrage of letters at the Albany officials who had so inexcusably downgraded City College, and they succeeded in changing the offensive ruling. Some years later, when a CCNY graduate was denied admission to the Harvard Law School, Finley immediately protested to President Lowell and succeeded in gaining assurance that City College graduates with good records would be welcomed at Harvard's professional schools.

But sometimes the attacks against the vulnerable institutional prestige of CCNY came from within the college community. A trustee in 1908 expressed concern about "extravagant" expenses, which, he said, were only allowable in a very extensive and profitable business, but should not creep in in the running of a free college." Trustee Miller, a Brooklyn banker, admitted that "wiley [sic] enemies" of City College were raising the cry of extravagance, but he felt that there was

justice in these charges. Finley's reply was a tactful but firm
defense of the college's budget. He refused to agree that the
municipal sponsorship of CCNY necessitated any special
frugality. He generally regretted the rise in expenditures, but
he held this rise to be necessary and not at all extravagant.

Much of the ill will directed against City College during
John Finley's administration originated in resentment of the
connection between the college and Townsend Harris Hall
preparatory high school. Students at CCNY resented the presence of hordes of little boys on campus, seemingly belying
the institution's claim to collegiate status. Others professed
not to understand why the college had to maintain its own
preparatory department administratively distinct from the
high schools of the city. Townsend Harris Hall was particularly repugnant to New York school officials, who saw the
school as an obstacle to their creation of a respected four-year
high school system. They directed their fire against the three-
year course of study at Townsend Harris Hall and, with allies
in Albany and elsewhere, disparaged the City College generally.

This dispute threatened to get out of hand and jeopardize
the future of municipally supported higher education in New
York. Finley handled it with consummate skill, making
maximum use of his personal qualities of warmth and genial
enthusiasm. For example, when criticism of CCNY's policy on
this matter came to him by mail from so influential a figure as
the president of the Carnegie Foundation for the Advancement of Teaching, Finley did not immediately leap to the
passionate defense of his institution; instead he replied with a
request for a personal meeting where the matter could be
discussed congenially. He followed up such meetings with a
series of friendly letters, each of which gently urged an upwardly revised estimate of CCNY's worth as an educational
institution.

Although he stuck firmly to the policy of support for the
Townsend Harris Hall preparatory department he was committed to defend as executive officer of the City College,
Finley was disarmingly courteous to the avowed enemies of
that policy. The most doughty of these was New York City's

autocratic superintendent of schools, William Henry Maxwell. So bitter was Maxwell's resentment against City College that he was believed to have denied to its graduates licenses to teach in the city. Despite such provocation, Finley sought to maintain cordial relations with the superintendent. He commended Maxwell's work and deprecated "all our little differences and clashings."

Meanwhile, Finley went over the head of the superintendent to appeal for better appreciation of City College by the principals, teachers, and students of New York's high schools. He did this in a disarming and highly effective way, making use of the impressiveness of the college's new Saint Nicholas Heights campus. Not only did groups of high school students periodically arrive there after 1908, when the buildings were ready, to admire the imitation Gothic architecture, but the inspirational message of City College was brought to the schools themselves. This Finley accomplished by causing hundreds of copies of Charles Blashfield's Great Hall mural (depicting the noble and heroic quest for knowledge, with John Finley himself shown as the prototype of the young student) to be circulated in the city high schools.

Finley's great success in deflecting attacks on CCNY, and neutralizing adverse criticism, was recognized by the faculty when they commended him in 1913 for "converting unfriendly critics into enthusiastic adherents" of the cause of City College. Perhaps an even greater mark of his success in winning over New York City's educational establishment to the support of CCNY is to be found in the appearance of William H. Maxwell's name among the prominent candidates to succeed Finley in the City College presidency when he stepped down in 1913.

In this unique campaign to accomplish what would now be called "enhancing the image" of CCNY, the personal qualities of President Finley came into active play. To the extent that there was a spiritual transformation there in the early years of the twentieth century, the credit may be fairly assigned to him. But the changes for which he was primarily responsible were accompanied by others which called forth the energies and imagination of Finley's associates at City College.

One of the most effective of these associates was an instructor in political science, Stephen P. Duggan. Duggan wished CCNY to become less "a cloister of learning [where] . . . the minds of young men [are filled] with an unusable something, vaguely called culture," and more a school adapted to "the real affairs and practical business of life." One means to make the college a center of practical learning was the proliferation of extension courses. Duggan was active in developing such courses for New York City teachers. His more ambitious plan was to offer a full range of college work in the evening so that otherwise qualified young men, forced to work by day, could continue studying for a college degree. There was opposition among both the faculty and the trustees. Duggan did have President Finley's enthusiastic support for the scheme, and in the fall of 1909, City College began to offer the first college courses leading to a baccalaureate degree at night. The first student to take such a degree graduated in 1917.

Again on the initiative of younger men of the faculty, a curriculum reform was carried through under John Finley's presidency. Years of wrangling at faculty and trustees' meetings finally issued in a new curriculum, based upon Harvard's Group Elective System. Finley did his best to steer these reforms past the obstacles raised by the old-guard opposition, which stood against any attempt to tamper with the classical curriculum. The aim of these new changes, it was feared, would be to introduce vocational training into the sacred groves of academe. And despite President Finley's frequent fulminations against mere vocational training, the proposals were in fact a step away from the educational cohesion and spiritual unity of the old-fashioned classical curriculum. But the advocates of new departures (including Finley, whose own undergraduate education had been strictly classical) had their way; a new curriculum was introduced in the spring of 1913. Its "keynote is efficiency," wrote one of the young faculty enthusiasts of change. The student was to be refined by it into a socially useful "product"; he was to be helped to "*find his place in the complex social organization.*"

It may have been a calculation in Finley's passive educational leadership that the trend to vocationalism at CCNY would be countered by recruitment of faculty who would not lend themselves to the debase-

ment of traditional college standards, or by the resistance of students themselves, who, whatever their career aims, were not prepared to dispense with what Duggan called an "unusable something, vaguely called culture." CCNY's devotion to culture was not exactly that of a leisured, aristocratic institution; it was more fiercely held and more intense. It was what made CCNY the stimulating place it was, far beyond the impact of administrative decisions and policies.

A college moving toward specialized training for what was elsewhere being called "life adjustment" needed a faculty capable of teaching the specialized courses. Faculty recruitment was a major area of presidential responsibility at City College, and Finley used all his charm and influence to bring able men to the college and make them pleased that they had come. He was successful in getting Harry A. Overstreet from the University of California to fill a chair in philosophy, Thomas A. Storey of Stanford to take charge of work in physical instruction, Charles Baskerville from North Carolina to head the chemistry department, and Carleton Brownson from Yale, who eventually became dean. The problems of a heavy teaching load, emphasis on undergraduate work, and low salaries kept many away. But even a salary increase came forth from the trustees during Finley's administration.

Recruited from the outside, and promoted from within the ranks of the college alumni, a faculty of some distinction gathered at CCNY. As with the students, President Finley worked hard to exert his personal charm on these men. For example, a young history instructor was called to the office one day, fully expecting to be fired. Instead, Finley observed: "I see you have a free hour, Schapiro. Well, so do I." The two subsequently met and talked regularly. (J. Salwyn Schapiro went on to a distinguished career in teaching and writing in European history.) Another young faculty member, whose hobby was "tramping and mountain climbing" in Greece, found in the college president an enthusiastic Hellenist. As we have seen, others still could enjoy with him a manly game of handball. Finley supported the applications of a number of City College professors for membership in the fashionable Century Club. The president could be counted upon for support, sympathy, and counsel. He would visit faculty members ill in hospitals (as he did with the students), dine with them, offer advice and encouragement. An undercurrent of animos-

ity toward Finley, perhaps motivated by resentment of his
popularity with students, was barely perceptible in a part of
the faculty. But the overwhelming majority "developed an
attitude of positive admiration for . . . [President Finley], akin to
hero worship."

> The first, and very likely the only and last, time I set foot in the
> prestigious Century Club on West Forty-third Street was when a Finley
> invited me. Enjoying the hospitality of one of John Finley's sons, I knew
> at once I was out of place in the Century Club. The deferential black
> workers, the plush chairs, and the copies of the Wall Street Journal and
> Barron's scattered about were signs of alien turf for a Bronx street-boy
> turned socialist professor. Yet my hostility to the upper-class life-style
> represented by the Century Club did not quite blind me to the lure of
> congeniality and ease into which a Finley naturally fit, and toward
> which aspiring CCNY academicians in the early twentieth century, if
> not now, would reach.

During the decade that he held the City College presidency, Finley himself gained prominence and distinction. His
long list of honorary degrees was lengthened, and each time
some honor descended upon him, Finley took pains to associate the college with his own success. He delighted in
permitting members of the CCNY community to bask in the
glory reflected on their institution when, for example, its president "receives a degree along with the president[s] of Harvard, Yale, Princeton, Columbia, and Cornell."

A number of times Finley was openly "mentioned" for local
political office in New York City. On the level of national
politics, he had twice supported McKinley and in 1912 swung
to the support of Theodore Roosevelt's Bull Moose Progressive candidacy. This modest political activism gained Finley
prominence, during the City College years and afterward, in
independent Republican circles. His support was solicited for
a number of political causes, among them the important
League to Enforce Peace. His name was brought forward in
many national discussions about presidential nomination and
choice of ambassadors.

But Finley did not receive, and neither did he energetically
seek, political office. His major prominence and achievements
came in the field of education during the early decades of the
twentieth century, and he generously permitted CCNY to bask
in its president's reflected glory. A notable honor that came to

Finley was the invitation to deliver the Hyde Lectures at the Sorbonne in 1911. He followed in this endowed lectureship such distinguished scholars as Barrett Wendell, George Santayana, Bliss Perry, and Henry Van Dyke. En route to France on his first European trip, Finley expressed "terror" at the distinction that had come to him. "Who should have believed a year ago that I should be going on this errand—with a commission from Harvard [sponsor of the lectureship], a letter from the president of the United States and the affectionate confidence of Henry Van Dyke? It's rather too much for me."

After he had heard about his appointment to the Hyde Lectureship, Finley lay awake at night until he hit upon an appropriate subject—the French in North America. He researched his subject in various midwestern and Eastern libraries (but finally relied mostly on Francis Parkman's classic, multivolumed *France and England in North America*), and he revisited the prairies where in childhood he had paddled or poled a boat "in the rivers that once carried the canoes of the French explorers." Charged with local color and his own personal empathy with the French explorers, Finley's Paris lectures (delivered in English) were filled with whimsy and distinctly lighthearted scholarship. Despite this, or because of it, he was a great success, finishing the series in February, 1911, just as a ministry fell. Accompanied by his wife and family, Finley repeated his well-received lectures at many other French universities, enjoyed a tour through Switzerland and northern Italy, and only returned to New York in early May. Serialized in *Scribner's Monthly* in 1912, the lectures were finally published in 1915 as *The French in the Heart of America*, followed by a French translation the following year.

The City College community participated vicariously in Finley's triumph in many ways. A public meeting was held to wish him well the day before sailing, and the next day (when an icy November gale lashed New York Harbor), a cheering delegation of enthusiastic students went aboard one of the tugs leading Finley's liner, *La Provence*, out past the narrows. When he returned, there was another round of meetings at CCNY to celebrate the homecoming. Having visited the homeland of some of his City College boys, Finley found on return that he could even more compellingly exercise his unique personal gifts as president. A graduate of Italian ancestry vividly remembered decades later the story of a walk Finley had taken in the Catskill Mountain region in New York.

Many miles in the hot sun had made him thirsty, and he gladly stopped at a spring.... He uncorked his borraccia (canteen)and, as was his wont, shook it to make sure that no water was still in it. Some drops did fall... into the spring. He then remembered that he had last used that borraccia at a spring or fountain in Assisi. Those drops and the spring, he said, symbolized the absorption of the Italian immigrants into the population of the United States.

John Finley's unabashed sentimentalism was the product of an era of innocence. It was no mask put on merely for ceremonial purposes, but the genuine expression of a personality in harmony with its age. The students at CCNY, who were the major recipients of Finley's influence, knew his sincerity. It was important to many of them, awkward adolescents mostly, some of whose parents may have only recently survived the searing experience of being uprooted from rural Apulia, or driven from bloody pogroms in Bessarabia. To these ardent and ambitious boys, Finley was a symbol and an image of a hospitable America, eager to accept and assimilate immigrants. How much, or how little, reality underlay that image many CCNY lads would soon discover.

Chapter 19

Attic Democracy and Public Service:

The Rhetoric of College Uplift

Mitigating and qualifying my posthumous criticism of Finley and his role in the shaping and justifying of modern America is my feeling of affinity with him on the level of a common commitment to the spoken and written word. Rarely am I in sympathy with the content of his rhetoric; what I do however identify with is his effort to use words as a means of persuasion and exhortation. He put his rhetorical powers to use in defending a capitalist order for which, it should be admitted, there was better prognosis for survival then than now.

In 1912, at the opening of his tenth and last year as president of City College, John Finley considered the tasks that remained for him to complete. There were a number of matters: increasing faculty salaries; erecting a library building on Saint Nicholas Heights; obtaining a stadium for sports events and outdoor musical concerts; arranging the financial backing for a college of commerce; and a host of minor matters, including finishing his projected biography of Grover Cleveland.

Except for the book, which he never completed, Finley attained most of what he set out to do. Yet even these considerable tangible achievements were not his main work at CCNY. Rather, his chief concerns were the creation of an atmosphere, the advocacy of certain principles, and the advancement of high ideals.

To accomplish what he felt were these deeper, more essential tasks of an educator, John Finley had two great talents. There was his immense personal charm, enhanced by his ability to exercise it among all manner of men. We have seen in a previous chapter what this quality won him at CCNY in student affection and faculty trust. But there were also his

forensic gifts that had become apparent early, in the undergraduate oratorical contests of the prairies in the 1880s. As
president of the City College of New York, Finley was called
upon to use these gifts frequently—on the CCNY campus and
elsewhere. In the course of these many oratorical efforts, he
made a great reputation as a public speaker. (British ambassador James Bryce remarked that the CCNY president had "a
tongue of which we would say in Scotland that it would wile a
bird off a bush.") On these occasions Finley also expressed a
set of ideas that (with qualifications we shall see in the next
chapter) may be called an educational philosophy.

Finley was a man whose actions were usually magnificently
consistent with his public statements; but in one area at least
there was a slight discord between theory and practice. This
was the sensitive one of ethnic and race relations, in which his
ideas formed an interesting counterpoint to his actions.

Since Jews were the most numerous and visible "minority"
at CCNY in Finley's years, his ideas on what he and his fellow
WASPs called "Hebrews" are of particular significance. Finley moved in a social circle that, as E. Digby Baltzell shows in
his book *The Protestant Establishment* (1964), was well on its
way to retreating to a narrow ethnic exclusiveness. America
had just been launched upon its imperialist adventure, and in
his justification of this course Finley voiced a breezy confidence in Anglo-Saxon superiority. On occasion (before such
selected audiences as the members of New York's posh Quill
Club) he might even be heard making condescending references to "Ikey Goldstein" and his tribe. But surely the major
thing to notice about Finley's attitudes is not that he retained
some of the residual racism of his milieu, but that he rid
himself of so much of it.

Finley explained his own attitude toward the Jews by admitting he might have been an anti-Semite if it were not for his
early experiences. First, his childhood reading on the Illinois
prairie gave him an early familiarity with Moses, Joshua, and
other Hebrew notables of the Old Testament. As a freshman at
Knox College, young Finley's first appearance in print was
with a generally laudatory essay on the Jews. He claimed also
to have had a Jewish friend in "college," who boasted of

descent from King David. A refugee from Russia, young Finley's Jew—

> had one of the sweetest, noblest natures I have known in man. Though
> hordes of dirty, ill-smelling Hebrews may come out of steerage and from
> their sweat-shops into the streets and pierce my ears with their shrill
> speech they are still the people of my friend. To me the Hebrew is that
> man.

It is easy to suspect that Finley concocted this "good Jew" for rhetorical purposes. That such devices were necessary reveals that he was not quite free from a touch of racism. Yet it never interfered with the task he set for himself, which was almost literally to embrace the population of the college. Finley did not allow himself to be diverted by its ethnic heterogeneity. The school whose student body was largely Jewish, but included many boys of Italian and Irish extraction, flourished in the warmth of its president who often prayed, "Lord keep me to remember that these thousands of boys from every nation of the earth are not men, [or] awkward pieces of clay, but immortal souls."

When he moved from the practical business of maintaining a nurturing and hospitable milieu at CCNY to the theory of race, certain ambiguities appeared in Finley's thought. For one thing, he refused to condemn racial antipathy in any thoroughgoing way. In his view, it had certain positive aspects.

> [It is] the reverse of a beautiful coin, on the obverse of which is stamped
> the symbol of loyalty to family, to country, or to the particular race;
> [prejudice] . . . is the negative of an egoism on its way through the love of
> family, state and nation to the love of mankind.

Putting something in such an evolutionary framework legitimized it in Finley's eyes. Also, racial prejudice gained justification because it seemed rooted in the nature of man. His study of biology testified to the existence, even among infants, of "congenital antipathy toward the stranger." Finley discerned "some pre-natal listening of the likes and dislikes of ancestors which the child and man do not forget, and must whisper on through generations to come."

Racial antipathy was thought by Finley to have had great value in the past, in allowing special group characteristics to

emerge—"strength, skill, prescience, skill of hand or tongue."
But in the twentieth century, technology had rendered such
prejudice obsolete. "World dispersion and intercom-
munication" had made it no longer necessary or feasible
to cherish racial antipathies. Besides, Finley added, was it not
a shame that cultured Negroes were excluded from certain
associations!

Education was seen as a primary weapon in the struggle
against prejudice—particularly the kind of education obtain-
able at such a school as CCNY.

> Think how racial barriers are to be broken down [Finley said] when
> Smith and Schmidt and Cohen and Olson and Jackson (colored) and
> Agramonte ["Bounarotti" crossed out] and O'Brien ["Finley" crossed
> out] journey through the Parasangs of the Anabasis, or march with Caesar
> into Gaul, or compute a parallax, or follow a premise to its conclusion, or
> build an arch—or any one of the thousand other things that have no
> national or racial boundaries.

Those who could not taste the ethnic diversity of CCNY were
urged to seek substitute experience.

> I have often said that if every man of boasted American stock in this city
> [New York] were to bring into his acquaintanceship and friendship a
> descendant of King David, a descendant of Dante, a descendant of the
> rugged Norsemen, an heir of the Japanese Samurai and of an African
> King, the best that these races produce—he would find his prejudice
> giving way to fairer opinions and probably to admiring opinions and his
> citizenship growing into something of a finer spirit than was ever con-
> ceived by a protective tariff economist or an imperialist statesman.

These widened contacts would make different groups in
pluralist America better acquainted and render their relations
more harmonious. But, Finley added, the relaxing of prejudice
would not mean a general "razing of all barriers" between
groups. Those should be maintained "that preserve the integ-
rity of certain vital virtues in a people."

The feature of City College that made it a place where
prejudice broke down was its democratic atmosphere. Finley
expressed recognition of this special characteristic of CCNY in
his installation address of 1903, in which he committed the
college to the further pursuit of democracy. During the fruitful
ten years that followed, there was ample occasion to elaborate
and expound the ideal.

The consideration of educational democracy brought Finley

about as close as any topic treated in his college rhetoric to an analysis of fundamental political questions. He was a conservative Republican who had worked for McKinley in 1896. His later support of Theodore Roosevelt reveals not so much a change in Finley's outlook as the conservatism of Bull Moose progressivism. His utterances on democracy reflect the same conservatism as that of the political leaders Finley supported.

He once warned: "We have assumed that pure democracy united with *any human nature* would produce a beneficent political result. I don't say we shan't always get it but I know that there *are* combinations of *benign and sweet substances,* so reckoned, that sometimes produce nitro-glycerine. We simply ought to procede *slowly* and *carefully* in our political laboratory or we may blow the roof off." Finley was glad that egalitarian social experimentation had not gotten out of hand in America.

> Democracy [he observed] has let her children go their free ways in the conquest of the continent upon which we live. She has given them as full freedom as their increasing numbers have permitted. She has even helped them with money from her own purse, now and then, to build a railroad or dig a canal. She gave the pioneer title to her lands and she has permitted that title to descend from father to son. She let the intrepid precursor stake out his oil or mining claim and she has confirmed to him and his heirs the millions of treasure that lay beneath it. She has given to the individual perpetual lease of her lands and eternal franchise to most of her resources. Generous mother that she is she has kept little for herself. She has exacted only slight revenues for her own support and their common good. Wise mother that she is she has given every stimulus to individual enterprise on the part of her children even at the risk of great individual inequality.

And if "she" had tried to distribute wealth equitably, Finley thought it would very likely "come back to the hands that now hold it."

> *How many times, with students and others in debate, have I been presented with the argument that an immutable "human nature" prevents the achievement of socialism? It is an argument that Finley would have used in such a discussion, were there any record of his having had one. How do we socialists answer this objection? It's not easy. First, it is necessary to inquire if the believer in immutable human nature has any broad experiences with persons of different viewpoints and outlooks, or whether he or she knows only a limited range of similar people from the same culture or, worse still, the same neighborhood. Once the point has been conceded that a conception of human nature has been drawn from too narrow a selection of cousins and uncles or kids from the corner*

*candy store, then it is possible to introduce the liberating vistas of
history and anthropology, which show men and women in other times,
other cultures, unlike in important ways the human beings nurtured in
late capitalist environments. In short, education can commence. Yet,
not every educated and well-traveled person is an incipient socialist; for
there is the matter of class interest and ideology that, far more than
rational argument, shapes people's deepest social convictions. That is
why the present epoch, with the unmistakeable signs of capitalist decay
and stagnation, provides such a great opportunity for a socialist revival
in the United States, an end I hope in a small way to hasten with this
book.*

Distributive schemes, Finley thought, were folly; and individual enterprise in America had created legitimate inequalities. But the nation's educational policy, he believed,
was an enlightened departure from laissez-faire.

She has been continually careful that the intangible state which she
inherits from the past should have more equal division among her children. . . . Material inequalities . . . have always existed and will always
exist as long as men are as they are.

But the sort of educational experience available at City College transcended the inevitable inequalities of life in the metropolis. CCNY was the place—

where rich and poor shall strive and study together, where new and old
Americans shall each come to know the worth that is in the other, where
the descendants of those who gave us our [ten?] commandments of civic
and individual righteousness, and the descendants of those who have
painted the world's best pictures or have sung the world's best longings,
and the descendants of those who got our political liberties for us, shall
meet, and in the blending of their purposes, not only make a more
beautiful, a safer, a more habitable city—an American city,—but preserve that honest spirit of democracy which is essential above all things
to the better life and happiness of those who are on God's earth.

Without risking the dangers of trying to equalize wealth, "the
safety of the republic" can be ensured, Finley asserted,
through education. It equalizes "the *gifts of the Past* by assuring to *rich and poor* alike a competence in those things which
are the real riches of the human being."

Finley perceived that democracy is threatened by the setting in of social, racial, or religious stratification. The remedy
was to be found by simply providing places where members of
the separated groups could come together on a basis of
equality. Finley suggested at various times that a theater and a
road could serve this purpose. But most often, and most per-

suasively, he argued for the school above all other social institutions as a breeder and sustainer of democracy. While sending his own sons to prep schools and Harvard, he lavished praise on "the courage and good sense" of parents who sent their children to public "schools in which Protestant and Catholic, Jew and Gentile, Oriental and Westerner come together in a true democratic spirit." The ceremonial occasions at CCNY gave Finley frequent opportunities further to expostulate on how schools in general, and the college on Saint Nicholas Heights in particular, served to safeguard the democratic ideal.

> *Parts of this book were drafted in the Manhattan public school our children attend, whose atmosphere has been well captured in Phil Lopate's* Being With Children *(1975). In 1976 the Board of Education attempted to close the school early two afternoons each week, and, with a phalanx of militant parents, I held the school open twenty-four hours a day, seven days a week for three months! We were impressed with the determination of parents to fight for the public schools and not succumb to the prevalent middle-class revulsion from them. Some mornings, kindergartener Rebecca Gettleman and her first-grade sister, Eva, would come to school in the morning and wake me up in the occupied administrative offices with its sleeping bags strewn on the floor. It was a highly educative experience for the girls. Later still I became Parents Association president at this school, P S 75, The Emily Dickinson School on West End Avenue. An exciting educational institution, it provides far better elementary education, I am convinced, than New York City's private schools, which are primarily training grounds for class snobbery.*

These paeans to democracy were made in the manner of the "voluble and voluminous" nineteenth-century college presidents, many of whom presided over institutions that did in fact achieve "a certain internal cultural democratization."

> In the old college [Professor Richard Hofstadter observed] the sons of plain farmers had often rubbed elbows with the sons of the upper middle class; applying themselves to a common curriculum in the intimate atmosphere of a small school, they grew somewhat more alike because they had something in common, both social and intellectual.

Because of the lowly status of some of the students, and its municipal control, CCNY long retained democratic features usually associated with old-time colleges. Finley's rhetoric thus had relevance.

But it was a diminishing relevance. The forces that sustained democracy in the old-time college were everywhere

weakening. Intellectual unity and a common focus were sac-
rificed to the rise of electives and preprofessional specialization. The social heterogeneity and snobbery of the outside
world were gradually being reproduced where before there
had been, in many colleges, a large measure of social equality.
If CCNY, by reason of the ethnic marginality of its students,
escaped the danger of elitism, its curriculum did succumb to
careerist diversity. We have seen that by 1913 there was no
longer a common core of liberal study. Finley could no longer
be sure that his students were journeying collectively through
the parasangs of Xenophon's *Anabasis,* or together computing
a parallax. Yet his notion of democracy depended upon a
common spiritual purpose. If this common purpose could not
be located in the curriculum, Finley would have to find it
elsewhere—among the competing educational ideals of the
day.

   Historians have come to perceive that the world of higher
education in the late nineteenth and early twentieth centuries
was not simply riven between secularist supporters of
rationalistic science and old-fashioned champions of religion.
(Particularly convincing demonstration of this point may be
found in the researches of Professor Hugh Hawkins, whose
1964 essay in the *Journal of American History* on Charles W.
Eliot and university reform is a seminal interpretation.) Finley's career as college president, as well as that of a number of
his contemporaries, reveals a more complex pattern of differ-
ing collegiate ideals. There were a dwindling few advocates of
old-fashioned piety and discipline, champions of the practical
utility of universities, and supporters of the slightly different
goal of pure research. There was also a group of eclectic
college presidents, who favored the educational ideal of "liberal culture." Finley was among the most eloquent of these.

   His best exposition of this ideal was delivered to an "over-
flowing" audience gathered in CCNY's Great Hall to hear the
baccalaureate address of February, 1913. Finley began appropriately by quoting remarks that U.S. President Woodrow Wilson had recently made at the college about the strongly felt
"presence" of New York City in its municipal college. Then he
suggested that the deeper significance of this "presence" be

considered. Finley recognized the "reducing heat of business zeal" as one of the forces that held the city together but considered this a "soulless" force. Another such force was the "spiritual [and] intellectual aspiration whose fusing fires would burn more fiercely and effectively" to knit the city together.

The "liberal culture" that would serve the high aspirations of New York was no ivory tower ideal to Finley. "Undisturbed, cloistered conditions are needed for the development of certain temperaments, perhaps for certain tasks of scholarship," he admitted. But he discerned a deeper—

> need of a learning that is kept from pedantry, and dilettantism and selfishness and exclusiveness only by its daily converse with the world about, that it does not lose the human sympathies with which it started, that looks often from its book to see the life that it is some day to try to better. . . . This intimates what I believe is to be the new liberal culture; not one that covers superficially the ever-widening field of the human knowledges, but one that liberalizes a disciplined mind by giving a social,—an unselfish[—] purpose.

To bring this educational ideal more graphically to City College audiences, Finley used Greek imagery that was doubly appropriate—in accord with the theme, and a fit imagery for a student of classics. He likened CCNY's Saint Nicholas Heights campus to "the city's sacred enclosure, the place of its worship and defense, and so, in a very accurate sense, [its] Acropolis." The "advantages and delights of study" in some such idyllic country retreat as ancient Delphi were acknowledged; but Finley observed that "the city needs the defences of the nearer and more intimate ministries. She needs her Acropolis, the visible sign of the continuing presence of her own best aspirations."

Not only did Finley invoke Attic civic virtues on rhetorical occasions, but he enlisted the entire college in his reverential attitude toward liberal culture on the Hellenic model. He did this by devising in his characteristic way a ceremonial by which CCNY boys could symbolize their allegiance to this educational ideal. The "Ephebic Oath," written by Finley, was first administered in 1913. City College graduates then, and ever after, pledged "after the manner" of the Ephebes, "Athenian youths of old about to enter public life," that—

we will never bring disgrace to our city by any act of dishonesty or
cowardice; nor ever desert our suffering comrades in the ranks; we will
fight for the ideals and sacred things of the city, both alone and with
many; we will revere and obey the city's laws and do our best to incite a
like respect and reverence in those about us who are prone to annul
them and set them at naught; we will strive unceasingly to quicken the
public's sense of civic duty; and thus in all these ways, we will strive to
transmit this city not only less but greater, better, and more beautiful
than it was transmitted to us.

Finley was close enough in spirit to the students of City
College to know instinctively that such idealistic sentiment
would likely be acted upon by a portion of them. One graduate, who later sponsored meliorative social legislation in the
New York City council, wrote to him in 1929, "The precept of
the oath of the Spartan [sic] youth, taught me at CCNY in the
days of your presidency, has prompted me to give thought, as
one of the members of the Board of Aldermen, to the matter of
improved tenement housing in New York." Others too recognized in Finley's Ephebic Oath a stirring invitation "to fight
for the ideals and sacred things."

The City College years gave to John Finley a golden opportunity to kindle in others the same devotion to the cause of
public service that he shared in good measure. Before leaving
City College, he would himself be called upon to serve the
public interest in a labor arbitration case of 1913. Afterward, as
he gained in distinction, there would be much more such
activity on his part, both in the United States and abroad. It
was therefore from firm personal conviction that John Finley
preached the gospel of public service and, insofar as it was in
his power, dedicated City College to that ideal.

Finley's noble exhortations on public service, which pervaded several of his baccalaureate addresses, were hardly
original with him. With its roots in softened and socialized
Calvinism, the doctrine of service to society was an intellectual commonplace in the late nineteenth century, and advanced skeptics were already beginning to run it down. For
Finley however the doctrine was an inner compulsion, the
natural result of ancestry, upbringing, and education. It was
also an appropriate affirmation for the president of such an
institution as City College.

He found many occasions to refer to public service. A baccalaureate speech in June, 1909, was one such effort. He addressed the graduating "Sons of the City" as beings transformed.

Fifteen years of teaching by this city have transformed you, have recreated you, have made you her sons, whether you were first born son of an Irish cotter, a Russian gun-maker, an Italian stone-cutter, a Scotch shepherd, a New England farmer, or a New York merchant. Memories of linden trees, of mountains of gold, of fields of grain and roses, or high perched mediaeval castles and of the tabernacle in the wilderness are in your name, but in your nostrils is the breath of this city's desire for her children. You carry in your very being the fire of her hopes, the flame which she has lighted in her search for a good that is beyond the present good.

At this time Finley characterized the city's hopes in spiritual terms transcending mere service. He refused to admit that the metropolis trained young men "merely to get [their] . . . living more easily and cleverly, or even to help [them] . . . to make others' bodies a little more comfortable and lengthen their lives." These "practical endeavors" were worthwhile, but the graduates ought to pursue a more spiritually refined, moral goal. Finley did not bother to define this goal, apparently assuming a general understanding of these matters among his audience.

On later occasions Finley did not so disparage the ideal of public service. On the contrary he most frequently commended and treasured it. He endorsed as "the hope of the democracy" the efforts of young men and women to get college training, which should not only bring "self-culture" but also provide "a special service to the city." In a midwinter baccalaureate address, "The Spoken Word," President Finley outlined the service rendered to democracy by the—

lovers of pure speech who can teach her children, who can write her laws for her, who can compose an amendment to the Constitution that needs not to be interpreted, who can discover to others in plain unambiguous English the good from the evil which they have themselves discerned.

At the next CCNY commencement in 1910, Finley again turned to the subject of public service. His address "The Man and the Job" was one of those characteristic feats of oratorical wizardry that apparently dazzled audiences but left them wondering afterward what had actually been said. The theme was apparently an attack on the notion that education should "make the man fit the job." After reference to the sons of Lamech, "the grandson of Adam, five times removed," Finley denounced the job-centered, "Ptolemaic" theory of education as an attempt to define man by the accident of his vocation. It was a primitive method of definition, reminiscent of the pre-patriarchal age, and it also denied man's spiritual nature as well as being undemocratic. In a democracy the "social position" of a citizen must not be "tyrannically proscribed" by his manner of earning a living.

Finley substituted for the job-centered conception what he called an "anthropocentric" or "Copernican" theory of education, which placed "the man or woman or the boy or girl" at the center of his fanciful universe, rather than simply allowing him to become a "soulless satellite revolving around a terrestrial world of salary." Finley did not, in his address "The Man and the Job," advocate the elimination of vocational training. Indeed, we have already seen that the curriculum that took shape under his presidency enshrined the vocational principle. In such oratorical exercises as his CCNY baccalaureate addresses, Finley instead sought to supplement the careerist goals of the students with a higher order of aspiration. Spiritual aims, central to any "Copernican" theory of education, were stressed. Finley's "young jobless idealists" were urged to look upon choice of trade or profession as enlisting in the cause of the community, as service to the "collectivity," rather than the pursuit of private ambition. It was this transformation of outlook that Finley was "trying to make the dominant one" at CCNY.

It is too easy to dismiss these rhetorical glosses on the homely realities of the workaday world as mere mystification. To some extent they were mystifying, but they also expressed the sense of its own significance of a new stratum of the middle class that was just coming of age at that time. Seemingly counter to the Marxian hypothesis of the obliteration of all strata between the lords of capitalist enterprise and the oppressed proletarians, a vigorous and self-conscious middle class was maintaining itself. It is true that Marx's original predictions were based upon the model of a predominantly laissez-faire capitalist state, but after Capital, *Marxism remained a growing, flexible body of theory, quite capable of absorbing and integrating fresh data. A recent work of Marxian scholarship, charting a cogent interpretation of the rise of a so-called new middle class, is Harry Braverman's* Labor and Monopoly Capital:

The Degradation of Work in the Twentieth Century (1974), a work truly deserving the status of a classic, and one which provides a firm empirical and theoretical basis for evaluating John Finley's rhetoric about work and career in twentieth-century America.

In one of his most widely noted public speeches, the City College baccalaureate address in June, 1911, Finley offered another elaborate exposition of the ideal of public service. To the students, gathered with their families and teachers in CCNY's Great Hall, Finley recalled the story of "the ancient prophet who walked one day many centuries ago out over the Judaean hills to anoint a young man who should some day be king." He fancied the assembled graduates as the future "kings of whom democracy is dreaming," and perceived as "one of the peculiar offices of this College . . . the training and anointing" of young men for public service. To Finley democracy meant largely the spread of noblesse oblige to all strata of the population.

Necessity for the expansion and dispersal of the ideal of public service was manifest. Finley observed in this baccalaureate address that "in thickly settled communities one in every thirty adults is a public servant." This category was a broad one. The Thirtieth Man (often a *woman*), said Finley,

sweeps the streets of the city. He is pontifex of the country roads. He lights the lamps when the natural lights of heaven go out, and extinguishes the fires of the earth. With one hand he gathers our letters of affection and business and with the other distributes them in the remotest cabins on the mountains. He weighs the wind, reads the portents of the clouds, gives augur of the heat and cold. He makes wells in the valleys, he fills the pools with water. He tastes the milk before the city child may drink it; he tests and labels the food in the stores and shops; he corrects false balances and short measures. He keeps watch over forest and stream; gives warning of rocks and shoals to men at sea and of plague and poison to those on land. He is warden of fish and bird and wild beast; he is host to the homeless and shelterless; he is guardian and nurse to the child who comes friendless into the world and chaplain at the burial of the man who goes friendless out of it. He is assessor and collector of taxes—treasurer and comptroller; he is the teacher of seventeen million children, youth, men and women; he is public librarian and maker of books; overseer of the poor and supervisor; superintendent, doctor, nurse and guard in hospital, prison and almshouse; coroner and keeper of the potter's field. He is mayor, judge, public prosecutor and sheriff (who may summon all the other twenty-nine as his posse comitatus). He is a soldier in the army and a sailor in the navy, general and admiral, legislator, justice, member of the cabinet, Governor and President.

Some of these tasks of public service were unromantic and unrenumerative. Finley perceived a necessity to uplift and glorify such lowly services as the teaching of children. His use of rhetoric for these purposes was one of the most important features of Finley's own presidential service at City College. The municipal institution, with its students of marginal status, lacking prestige and tradition, sending many of its graduates into prosaic civil service positions, needed the increment of sentiment provided by its eloquent president.

> As rhetoricians (whether of the spoken word, as in our college lectures, or in books and articles), we academicians are vulnerable to the charge that our actions do not conform to the ideals we espouse in our rhetorical exercises. Judged in this way, Finley is an admirable model of consistency. As a later chapter will show, Finley was ready when called upon to perform public service, in his case to serve as arbitrator in a labor dispute. Few of us on the contemporary left would score as well on a test of our willingness to act on the basis of our beliefs; there are many more theoretical advocates of socialist revolution than there are people willing to staff a literature and propaganda table on Broadway, or hand out leaflets at the subway. Particularly for the left, public, political involvement is subject to a cruel cultural paradox: in part the repudiation of capitalism springs from the urge to liberate ourselves and others from oppression. Yet the left's effort to organize itself involves long, boring meetings, commitments of time that otherwise might be spent more enjoyably or more profitably elsewhere. For mainstream conservatives like Finley, the commitment to public service is usually eased by the willingness of the institutions that employ them to continue to pay them. For radicals, the sacrifice demanded is usually greater, and few of us are prepared frequently to make it.

Only on rare occasions would there be any explicit dissent from the rich idealism in Finley's rhetoric. One of these moments came in the fall of 1909, when two practical-minded CCNY boys formed a committee to bring to the college lecturers who would speak on frankly utilitarian subjects. "Facts and not ideals are to be spoken about," declared the announcement of the lecture series. "In these lectures the CCNY man is not to be regarded as a regenerator of society, but as a fellow in search of a job."

Finley rejected such a polarity. To him, fellows in search of a job might at the same time be Public Servants and Regenerators of Society. To accomplish this simultaneity of goal, it was merely necessary to redefine reality slightly, as a poet would. An epic poem on public service to rival Homer's work might be written from New York City's payroll list, Finley believed. Walt Whitman could have produced noble verse to celebrate the civic heroes who extinguish tenements, fight bacteria in the air, struggle against "ignorance and laziness and passion in the thousands of public school rooms," and fight "uncleanness and uncleanliness and corruption and waste with brooms and statistic and lens and meter and honest expert and eyes." In the absence of a twentieth-century Whitman (who might not have relished the assignment in any case) Finley himself undertook, both in verse and especially in the prose of his baccalaureate addresses, to provide that redefinition of reality that would convince the graduates of CCNY that their vocational training was also a preparation for idealized public service.

The reinterpretation of unflattering aspects of reality also had political consequences. In his baccalaureate address, "The Thirtieth Man," Finley observed that democracy in America had certain unpleasant features—selfishness, dishonesty, venality, voters who respond to " 'outward appearance' and [who] take the man who puts himself forward first." But transcending the blemished actuality of democracy was a more fundamental tendency to transform citizens into "kings in the sense of men who are monarchs of themselves at least, clear visioned, strong willed, clean virtued, sovereigns." Finley apparently believed that such a transformation could be effected by sheer rhetoric. He referred often to Gilbert Chesterton's idealized descriptions of the ordinary things of life. The railroad signal box, for example, was verbally transformed into the instrument by which men, "in an agony of vigilance, light blood-red and sea-green fires to keep other men from death." Similarly, a mail box, "a most unpoetical name as one sees it written in reports and a most inartistic object as one sees it attached to a street lamp," becomes transformed when it is seen instead as a "sanctuary of human words."

The political significance of this rhetorical principle was obvious to Finley. "If someone of like insight could make the definitions of other everyday realities about us," he observed, then "democracy might appear the glorious thing which in its intending it really is." In a like way those CCNY graduates, many of whom would find employment in various public agencies, were urged to look upon their bureaucratic futures as glorious opportunities for devoted public service. By means of embracing the ideal of public service, Finley was able both to endorse the vocational drift at City College and to shrink from the crass attitudes connected with vocationalism.

Chapter 20

The Notion of "Presence":

Substitute for an Educational Conviction

The essence of this chapter is an attempt to demonstrate that John Finley had no realistic intellectual grasp of the educational process, yet kept expounding his hazy conceptions through the CCNY years and afterward. What protected him from the consequences of this was his solid anchoring in New York's educational structure. Instead of suffering professionally for his inadequate conceptions, Finley climbed to higher and more distinguished positions.

Finley's rhetorical vision, focused on the concept of public service, enabled him to claim to see in the college—beyond the curriculum, the physical plant, and faculty deliberations—the presence of New York City's deepest aspirations. This notion of an intuitively grasped *presence* beneath ordinary reality also provides a key to the understanding of that collection of notions that Finley substituted for an educational philosophy.

Having little relationship to the mechanics of school organization or the choice of subject matter, Finley's educational belief focused almost exclusively on the encounter of teacher and pupil. Education, he stated in 1915, is "likely to be valuable directly as the square, or other power of the [teacher's] personality." Often did he repeat this invocation of the sheer potency of a pedagogue's influence, especially at gatherings of members of that underpaid profession.

He elaborated the notion of *presence* in other metaphoric forms. In his poem "Life Is a Lamp," (explicated—if one can use that word—in an earlier chapter) education was equated with the light radiating from some edifying source, which by its very *presence* exerts a transforming power. Only in one baccalaureate address did Finley allow himself to doubt before a CCNY audience the adequacy of this metaphor, and the philosophy behind its use. He wondered if the symbol of the lamp were anything more than a "fancy," a "conceited rhapsody," an absurd magnification of the power of education.

> Is it after all [Finley inquired of the graduates] more than a vessel of *unpractical* light that you carry at best . . . down this hillside into a modern city in whose electric blaze your flame is as a shadow, in whose gusts of passion and avarice it may soon be blown out; or if it last, will but cook your food and give you light till you can come into the circuit of the industrial dynamo or other lighting systems, when you will throw it away as something for which you have no use, an academic, sentimental ideal?

But Finley was not the man long to sustain such pessimism; and in this and countless other academic addresses he remained confident that students who had stood in the presence of ennobling radiance would continue to emit the same light.

Another metaphor frequently used to illustrate the educational significance of the notion of *presence* was the scientific concept of the catalyst. "Violet crystals of a certain chloride," Finley observed, remain unchanged even when immersed in water for several days. But if only 25 millionths of a gram, "the mere breath" of a catalyst is added, the liquid is at once turned a deep indigo. Just as the catalyst effects the dramatic chemical change, so, in Finley's view, does the dedicated teacher, by a power that is ultimately divine, incline students toward noble pursuits.

Whatever the obvious shortcomings of this conventional and threadbare notion of *presence,* Finley himself was easily able to exert the kind of influence it prescribed as presumably the potential of all educators. His poetic imagination seized upon appropriate metaphors to express the idea of *presence*—the lamp, the catalyst; and in the ideal of public service he found a fit subject for the exercise of his rhetorical talents. The breathless inspirational earnestness of Finley's baccalaureate speeches at City College, backed up by his warm personal contacts with students, was rendered credible, not only because his rhetoric was magnificently consistent with his action, but because he himself was so supremely conscious

about the exercise of his own personal *presence*. Coming before a CCNY audience as president for the last time in June,
1913, Finley unblushingly declared:

> So I, a descendant of pioneers, who have come myself from the physical
> frontier, who have known the sensation of ploughing a strip of earth
> never before touched by human foot except of savage,—I meet you, the
> new pioneers, here upon what seems to me the newest frontier of the
> America which is in the spirits of men, where transformations more
> wonderful than those of the physical frontier are to take place in your
> day.

In shimmering rhetoric, Finley displayed a vivid awareness
of his own role in the creation of generous sentiments in the
college. And in turn the emergence of such sentiments was to
him the end and justification of education.

> *Obviously unconvinced by Finley's breezy notions of a realm of High
> Ideals floating above and presumably nourishing the nation's educa-
> tional institutions, I am obliged, if not to sketch in an alternate outlook,
> at least to indicate how a more adequate conception of education might
> take shape. In my opinion, such a conception would reverse the flow of
> influence; instead of ideals shaping actuality, it would be more useful
> and accurate to envision educational ideals taking their shape from the
> surrounding society, yet having something of an independent life of
> their own. Just as these pages were being written, two New England
> Marxist economists, Sam Bowles and Herb Gintis, published their
> long-awaited* Schooling in Capitalist America *(1976), which, though not
> free of defects, is the sort of alternate vision that I believe superior to
> the sentimental idealism of a Finley and his ideological descendants.*

John Finley's theory of educational methodology thus was
little more than rhetorical glorification of the teacher's *presence*. This position indeed was less a "theory" than a theme
for numerous eloquent exhortations. He showed little interest
in, or knowledge of, the contemporary ferment in educational
theory that was bubbling all about him. For example, one
evening in 1913 at the Player's Club in New York, Finley was
gathered with a number of his friends in journalism, including
Lincoln Steffens, John Phillips, and Frederic Howe. Steffens
recalled the conversation the next day in a letter to his sister.
He professed amazement "at what he [Finley] seemed not
only not to know—but never to have heard of—education
and—other things."

> [When] the conversation turned upon the subject of education and
> modern ideas, . . . the least informed man was the college president

who is [recently] promoted to be head of a state educational system. And,
for the rest, it seemed [to Steffens] as if all that the three others of us
knew or thought was amazing to F. We must really be radicals or
else,—well,—never mind. I like F. But he was a jolt last night.

Steffens recognized his friend's basic lack of interest in
educational theory. There were, however, points at which
Finley's educational viewpoint skirted close to the avant-
garde theory of the day—"progressive education." He and the
progressivists both endorsed the notion that the school should
aid society by training leaders. Yet, believing that education
should be a rigorous regimen, Finley was hostile to any such
permissive school atmosphere as the progressivists favored.
Furthermore, he was unfamiliar, as Steffens suspected, with
much of the literature of educational theory.

Finley's lack of any clear conception of the process of education beyond the poetic but limited concept of *presence* was
matched by the meagerness of his ideas on the substance of
education, the question of what should be taught in the
schools. Most often when faced with the opportunity to offer
substantive ideas on the subject, Finley would beat a hasty
retreat. "I shall not attempt to speak" about "the machinery of
education," he said on one occasion: "It is complicated." On
another, when faced with the challenge of defining his educational ends, he cast up a haze of vague images about "a limit-
less sea or a pathless plain or summitless mountain." Yet,
toward the close of his City College career, Finley began to
speak in behalf of an educational conception that, if it did not
clarify the subject, certainly dramatized it. This conception
was drawn from a series of literary lectures by Columbia
University professor George Edward Woodberry, which was
published in 1912 under the title *The Torch*. Woodberry promoted the idea of the "race mind," which Finley eagerly
seized upon.

In Finley's hands this notion was used to complement public service. In glorifying public service he was celebrating the
"local" utility of the colleges. The image of the race mind
invoked the complementary idea of education's "illocal" and
universal aspects. Finley set forth a vision of a unity of mankind that could be brought about by somehow collating all

curricula and eliminating what was merely "national and local." Then, said Finley, we should "reach the race's educational foundations"; colleges teaching this core curriculum would function as centers of mankind's unity, as "the place[s] of entering the race-mind."

> [Education would] include the languages and literature of ancient and modern civilization, their humanities and gracious inspiration, the rigorous reasonings of mathematics and its beautiful and world ruling applications, the sciences of mankind and of the earth beneath and of the heavens above, the share which the arts of beauty ought to have in the life of the educated citizen, the histories of the living past with lessons to the living present, the field of government and laws and the economics of man's subsistence, and the reasonings of divine philosophy herself.

This ornate enumeration of almost all the subjects that could be taught marks the closest Finley ever came in his long career in education to identifying the specific content of his educational ideals.

Inspirational rhetoric, backed up by his own personal *presence,* substituted for a clear educational policy. This substitution was recognized and praised by Finley's contemporaries. Writing what was intended as a sympathetic account, a Boston author admitted that Finley was no educational "expert," standing for some clearly delineated pedagogical theory. Neither was he "an iconoclast and propagandist as Eliot was, nor the creator of a new type of urban university with new methods of administration like Harper, nor the exponent of a philosophy of education like Dewey." Finley's strength was in his personal influence and contagious idealism. Faculty members at CCNY, who saw his "great spiritual power" exercised at close range, acknowledged that this power "constantly sends forth currents of civic idealism to strengthen those who are toiling for a better and nobler New York." A perceptive young historian told Finley: "Fortunately you have the rare gift of an educational imagination [which] . . . means everything you have touched immediately took the form and color of an ideal, and so enlisted the enthusiasm as well as the approval of your co-workers." Another faculty member not writing for Finley's eyes described how the president "transformed . . . the atmosphere" of City College. "With the students Mr. Finley is at his strongest and best. His temperament is the poetic one, expressive, with ideals that appeal at once to the youth." Much more similar testimony could be marshaled.

The shortcomings that went along with Finley's strengths were not so widely noted. A young instructor suspected that the president's "weak point . . . is in the management of details, getting the most efficient service from subordinates, choosing committees wisely and getting from them wise and reasonably timely action." Another, far more weighty, appraisal came at the same time (1909) from Princeton University president Woodrow Wilson. Wilson wrote with great candor about his former student, who was being considered for the presidency of a mid-western state university.

> I know Dr. John Finley, President of the College of the City of New York, very well and entertain a very warm admiration for him. So far as engaging character is concerned and great power to please and, therefore, to lead, and unusual social gifts, making him everywhere a much desired guest and speaker, he is an ideal man for such a post as you now have to fill. But my association with him has led me to the judgment that he has no great constructive power. He does not seem to me a man who can make large plans or carry them out with consistency, and he lacks, I should judge, the aggressiveness and clearheadedness necessary to lead public opinion and carry his policy forward in the debate of committees and legislative bodies. His administrative ability, in other words, is better suited for the conduct of a completed institution, I should think, than for one that has constantly to be adjusted to the growth of circumstances and the changes of the time.

Finley had something like a perception of his own talents and limitations. He wrote to his brother-in-law, who was calling attention to a vacant presidency at the University of Minnesota, that he would not be suitable for the post; the school was a well-established institution and had no need any longer for a "missionary" and "creative" president. Later in its development an institution can do with a man primarily concerned with "the internal administrative task. In that particular sort of a job," Finley observed, "I am not supremely interested."

There is a revealing discrepancy between Finley's self-appraisal and the judgment of Woodrow Wilson. Wilson implied that it was just in its early stages that a college needs a bold, decisive president (but that his former student was not such a man). For his part, Finley seemed to believe that a developing college could be sustained by the buoyant vision of an inspiring president. It may be that, had he been put into a situation that demanded vigorous leadership, other qualities unsuspected by Woodrow Wilson would have emerged. But the fact was that Finley at City College presided over an institution whose foundations were already laid and whose direction of growth was already charted—"a completed institution," in Wilson's phrase. In this capacity he did not feel called upon to carry out any sweeping reforms or organizational overhaul at the college. Finley brought instead, by the twin means of abundant rhetoric and personal *presence,* a rich dose of uplifting idealism. He could easily have accepted the judgment of Charles Thwing, who described the college president as "a prophet . . . not in the narrow sense of avoiding danger, but in the sense of having a far-off look." Finley's gaze was directed at the far-off realm of noble ideals. It was his great power to be able to focus the attention of others in that same, somewhat hazy direction.

The uplifting of the spirit that Finley accomplished at CCNY, and the raising of its prestige, were made possible by widespread support in the metropolitan community for expanded, free, higher education. A welter of motives, intentions, and ambitions made up the fabric of this support, and it became Finley's task to translate this generalized feeling into specific administrative acts. He chose to seize upon the golden thread of noble intent among the many strands of community support for City College and weave of it a shimmering image of aspiration. With great imagination and warmth, he identified the college, both in the public mind and in the students', with this noble aspiration.

Other men would have found different ways to discharge the responsibility of presiding over such an institution as CCNY. Finley's was to use rhetoric, ceremony, and personal influence in behalf of high ideals. He endorsed, aided, but did not initiate the large changes that took place during the decade of his presidency—the erecting of a new campus, the development of a new curriculum, the launching of an evening college. These changes were responses to a transformation of

American society that was rapidly underway during his CCNY tenure. Social harmony and the need to integrate potentially dissident elements into a broad consensus were dictated by the changes in American capitalism as it became a world industrial and financial power and a dabbler in imperial adventures. In his characteristic way, John Finley cast a haze of sentimental rhetoric over these changes, few of which he clearly perceived, but the main drift of which he enthusiastically endorsed.

Book 6.
Empire State Education

Chapter 21

The Call to Albany, 1913

In the later phases of Finley's career (chronicled in the next chapters), the same energy and vitality he showed as a young man are evident. On the personal side this is, I think, admirable and a contrast to the situation I deplored in my early academic career, when I overheard time-serving professors admit that once they achieved tenure they would exert themselves no longer. Of course, there are aspects of the inner-directed achievement drive (to use a bit of sociological jargon) that I find less attractive, particularly the striving for power as a means to dominate others (a tendency I find in neither Finley nor myself). More subtle is the devotion to professional work as a means of avoiding the less structured and more risky contacts with people we call friends.

Andrew Sloan Draper and John Huston Finley were both college presidents on the Illinois prairie during the 1890s. Finley, as we have seen, was busily making a modern institution of the college in Galesburg; Draper at the same time was transforming the state institution at Urbana into a university. There were many occasions for the two men to meet; at one of these Draper expressed the hope that Finley might succeed him as president of the University of Illinois. But events did not work out that way. Finley was already settled in the CCNY presidency when Draper finally left Urbana.

In 1904 Draper was elected by the New York State legislature to the educational position he coveted above all others—Commissioner of Education of the State of New York. This post had been newly created, and Draper perceived the opportunity to put his considerable talents to work in it. Immediately Draper hastened to clarify the relationship between the Office of the Commissioner and the Regents of the University of the State of New York. He put the State Department of

Public Instruction itself in order, creating a well-organized and smoothly working agency. In 1912 Draper crowned his labors by obtaining from the legislature and governor a magnificent new building in Albany to house the department's operations.

Commissioner Draper died on April 25, 1913, and within a month Finley had been sounded out as a possible successor. At first he responded by suggesting others for the Albany vacancy. But in June, the regents, sensing Finley's interest, pressed him further. "The time is ripe for great conceptions and great beneficent achievements" in education, Finley was told—

> and nowhere else in the world is there, today, such a favoring vantage ground . . . as in this great Empire State—truly an empire in extent and in population, and possessed of unparalleled wealth which its citizens, a people of already generally highly developed cultivated intelligence, are more than willing to have used in almost unrestricted measure for furthering and bettering the means of public education.

Though Finley may well have discounted so rosy a prognosis of potential public support for educational pioneering, he could not ignore the plea of Regent and Vice-Chancellor Pliny T. Sexton: "Here the greatest of all existing opportunities awaits the devoted leadership of a great educator, and we believe you to be the man for the place." Speaking for the regents, Sexton asked Finley to "come to what seems to us to be, for you, a divinely appointed mission."

> *It is easy to suspect that such talk about divine missions, great opportunities, etc., comprised code words in the esoteric vocabulary of professionalism that was taking final shape in early-twentieth-century America. It was to become an obscurantist vocabulary of indirection, evasion, and bureaucratic distortion, picturing events taking place, not according to choice and volition, but through operation of mystifying impersonal forces. Finley, thank goodness, never succumbed to this debased language, perhaps because of his early training in classical languages and his flair for vivid and direct writing.*

Before he could accept this call, Finley had to clear up a number of matters. There was opposition to him in Albany; some of the regents and Gov. William Sulzer were hostile. The governor had no official voice in the choice of the education commissioner, but Finley would accept no offer from the regents that was not unanimous. Another thing that was troubling him was the title of the office for which he was being considered. Finley did not care for the prosaic, bureaucratic "Commissioner." Anxious to please him, the regents considered relinquishing to Finley the title "Chancellor," held by the senior regent. They accepted the candidate's alternate proposal that he be appointed both commissioner *and* "President of the University of the State of New York." Finally, Finley asked that he be given time to finish his work at CCNY.

The Board of Regents officially accepted most of Finley's conditions at a meeting on July 2. The office of the president was duly created. The incumbent would enjoy the—

> power and duty of general supervision over all educational work and activities in this State, and it shall be his duty also to devote himself to educational research, to the study of the educational research, to the study of the educational work . . . of other jurisdictions, and selectively and reflectively, with the approval of the Board of Regents, to introduce and originate . . . better methods of education, and especially to endeavor in every feasible way to bring about the improved development and greater usefulness of the common schools of this State. . . .

The regents then sent a telegram to Finley, who was vacationing in Tamworth, New Hampshire, informing him of their unanimous action in electing him to the two posts at the salary of $10,000 a year, the same as he was receiving at CCNY. Finley accepted immediately.

Reaction to this development varied. A great cry of anguish went up from City college. Finley was urged to refuse on the grounds that he would be a "mere functionary" in Albany, "at the mercy of the Legislature." It was feared that at CCNY "the devilish side" would come to the fore with Finley gone. The departing City College president corrected some of these extravagant suppositions and calmed the exaggerated fears. The bulk of the responses, however, was warmly congratulatory of the honor that had come to Finley and of the great educational work that lay before him. (Some of them have been cited in the introduction to this book.) It was acknowledged that Finley by 1913 had come a long way from rural Illinois; many expected even greater things to come.

Chapter 22

Labor Peace:

The Obligation of a Progressive, 1913

The term Progressive *is riddled with ambiguities that necessitate care and precision when it is being used in a historical context. Most familiar to Americans from a series of presidential campaigns in which candidates as diverse as Theodore Roosevelt, Robert La Follette, and Henry Wallace assumed the label "Progressive" for their unsuccessful campaigns in 1912, 1924, and 1948, it has also been used by the Communist Old Left to refer to supposedly beneficent tendencies in history—namely, socialism. But since the first state claiming the "socialist" label was Bolshevik Russia, a society precisely the opposite of a technologically or politically advanced nation, the association of the USSR with "progress" was bound to produce confusion. (In my next book, a study of the American Communist movement, I will explore some of the features and consequences of this confusion.) The chapter that now follows will cover Finley's involvement in a characteristic episode of reform during the era—roughly the first decade and a half of the twentieth century— that is known as "the Progressive Period" in U.S. history. The chapter will also provide an opportunity to explore further aspects of the ambiguity of Progressivism.*

Before he could take up the challenge that education in the Empire State presented, Finley was called to do temporary but important service for the nation. In late August, 1913, while he was attempting to wind up affairs at CCNY, requests came to Finley that he accept appointment as arbitrator in a railroad labor-management dispute of considerable significance. The assent of the regents was necessary if Finley was to postpone the assumption of his duties in Albany. Their agreement was quickly obtained; Chancellor Pliny T. Sexton continued to exercise the duties of commissioner of education while commissioner-elect Finley deliberated on the railroad dispute.

Labor-management relations in the railroad field had entered a new era with the passage of the Erdman Act of 1898. Under this legislation, the national government undertook to promote industrial peace through the techniques of mediation and arbitration. Although scores of disputes had been settled under the Erdman Act procedures, most of them by binding arbitration previously agreed to by the disputants, new approaches were called for in 1913. Three-man arbitration boards were believed to be inappropriate bodies to deal with complex labor controversies. Inordinate power rested with the odd member; and the public interest was not considered adequately represented.

> *The assumption that there is a "public interest" over and above such partial and particular interests as "labor" and "capital" is a staple feature of liberal ideology. Academic social science often supports this notion, telling us that advanced industrial societies supply so many "roles" that we can choose among them as if switching clothes at will in the fitting room of a department store. The implication is that a Finley, who all his life identified with the established order of capitalist domination, could at will transform himself into a champion of not the capitalist interest but the "public interest." There is no simple refutation of this notion, but the Marxian approach itself can be used as a flexible tool to illuminate social transformations, taking account of periods of relative stability such as the Progressive Era when class forces in tenuous balance give semblance of reality to the idea of a "public interest."*

During the summer of 1913 a wage dispute was smoldering between a group of Eastern railroads and two unions—the Order of Railway Conductors and the Brotherhood of Railroad Trainmen. The National Civic Federation, headed by Seth Low, after wide consultation with unions, management, and government officials, proposed a method of settlement. Legislation to enlarge the Board of Arbitration to six was called for. A bill to this effect was introduced by Sen. Francis G. Newlands; a day of hearings was held before Newlands's Interstate Commerce Committee; the bill quickly passed the upper chamber, and the House of Representatives voted its approval on July 15. President Woodrow Wilson signed the measure on that same day.

The enlarged Board of Arbitration permitted by the Newlands Act (as it was called) included John Finley. Chairman of the board was National Civic Federation president Seth Low.

Two brotherhood heads and two railroad management officials completed the membership. So constituted, the arbitration board began its hearings in mid-September. Held in Manhattan, they lasted for more than a month. During this period Finley was able to spare little time for educational matters. He did travel to the upstate New York community of Oneonta, probably to give an address, and he managed to come to New York City Hall to testify in behalf of a CCNY budget request. But his main duty was to attend day after day of exhausting conferences in Manhattan. After one of these conferences Finley, needing respite, took the ferry to Staten Island at 9:00 P.M. He reached Tottenville after midnight and took a ferry from there to Perth Amboy, New Jersey. It was a "beautiful moonlight night" according to his diary. He slept briefly on the porch of an unoccupied house and had breakfast at 4:30 A.M. in New Brunswick. He was en route to visit friends and family in Princeton. Finley's diary does not record the precise time of his arrival there.

It is not known what devices the other arbitrators used to escape temporarily from the highly technical, complicated issues of the dispute. One of these was the question of standardization that had been raised in earlier arbitrations. Western railroads were paying higher wages in 1913 to conductors and trainmen; the Eastern brotherhoods wanted a standardization of wage rates that would bring their pay in line with that of their Western brethren. The railroads refused to honor this contention because they claimed the higher Western rates had been unjustly gained by coercion. The arbitrators also rejected the principle of standardization. "This Board does not intend to open up any [new] questions as to standardization of rates," they declared in the published *Arbitration Award.*

The brotherhoods also demanded wage increases for the many classes of service (conductors, baggagemen, flagmen, brakemen, etc.) of about 20 percent, or $18 million yearly. The arbitration award scaled down these demands to an average increase of about 7 percent, or $6 million. The contention that greater productivity of train crews was due to the workers' efforts was rejected; management efficiency was credited with the rise in productivity. The board also rejected the argument that workers' risks had increased, although it was conceded that trainmen's responsibilities had mounted. It perceived no relationship between wages and railroad rates that justified any great increase in the former. The formula hit upon to arrive at the precise amount of increase was that the cost of living had gone up about 7 percent, and wages should go up accordingly.

The general issues disposed of, the arbitration board turned to a detailed consideration of the complex problems of railroad labor. Finley became familiar with such recondite matters as double heading, size of crews, classes of freighthandling, and the definition of a working day. Informed observers considered the resolution of these matters constituted something of a victory for the workers. Soon afterward, however, some of the union leaders would have second thoughts about their alleged gains in the 1913 arbitration. Three years later, one of them, A.B. Garretson of the Order of Railway Conductors, confided to the *Boston Evening Transcript* (August 11, 1916) that Finley and the other "neutral arbitrators" were men—

> of high standing and intelligence. [But] . . . no matter how honest their intentions they could not bring to bear on the questions at issue the disinterestedness necessary. Finley's future relies entirely on the direction of corporate influences. . . . The appointments of neutral arbitrators in the past under the provisions of the Newlands Act ha[s] damned arbitration as a practical proposal in the minds of the [working] men.

A sensible expression of class consciousness that is too rare in the American labor movement.

> *Celebrated by some as a wonderful cultural by-product of the success of American capitalism, the relative lack of proletarian class consciousness in the United States poses some serious historical and political problems. For one thing, there were dramatic episodes of class struggle accompanied by vivid perceptions of class differences in American history, but the genial consensus that virtually blankets popular understanding of the American past hides these episodes from most people. So, radical scholars have the task of informing their fellow citizens of the rich heritage of struggle in such periods as the heyday of the Industrial Workers of the World in the early twentieth century, or the CIO organizing drives of the thirties. But the very unfamiliarity of this past is the result of a variety of factors that has divided sections of the working class from their rational allies: the heterogeneity of the working class deriving from the various ethnic strains in American immigration; the prevalence of racism; the size and diversity of the continent. But now, as the future of capitalism looks less and less rosy (even to its defenders and supporters), the need arises to overcome these differ-*

ences, and especially to bring blue- and white-collar workers, men and women, black and whites, along with other minorities, together in a creative political alliance to replace capitalism with its only conceivable (beneficial) alternative, socialism. It would, however, be virtually impossible to exaggerate either the difficulties in this task or the necessity of the attempt to achieve it.

The Newlands Act, and the arbitration it authorized, were landmarks in the abandonment of laissez-faire during the Progressive Era. A congressional supporter, Congressman Kelley of Pennsylvania, declared in July that the measure deserved the backing of "everyone who believes that the function of the government is to promote the general welfare. It is a measure which seems to me, at least, to prove that the old philosophy of political economy. . . , [suitable for the age of] the stagecoach and the tallow dip. . . , no longer serves the purpose of this day of 1913." The purpose that was to be served by such arbitration was well stated in the social work journal the *Survey* (April 18, 1914): "There is a chasm here between capital and labor that must be bridged. Only men with great social vision can help bridge that chasm. But the[se] men can be secured. There never was so much social spirit in the world as there is today."

The celebration of undifferentiated "social spirit" was an accurate reflection of a popular mood that sustained Progressivism during the early twentieth century. This socially conscious attitude had authentic sources in experiences and perceptions of injustice. But recent scholarship has demonstrated that much of this "social spirit" was translated into a new form of ruling-class hegemony sometimes known as corporate liberalism. The endorsement of Pennsylvania legislator "Pig Iron" Kelley of this abandonment of laissez-faire raises the question of what new procapitalist ideology would take its place. During the past decade and a half, a sophisticated group of historians has attacked this question. The leading studies are Gabriel Kolko's Triumph of Conservatism *(1963) and James Weinstein's* Corporate Ideal in the Liberal State *(1968), which show how some business interests seized upon this new "social spirit" and used it for their own ends. Not all businessmen, however, celebrated the demise of laissez-faire and the advent of the interventionist state, and such dissenters lingered on to join the anti–New Deal Liberty Leagues of the 1930s and even to vote for Barry Goldwater in 1968. But the short-run future was with progressive businessmen who found in the state apparatus both the basis for their own collective and individual enrichment and a means to offer concessions to a potentially rebellious working class.*

John Finley's life and career formed an admirable example of the Progressive social spirit. But his participation in the solution of this labor dispute also suggests that the content of Progressive conviction was essentially conservative. The National Civic Federation, whose hand is evident in these proceedings, represented that segment of the Progressive business community that welcomed the advance of positive government and the incorporation of segments of the labor movement into the national consensus. Finley may not have perceived clearly the long-range goals he was serving as arbitrator in 1913, but he was in sympathy with a social program based upon the generation of class harmony and the willing use of the power of the state. Furthermore, his own service was an example of the willingness to donate one's energies to what was generally recognized as the public good—the same attitude Finley hoped to transmit through his educational activities.

Chapter 23

Romanticizing the New York State
Educational System, 1913–20

Romanticism *is one of the slippery terms in the scholarly vocabulary,
and the historian of ideas Arthur O. Lovejoy has discovered multiple
meanings. In this study the term shall be used to mean the attempt to
transcend routine administrative matters in favor of a search for an
inspiring spiritual purpose in education. In adopting this "romantic"
style, Finley was merely finding one more set of ways to project his
personal* presence.

By the end of November, Finley's work with the arbitration
board had come to an end, and he was free to turn his attention
to the tasks that faced him in Albany. He recorded his attitude
toward the new responsibility in a note drafted during his first
day in the commissioner's office overlooking the state capitol.

I am taking the first step on a path which leads away from the old one. It
is not clearly marked beyond the reaching of this first day. I shall have to
use a compass to follow my instinct of direction. I only know in what
general way I am to go. It will be a hard journey I have no doubt; but I
shall try to keep the direction and my courage even when goose ponds
and moose mountains lie in the way.

In some ways Finley's new position was something less
than a sharp break with the City College years. At Albany, as at
Saint Nicholas Heights in New York and at Galesburg, Illinois, his administration was marked by nothing so much as
the force of his personality. Also, in each new position he
endeavored to exercise the talents of academic showman; his
own inauguration was always the formal beginning. In Albany
the inauguration took place the day after New Year's, 1914.
Apparently little of the responsibility for staging the cere-

monies that day fell upon Finley. Nothing more than a round
of speeches marked the accession of the new commissioner.

In his own address, Finley characteristically did not intimate *how* he intended to care for the educational system; "I
shall give no intimation of policy or detail of purpose," he
said. What he did try to accomplish in his inaugural peroration
was a redefinition of the spirit of New York State's educational
enterprise.

Finley was willing to concede that the tone of the operation
was prosaic and uninspiring. The University of the State of
New York, with no campuses of its own, seemed little more
than "a standardizing, policing, appraising agency of the State,
making children go to school, punishing parents who try to
keep them from doing so, conducting examinations, settling
disputes, deciding who should be allowed to study for the bar
and medicine." It was an institution "with no more romance
than the Department of Public Instruction." The lack of romance was intolerable to Finley; but it could easily be overcome by the use of characteristically inspired rhetoric. The
state's elaborate educational bureaucracy was redefined in
terms of what Finley happily perceived as its "inner significance," the tendency to link up and consecrate the noble
thoughts and ambitions of New York State's widely scattered
school population. The "collection of administrative machinery" under the new president-commissioner would become—

> a little state, a polis that has at heart the good of every citizen in the
> making, [and] that has within its horizon the whole range of educational
> problems, from those which the newest immigrant brings in his alien
> speech and tradition up the harbor of New York to those which remain in
> the mute hearts of the descendants of the aborigines upon the other
> border.

Finley concluded his inaugural address by stating that in
the Albany position he had reached the apex of his career in
education: that there could be no higher ambition for him than
to serve the needs of New York State. These initial, vague
statements of purpose were greeted with enthusiasm from all
corners of the state. The "obscurity" that had surrounded the
education department and the university appeared to be lift-
ing.

Finley's inaugural address, in all its vague idealism, promised a continuation in Albany of the same qualities that had made his City College presidency such a success—exertion of his personal *presence*, exploitation of ceremonial opportunities, and the liberal use of inspirational rhetoric. As one former CCNY associate put it, "Before long the Finley atmosphere will envelope the school system of the State and a new meaning will be given to popular education."

The nature of the new office, however, made it difficult to exercise some of these qualities. From his office in the imposing but remote education building, Finley could not readily make his *presence* known to students, teachers, and school officials scattered all over the state. Therefore, at every opportunity, and sometimes in unorthodox ways, he went to them. For example, in the fall of his first year as commissioner, Finley took a walking tour of the south central counties with another official of the department. "We walked," he said, "to catch the atmosphere, to feel the pulse, not to spy." The academic hikers carried cooking utensils in sacks on their shoulders and generally slept in country inns, except for one night in a barn. Much later, his secretary wrote warmly of discovering Dr. Finley traveling incognito, "visiting country schools. He played with the children, photographed them, queried them about their homes and their parents, asked them what they had to eat in their dinner pails." Although stodgy officials "expressed apprehension concerning . . . proper regard for the dignity of his office. . . , Dr. Finley knew that the top of the education department at Albany needed to get in touch with the bottom."

Ceremonial occasions also helped maintain a spirit of common purpose within the sprawling state educational bureaucracy. Finley was a past master in these matters, and some of the academic pageants he staged in Albany were adaptations of the same sort of events he had brought about in Galesburg and on Saint Nicholas Heights. A ready-made vehicle was the traditional annual convocation of the officials of the education department, which generally included dreary rounds of speeches. Finley did not at once depart from the customary format. But in the convocation of October, 1916, Finley's imaginative conception is evident.

The central theme of the gathering was "the word." Finley

composed on this theme what he called a "trilogy," with sessions devoted to the written word, the pictured word, the spoken word. To be sure, there were scattered through the two-day proceedings conventional educational addresses on such topics as "The Importance to Health of Physical Training in the Schools" and "Possibilities of the Junior High School." But there was a central and possibly inspiring design to the whole proceedings; the addresses by eminent persons were grouped about the appropriate subthemes, and there was a dramatic technological climax with a national telephone hookup (compliments of A. T. & T.) by which the delegates to the convocation spoke with absent pedagogical dignitaries in such places as Oakland, California, and Lyndonville, Vermont. The meeting wound up on a lyrical note as President Finley awarded the degree of Doctor of Laws *honoris causa* to Thomas Alva Edison, by telephone. A mid-twentieth-century temperament might tend to be skeptical of the vision of technological glory that animated the 1916 convocation, but at that time, guided by Finley's deft hand, the ceremony was appropriately awe inspiring and dignified.

Later convocations, although nothing to match the event of 1916, also showed an unmistakable Finley touch. The appearance of distinguished and unconventional people could be expected. In 1920, for example, the ceremonies at Albany were enlivened by the presence of the Archbishop of Baalbek, Syria, speaking in Arabic on the virtues of education (scholar Philip Hitti translated). Although Finley could use the convocations imaginatively as vehicles for the dramatization of the adventure of education, there were certain shortcomings. The meetings attracted mostly school officials. Audiences at the academic ceremonies Finley had staged at Knox College and CCNY included students and teachers, groups unrepresented at the convocations even though the state's educational policy ultimately concerned them. Thus, the Albany surroundings, although stately and impressive, were too far removed from the actual sites of the teaching-learning experience. What was needed was a device to bring the unifying, inspirational message of the commissioner to schoolrooms throughout the state: a device for transmitting his *presence*.

Finley found an answer in the semimonthly publication *Bulletin to the Schools,* which in inspiration and execution was an expression of the new commissioner's temperament and philosophy. Finley's early ambition had of course revolved about a journalistic career, and, although he had been involved in educational work for over two decades, journalism was never too far from his mind. It was therefore natural that, when it came to devising a method to bring a sense of common purpose to the school system, he would hit upon a *Bulletin* of news and inspiration, which could be posted in each schoolroom. The first number included specific instructions to the teacher on this posting.

The *Bulletin* was the major outlet for Finley's ideas on educational policy during his commissionership. These ideas were, in Albany, essentially what they had been earlier in New York, Princeton, and Galesburg: service to the state, Americanization, and patriotism. The vigorous action by Finley in behalf of these ideas was mainly undertaken in connection with the crises of preparedness and the First World War. The impact of the war on education in New York State will be the subject of the major part of subsequent chapters. It is only necessary here to sample the tone and content of the *Bulletin.*

For an official publication of the state education department, an agency whose printed matter generally included bulky reports written in drab bureaucratic prose, the *Bulletin* was unusually personal and intimate. Through it Finley spoke directly to the students and teachers of the state. He urged his traditional advice—"Read a book, take a walk, make a friend." He publicized some of his favorite authors. His own enthusiasm for academic ceremony was transmitted in detailed instructions and materials for tercentary pageants celebrating the Plymouth and Jamestown landings. Abraham Lincoln's birthday called forth in the *Bulletin* references to Finley's own nurture in Illinois. There were inevitable reminiscences of the plowing on the prairies with a volume of Horace strapped to the beam. His own experience, travels, and occasionally photographs, poetry, and correspondence made up copy for the *Bulletin.* When he left Albany on trips, as he did more and more often after 1917, editing the *Bulletin* fell to Finley's subordinates. At those times, only prosaic, routine notices appeared, with none of the edifying rhetoric with which Finley could surround almost every subject. Finally, after he left the commissionership altogether, the *Bulletin to the Schools* was no longer issued. It was recognized as his own personal project, a continuous inspiration to the state's teachers. A regent marveled over "what it is possible to do with a little printer's ink and a little sympathetic understanding of the schools."

> *Like Finley and Regent Adelbert Moot, I am occasionally capable of inflated views on what can be accomplished with "a little printer's ink." At this writing I am engaged in a collective attempt to bring about a socialist revival in the United States, and a major tool is a weekly newspaper called* In These Times, *which began publication in Chicago in the fall of 1976. In* These Times *aims at reaching a readership of ordinary Americans and helping them realize that the idea of socialism is relevant to their lives. The newspaper focuses on work, leisure, and sports as well as political analysis. (One of my contributions was an essay on fencing in a summer issue in 1976.) Militantly nonsectarian, In These Times aims at achieving a consistently socialist outlook, without being the kind of newspaper (there are too many) that can only appeal to the already convinced and those who prefer to finger the beads of some supposed doctrinal purity rather than build an actual socialist movement. Having perhaps less immediate political relevance than In These Times, but in the long run a force for socialist scholarship, is the venerable Marxist quarterly,* Science & Society. *Apparently the world's oldest Marxist journal in continuous publication, S & S invited me to join its editorial board in 1974, after I had contributed a number of articles. This work also constitutes one of my main political tasks in this period.*

Some of the duties of the office of commissioner of education bore little direct relationship to the qualities of sympathy and idealism that John Finley had in abundance. Prominent among these duties was (and still is) the judicial power dispensed under a legislative mandate of 1822. The commissioner exercised both original and appellate (appeals from decisions of local school boards) jurisdiction under what was by Finley's time a large body of statutory law and judicial precedent.

Most of the cases were routine. The first decisions handed down over Finley's name dealt with such issues as the com-

plaint of an Orange County taxpayer that local school officials
had redrawn school district boundaries in a way that was not
in accord with legally established procedures. The validity of
the complaint was upheld; Finley ordered the boundary line
"set aside and declared void." Another case decided at the
same time also related to a dispute between taxpayers and the
local school officials. Early in 1915 Finley decided a school
segregation case. Negro parents in Nassau County appealed to
him against the continued use of separate grammar schools for
their children. He turned down the appeal on the grounds
that, according to state law, the inhabitants of any free school
district could decide to establish separate schools. Furthermore, the school under question had been "exclusively maintained [for Negroes] without complaint to the Commissioner
for a long period." Finley would insist that the education
department uphold the equivalence of the separate facilities,
but he dismissed for want of proof the appellants' argument in
this case that the school building was inferior and unsafe.

One of the most widely noted of his judicial opinions, and
one that seemed to testify to Finley's warm humanity, was
rendered in January, 1915. Mrs. Bridget C. Peixotto had been
acting principal of Public School 14 in the Bronx when she
asked for leave on account of "some affliction of her ears and
nose." It later developed that Mrs. Peixotto's "affliction," if it
could be called that, was pregnancy. A baby was born in early
April, but she was dismissed a month later by the New York
City Board of Education for "neglect of duty." The mother
appealed to the courts, but got no satisfaction. She then took
the case to the commissioner.

Finley was under pressure to decide the issue "in favor of
the stork in education." Eminent women, such as Charlotte
Perkins Gilman, Fola La Follette, and Mrs. Frederic C. Howe,
had petitioned him to overrule the New York City Board's
regulation that teachers must be dismissed upon having a
child. Even Galesburg, Illinois, had its attention directed to
this case. In his decision, Finley declined to be diverted from
the "main issue by the Board of Education, which did not wish
to base its action on Mrs. Peixotto's concealment of her preg-

nancy." He pointed out that married women were regularly employed as teachers in New York City. Could the board then "dismiss a married woman teacher for that which is the lawful, natural consequence of marriage?" No, he ruled; it must accept the natural corollary of its policy of retaining married teachers and give "at least as favorable consideration to an absence for child-birth as is normally given to absences asked for [other legitimate] reasons." The board's decision was overruled, and it was directed to reinstate Mrs. Peixotto and other similar petitioners.

Finley's ruling was generally well received. The president of Princeton "was delighted to read [his] . . . recent decision regarding so important and significant a question." The *New York Times* only raised minor technical objections to Finley's decision. The Board of Education put up only feeble resistance. One member remarked, "Don't we know when we are licked?" By the end of the month, Mrs. Peixotto was offered her old position at Public School 14. Finley had won a "complete victory."

The significance of the Peixotto case lay in the limitation on the discretion of the local school board in the interest of teachers' welfare and on behalf of humane principles. At that time, Finley virtually apologized to the Board of Education for his interference, assuring them that the education department favored "the widest [local] discretion practicable." But in a case decided five years later, the next decision of Finley to receive wide public notice, the authority of this same powerful board was limited when it was found to encroach unduly on the professional domain of the superintendent of schools. Personnel transfers of clerical employees had been authorized over the head of the superintendent. Finley set aside the newly passed regulations under which these transfers could take place and upheld the prerogatives of the superintendent.

This decision too was widely hailed. To the editor of the *Journal of Education,* its "masterfulness places Dr. John H. Finley at the forefront among educational statesmen of America for all time." This somewhat inflated appraisal was echoed by an old friend who, "fresh from reading Beveridge's *Life of John Marshall,*" appreciated Finley's decision all the more. But rather than viewing the judicial powers of his office in Marshallian terms, as giving opportunity for creative educational statesmanship, Finley mostly relied on the recommendations of the legal division of the education department. He viewed the legal duties, along with signing diplomas, as drudgery, and presumably did not reserve much time or energy for them.

Chapter 24

School Consolidation and Departmental Power, 1913–15

The questions of administrative skills and abilities raised in this chapter prompted an examination of my own attitudes toward that whole range of human relations encompassed by the concept "administration." Initially I adopted the conventionally cynical attitude that administrative work is reducible to pushing papers, or worse still, pushing people, and is thus inherently inferior to the "creative" work I prefer. But gradually I have come to understand the shallowness of this view. Studying and writing about Finley's career in educational adminstration, as well as involvement in political struggles and community movements, have taught me the importance of advance planning, clearly defined agendas, procedures for evaluation and follow-through. In short, administration. But this new-found respect for administrative virtues exists side-by-side with suspicion of bureaucratic insensitivity and the dangers of too-complete identification with impersonal institutions so that human warmth and sympathy suffer.

An even less congenial responsibility that fell to Finley as New York State commissioner of education, and one that ran counter to his aim of "romanticizing" the school system, was the policy of consolidating the rural schools of the state. Begun long before Finley came to Albany, the education department's crusade against the small rural school districts had not gotten very far by 1913. According to historian John S. Brubacher (*The Judicial Power of the New York State Commissioner of Education* [1927]), any district that was financially and numerically strong enough and had the backing of a majority of its citizens could resist attempts to consolidate schools. But by the time Finley appeared on the scene, this situation had begun to change. In response to business and professional pressures that were forcing widespread rationalization of the nation's education, New York State committed itself to the replacement of the small, rural schools by consolidated grammar and high schools that could teach the complex skills thought necessary for life in an expanding, technological society.

The campaign for consolidation was kicked off by legislation in 1913 and 1914 that provided state funds for districts carrying out consolidation. To the carrot of state aid was added the stick of the commissioner's judicial power, which he wielded fairly consistently to bring about the desired change. When taxpayers, often a majority in the district, resisted the consolidation movement, Finley again and again dismissed their appeals. In early 1915 one such appeal was heard, and Finley took the opportunity to trace the historical evolution of the policy he was administering, as well as broadcast a full-scale defense of it. He pointed out that the laws of 1853 providing for the establishment of "Union Free School Districts" were intended to promote consolidation, as did legislation in 1896 and 1903. The legislation of 1913 and 1914 was even more specifically directed toward that end.

The end itself was a desirable one too, Finley maintained. The appellants, taxpayers in Erie County, objected to the annexation of four school districts, each with its one-room rural schoolhouse, by a larger Union Free district with an eight-grade elementary school and a four-year high school. The basis of the objection, Finley observed, was the same generally raised "throughout the entire country when the question of consolidation of schools has been under consideration." It concerned the rigors of climate and the difficulties of transportation. Such objections had been met in Wisconsin, Montana, and North Dakota, all of which decided *for* consolidation; *a fortiori* New York ought to go along. Transportation in trolleys and buses to the consolidated schools was no hardship. In the larger, graded schools, where the teachers could spend more time with their pupils, "interest and enthusiasm" for learning would be easier to foster, and instruction would be "much more thorough, comprehensive and efficient . . . than . . . in the separate rural schools." Strong financial reasons also impelled the process of consolidation; the tax base of the new combined district was $1 million in assessed valuation, which would support a good school without new burdensome taxation.

Departing from statistical and financial data, Finley concluded his rejection of the taxpayers' appeal with an invocation of the wider social purposes served by the policy of consolidation.

> The school maintained in the consolidated district [he suggested] may exercize larger and broader functions in this community than it would be possible for the separate schools to perform. Courses of study may be given which will be adapted to the needs of this community. Training may be provided for the boys and girls who desire to remain upon the farms and also for those who desire to prepare for business and professional life. . . . The scope of the influence and usefulness of the school may be made to extend beyond the enrolled children and to include the people themselves. The school may become an agency for developing a community spirit and . . . prove of far higher practical and moral value to the people of the united districts than could be given by the fine schools separately.

The taxpayers' appeal was dismissed.

Such a piecemeal, district-by-district policy for bringing about school consolidation, even though it was backed by the judicial power of the commissioner, was superseded by another approach in 1917, when the state legislature passed a bill to facilitate the process. Finley had been requesting such legislation for two years. He observed that voluntary consolidation undertaken at the initiative of district school superintendents had "proceeded slowly." Another, perhaps visionary scheme would be to redistrict the entire state and place schools in the "natural and social centers." Finley admitted that this policy was "ideal but also remote." He was aware of the "sentiment (most worthy in itself) which attaches" to the present rural schools, even though many of them served districts determined by social and economic conditions that no longer existed. For the education department, Finley asked the legislature to consider a bill that would neither be so drastic as redistricting by state fiat nor proceed at such a leisurely pace as the current, voluntary policy.

The proposed alternative centered around the Township Bill, which would widen the area of local taxation and school administration to coincide with the state's townships. The office of district school superintendent was abolished and all school property in the district was transferred to the board of education of the appropriate township. This board was assigned power to "determine in which school districts of the town school shall be maintained and the number of teachers to be employed therein." The financial responsibilities of the local boards were to be exercised under the close supervision of the State Department of Education. The unmistakable (but unstated) aim of the bill was to carry out a consolidation of districts that would mean the demise of the one-room rural schoolhouse.

This policy was a long-standing commitment of the state education department; it did not originate with Finley. He would have been far more inclined in his characteristic way to glorify the rural schoolhouses as "radiant, happy places." He had studied and taught in such a school many decades earlier on the Illinois prairie. But as commissioner, he was obliged to administer and defend a policy his underlings had convinced him was best for the state.

Here is a touchy problem in practical ethics, and one that has come up in our era with a vengeance. Finley was not exactly an underling carrying out orders of his superiors in this school consolidation struggle, but his situation bears more than a superficial similarity to those more weighty moral issues of obedience to orders and institutional imperatives vs. conscience. Issues like these surfaced at the Nuremburg trials, at the Eichmann prosecution, in the cases of U.S. soldiers ordered to perform acts of terror against civilian populations in Vietnam. Insofar as Finley's public life is relevant to this issue, he usually opted for authority over conscience and thus erred in a direction that has ominous overtones in a later era.

Finley was abroad in May, 1917, when the Township Bill was engineered through the legislature by Assistant Commissioner Thomas E. Finegan, who wrote to his superior in Paris of the legislative victory achieved in spite of the fact that the bill "got 'walloped' good and hard" by its opponents. The education department seemed to have overcome all opposition when Gov. Charles S. Whitman signed the measure later that month. However, opposition began to rise, even if belatedly; cries of protest went up from all over the state from two groups. Taxpayers whose taxes had gone up under the new assessments provided for in the Township Bill complained about rates that were sometimes doubled. In reply to this group, Finley admitted that the law fell heavily on small, rich districts that had not been paying their share before. Another group advanced a less selfish position, arguing—in terms that might have been borrowed from a Finley oration—that although the rural schoolhouses were "unpainted, draughty and ugly," they were nevertheless "radiating centers of intelligence and public spirit." As such, they were precious to the people of the state who would fight against any attempt to destroy them.

This popular opposition to the Township Bill quickly made itself manifest. Farmers in particular were rapidly mobilized against it, and they made their feelings known to local politicians. Opposition to Governor Whitman, who signed the Township Bill into law, was building up. In vain did supporters of the education department's consolidation policy urge the governor not to take "the back track in a good cause." Political expediency was a far more potent force, especially in an election year. Whitman, hearing that a move had begun in the legislature to repeal the Township Bill, himself made a widely publicized call for repeal. Public hearings in the assembly chambers in Albany became the occasion for a "furious attack" on the bill by embattled farmers from all over the state. One Sullivan County husbandman, convinced that the rural schools had been "Finleyized and Fineganized enough," demanded repeal. A former state official argued that, "While we are sending our boys to fight for democracy [in Europe], we are building an autocracy right here by this law." An Erie County farmer, "gesticulating with clenched fist," warned the legislature that if they did not repeal the bill they would "create a rural Bolsheviki."

Finley and the other supporters of the bill admitted that it had certain defects that could be remedied by amendments, but urged that it not be repealed. Their temperate and judicious arguments did little to mollify an opposition that was already speaking about revolution. When Finley rose to speak in behalf of the Township Bill, he was surrounded and drowned out by the shouted "Repeal! Repeal!" of the embattled farmers. The legislature dutifully repealed the bill. Finley had lost a major battle. Despite his considerable talent for injecting humanity into bureaucracies and bringing them close to the people they served, he did not successfully do it in this case. It was observed that the "human element . . . had been overlooked when this law was written, and passed and defended." The Township Bill had the flavor of arbitrary bureaucratic dictation, which Finley did little, and possibly could do little, to dispel. New legislation to effect the consolidation of rural school districts was passed in 1925, four years after he left the education department.

Far more congenial to Finley's temperament, but productive of no more success than the Township Bill of 1917–18, was the earlier attempt to cast constitutional protection over the education department's expanded powers. The state constitution, as revised in 1894, described the legislature's responsibility "for the maintenance and support of a system of free, common schools, wherein all the children of this State may be educated." In the years after these words were inserted in the constitution, the state education department and the University of the State of New York had been established, the role of the regents of the university had been defined, and this entire educational apparatus had vastly increased its powers. Finley asked the state constitutional convention that met in the summer of 1915 to write some of these changes into the new document they were preparing. The major textual revision sought was one that would have preceded the existing statement on free, common schools with the statement that "the State shall continue the supervision and control of the education of children as a State function and no powers in derogation thereof shall be conferred upon the local authorities of any civil division of the State."

What did this mean? Clarification of the proposed amendment came in the often acrimonious floor debate at the constitutional convention, in which Jacob Gould Schurman, President of Cornell, acted as "floor manager." In the debate more was perhaps revealed about the intent of the amendment than the framers wished. At first Schurman professed that only constitutional recognition of established policy was requested; "We ask for no change. We are for the *status quo*," he proudly stated. Eventually one of the delegates inquired, If there is so much satisfaction with things as they are, then why change the constitution? Supporters of the amendment then admitted that their intent was really to anticipate demands for "home rule" by New York City and to forever establish that education must be "an exception to the home rule program." The opponents (among them, Robert Wagner of Manhattan) pressed Schurman hard and forced the admission that some provisions of the amendment were legally ambiguous. This was the *coup de grace*; the amendment was soundly beaten. And what was more, in the fall of 1915 the voters of the state rejected the entire constitution as revised in Albany that summer.

During this entire sequence, Finley discretely stayed in the background. On the floor of the convention, it was stated that the state education department had "no responsibility for the proposed amendment." But Finley and other department officials *did* prepare drafts of the amendment. In addition the education department acted as sort of literary host to the delegates, entertaining them in the Education Building (across Albany Avenue from the convention chambers) and making library facilities available. Largely for the benefit of the delegates, but widely publicized, was a ceremony staged by Finley to commemorate the 700th anniversary of the signing of Magna Charta. In return for these courtesies, the constitutional convention unanimously voted their thanks to Finley and the staff of the education department.

Despite this token of regard, and despite the convention's formal acceptance of some administrative changes in the University of the State of New York, Finley wistfully regretted that the major amendment proposed was not accepted. But he was urged to take satisfaction in the convention's expressions of confidence. One of the regents pointed out that the convention's action (and inaction) really added up to an "appreciation of . . . the present administration of the educational systems of this State . . . as well as [satisfaction] with the Regents for calling such a man [as you] to this leadership." From another perspective, Finley's role in these schemes to consolidate the schools and reaffirm the powers of his department testify, not to leadership, but to lack of it.

Chapter 25

New York Reverberates to the Guns
of August, 1914

The disreputable dissenters who opposed World War I as a quarrel among capitalist powers, which the peoples of the various countries should resist becoming involved in, were subject to intense persecution. Even such a normally genial man as Finley (as will be shown in the next chapter) did not tolerate such dissent. Who could now convincingly argue that the dissenters were wrong?

When Finley accepted the position of state commissioner of education, it was agreed that he should not only devote himself to the local duties of his office, but also pursue "the study of the educational work of other jurisdictions." Finley interpreted this as the regents' advance endorsement of his plans to travel widely while he held the office.

The first opportunity came in the fateful summer of 1914. He was appointed by Secretary of State William Jennings Bryan as delegate to an international conference of educators scheduled to be held at The Hague in September. It became a family affair, just as the earlier European visit in 1910–11 had been. His oldest son was sent to a little French village, where Finley visited him sometime in July. They went on this occasion to nearby Dieppe for luncheon. Fifty years later, John Finley, Jr., remembered the day clearly. Dieppe was "a fashionable place, with gaudy restaurants then doubtless at the height of the season. We went to one, the Hotel Royal [which] had a simple meal, but were charged what then seemed a great bill." Finley did not stay long with his twelve-year-old son but returned to England, where he wrote to the lad on a postcard—

                    You'll need be economical
                        To keep yourself from want,
                    But can e'er recall one meal Royal
                        At cinquant francs cinquant.

The warm and affectionate father was not parted for long from
his son. On August 4, German armies crossed the Belgian
border, and soon Europe was plunged into war. Finley immediately hurried from his leisurely travels in the English
lake district, crossed the channel near Boulogne, and took the
train south toward Dieppe. Forty miles short of his destination
at Abbeville, the train was commandeered, and another was
not expected for twenty-four hours. Finley, the inveterate
pedestrian, set out on foot after his boy. He described the trek
in one of his most moving verses, which I quote in its entirety.

        Before I knew, the Dawn was on the road,
        Close at my side, so silently he came
        Nor gave a sign of salutation, save
        To touch with light my sleeve and make the way
        Appear as if a shining countenance
        Had looked on it. Stranger was this radiant Youth,
        As I, to these fair, fertile parts of France,
        Where Caesar with his legions once had passed
        And where the Kaiser's uhlans yet will pass
        Or e'er another moon contends with clouds
        For mastery of these same fields. Tonight
        (And but a month has gone since I walked there)
        Well might the Kaiser write, as Caesar wrote,
        In his new commentaries on a Gallic war,
        "Fortissimi Belgae." A moon ago
        Who would have guessed that dead would lie
        Like swaths of grain beneath the harvest moon
        Upon these lands the ancient Belgae held,
        From Normandy beyond renowned Liege!
        But it was out of that dread August night
        From which all Europe woke to war, that we,
        This beautiful Dawn–Youth, and I, had come,
        He, from afar. Beyond grim Petrograd
        He'd waked the moujik from his peaceful dreams,
        Bid the muezzin call to morning prayer
        Where minarets rise o'er the Golden Horn,
        And driven shadows from the Prussian march
        To lie beneath the lindens of the stadt.
        Softly he'd stirred the bells to ring at Rheims
        He'd knocked at high Montmartre, hardly asleep,
        Heard the sweet carillon of doomed Louvain,
        Boylike, had tarried for a moment's play
        Amid the traceries of Amiens,
        And then was hast'ning o'er the road to Dieppe

Through which I'd walked, with no companion else
Than ghostly kilometer posts that stood
As sentinels of space along the way.
Often in doubt I'd paused to question one,
With nervous hands, as they who read Moon-type;
And more than once I'd caught a moment's sleep
Beside the highway, in the dripping grass,
While one of these white sentinels stood guard,
Knowing me for a friend, who loves the road,
And best of all by night, when wheels do sleep
And stars alone do walk abroad. But once

Three watchful shadows deeper than the dark
Laid hands on me and searched me for the marks
Of traitor or of spy, only to find
Over my heart the badge of loyalty.
With wish for bon voyage they gave me o'er
To the white guards who led me on again.

Thus Dawn o'ertook me and with magic speech
Made me forget the night as we strode on.
Where'er he looked a miracle was wrought:
A tree grew from the darkness at a glance;
A hut was thatched; a new chateau was reared
Of stone, as weathered as the church at Caen;
Gray blooms were colored suddenly in red;
A flag was flung across the eastern sky.
Nearer at hand, he made me then aware
Of peasant women bending in the fields
Cradling and gleaning by the first scant light,
Their sons and husbands somewhere o'er the edge
Of these green-golden fields which they had sowed
But will not reap,—out somewhere on the march,
God but knows where and if they come again.
One fallow field he pointed out to me
Where but the day before a peasant ploughed,
Dreaming of next year's fruit, and there his plough
Stood now mid-field, his horses commandeered
A monstrous sable crow perched on the beam.

Before I knew, the Dawn was on the road
Far from my side, so silently he went,
Catching his golden helmet as he ran,
And hast'ning on along the dun straight way,
Where old men's sabots now began to clack
And withered women, knitting, led their cows,
On, on to call the men of Kitchener
Down to their coasts,—I shouting after him:
"O Dawn, would you had let the world sleep on
Till all its armament were turned to rust,
Nor waked it to this day of hideous hate
Of man's red murder and of woman's woe."

> Famished and lame, I came at last to Dieppe,
> But Dawn had made his way across the sea,
> And, as I climbed with heavy feet the cliff,
> Was even then upon the sky-built towers
> Of that great capital where races all,
> Teuton, Italian, Gallic, English, Slav,
> Forget long hates in one consummate faith.

As the poem intimates, Finley was arrested en route by French soldiers who suspected he was a spy, and who thought that his shaving stick was dynamite. His Legion of Honor ribbon, won for the publication of his *French in the Heart of America*, secured his quick release. By the morning of August 5, Finley was at Dieppe, from which he and the boy hurried back to England.

Finley sent his family to Scotland, where he joined them only for a few days at Andrew Carnegie's Skibo Castle. His main work in August was at London, where he was chosen by an U.S. citizens' committee to get in touch with Americans "marooned" in Germany. He was to travel there by way of Holland with a large sum of money for relief work. But this expedition was suddenly called off, amid "considerable mystery," by U.S. Ambassador to Great Britain Walter Hines Page. Presumably Finley's venture had noticeable anti-German overtones that appeared to compromise America's neutral diplomatic posture.

In early September Finley and his family returned home, not by the German ship on which they had originally booked passage, but on a small steamer to Quebec. The boy and father occupied "humble quarters virtually in the steerage," while Mrs. Finley and her daughter "gloried in something like the bridal suite." On returning to Albany he wrote to President Wilson expressing his delight at being back on American soil and his pride in being an American in those trying days. These personal experiences abroad proved helpful in his educational work, as we shall see.

Finley's immediate reaction to the outbreak of war in Europe was to underscore the lesson taught by peace advocates—that no sound national or international order can be erected on the basis of hatred and strife. He himself had earlier been one of these peace advocates. During the City College years he had served as director of the Peace Society of

New York and had often rhapsodized on the new hope for
mankind raised by the Hague Peace Conferences. In midsummer 1915 he could denounce war as a "hellish thing," a
"vocation of jealousy, envy and hate . . . which drags man
back to the savage . . . [and] which is strewing with stark and
rotting corpses fields already twice red with the carnage of"
battle. A month later he spoke of the great figures in the
history of German culture, and concluded:

> It is absurdly tragic that in this year of the world, we could be compelled
> to think of military preparedness against a people whose music we have
> sung, whose poetry we have learned by heart, whose science we have
> imported into our laboratories, whose philosophers we have welcomed
> into our universities, whose children we have loved;—it is the supreme
> travesty of civilization that we have to think of preparedness not against
> a pagan people but against a nation of Christian name.

> *Sustained involvement in the antiwar movement forced many of us to
> confront why we dissented from the prevailing American enthusiasm
> for cutting down the Vietnamese insurgents, an enthusiasm that of
> course began to wane by 1968. A commitment to Christian civilization
> turned out to be perfectly compatible with support of the murderous
> war, as American Roman Catholic sentiment was early mobilized for
> the anti-Communist crusade in Southeast Asia. (A good account of this
> is to be found in my book* Vietnam *[1965 ed., pp. 235ff; 1970 ed., reading
> No. 50].) To comprehend the Indochina conflict a less limited set of
> distinctions than the one between pagan and Christian was required. To
> be sure, some courageous Catholics spoke and acted against the war long
> before it became fashionable to do so, and, in one of the most dramatic
> episodes of antiwar protest in the United States, my* Vietnam *book was
> entered as evidence for the defense of fourteen Milwaukee Catholics who
> entered a Selective Service office to destroy draft files in 1969.*

Despite the tragic irony of it, Finley and many of his fellow
countrymen *were* beginning to think seriously about preparedness. The question had by the spring of 1915 become a
national political issue. Within a year President Woodrow
Wilson would gradually swing the nation and Congress from
antipreparedness to a point at which preparations for war
could not only be countenanced but could also be reconciled
with the domestic program of Progressivism.

Finley, never a rebel against what appeared to be the prevailing tendencies, went along with the growing support for
preparedness. As head of New York State's educational system, he effected its transformation to a wartime footing at a
pace neither ahead of nor behind the national preparedness
movement. The details of the New York State program will be

set forth presently. It is first necessary to see how Finley
sloughed off his superficial pacifism in order to develop a
rationale for preparedness that would do minimal violence to
his Progressive principles.

Finley came to Progressive doctrines of enlightened public
service through ancestral example, personal inclination, and,
what is most apparent from the documentary record of his life,
his training and education. As early as 1887 Finley used military metaphor in his valedictory address to describe the service that Knox College baccalaureates could perform. The
"free-floating militarism" expressed on this occasion was acti-
vated again at the turn of the century, when Finley mounted a
defense of Anglo-Saxon imperialism. When he elaborated the
doctrine of enlightened public service at CCNY, there was
also an undercurrent of militarism in his appeals.

In 1910 William James published his essay "The Moral
Equivalent of War." Finley read this essay with eagerness,
endorsing the proposition that even a nation at peace needed
arousing of its hardihood and valor. He lamented that sort of
peace under which citizens "degenerate into mild, peaceable
beings who will be [in] kindergartenland throughout life." By
1915 Finley had gone so far as to advocate the abandonment of
a "softened" vocabulary that proposed the tame ideal of mere
"public service" and timidly suggested just "doing good."
Finley began to call for a more forceful and militant appeal,
taking inspiration from the soldier: "Brave fellow, who hast
died for others' sake/In some wet, fetid trench, or blasted field.
. . ." The lesson to be learned was: "Shun softness, luxury
and paunched ease/Know the close comradeship of fearless
men."

In both poetry and public addresses, Finley began to draw
lessons in 1915 and 1916 that led him far from the sentiments
expressed in his poem of the fall of 1914, "To a Peace Advocate." The world war whose outbreak he had witnessed became to him something more than just a demonstration of the
brutality and folly of mankind. He lamented that the United
States had "so slight a share in the heroism and agony of this
most tragic, most significant struggle since man began to write
history." When he visited the English universities in August

of 1914, Finley witnessed the vast "mobilization of the spirit" that dissipated all effete talk of Milton, of science and philosophy as the manly Oxford and Cambridge students went forth "to prove the valor of their cloistered and unpractical learning."

> Am I being too suspicious to see an ugly and dangerous antiintellectualism here? The argument that real manhood proves itself on the field of battle, and any competing view is feminine? If so, then Finley was unable to escape the patriarchal antifeminism that the women's movement has only lately exposed and that, when overcome, will surely "liberate" men at least as much as women.

Two years after his memorable experience in France, Finley described to a large American audience what he thought were its lessons. He characterized the European mobilization as—

> purposeful, organized, destinated, collective mobility. . . , the liberation and effective use of every latent force—natural, economic, social, spiritual—that a nation has. [Mobilization] . . . means the elimination of every waste; the "conspicuous waste" of the rich, the waste of national vices, the wastes of inefficient government, the wastes of class struggle, and the supreme waste of unutilized talent and genius.

For the United States to achieve this noble consummation, Finley argued, it was necessary for every American to have an "imaginary uniform . . . in his wardrobe" to ready him for that "unquestioning, unhesitating, unboastful response" to his nation's call for duty. The key role of education in bringing this about was of course recognized by Finley. The imaginary garment, he pointed out, must be woven in childhood or youth.

As a prophet of collective mobilization, Finley did not intend to disparage "personal liberty." But he also perceived that a state could suffer from a "hard, intemperate individualism," which Finley believed was as bad as "a socialism . . . requir[ing] permanent wearing of uniforms by all." (Somehow he suggested that imperial Germany represented such an objectionable "socialism.") Finley acknowledged the attractiveness of the ideal of universal human solidarity, but in 1916 he found "more precious" a commitment to old-fashioned nationalism—"that complex of ideals, habits, beliefs and institutions that marks off nation from nation, people from people, that gives each people its soul." He added that "it is ultimately through the competition of these varieties that the human species is . . . to be enriched." Although a "terrible drama" was being enacted in Europe, it had its "sublime" side. In addition to the decimation, the bloodshed, the destruction, Finley discerned the birth of "new and greater nations."

> Nation after nation rises to unexampled heights of self-sacrifice and arduous toil, simple living, and uncomplaining dying. The spiritual as well as the material life of the nations at war is being transformed into something different and more precious.

Finley's virtual paean to war in this 1916 address, "Mobilization," reveals the ascendancy of a tendency that had long coexisted in his mind with more pacific notions. The change in outlook cannot be interpreted as any abandonment of the Progressive faith. Rather it followed in natural intellectual sequence from Finley's deep commitment to the ideal of public service, a notion shared widely by Progressives. As the nation prepared to gird itself for war, the commissioner of education readied himself to mobilize New York State for the struggle.

Once he had reconciled himself to war, the direction of John Finley's sympathies was a foregone conclusion. Although it is possible to find among his voluminous writings and addresses scattered expressions of respect for Germany, and in his correspondence an occasional pro-German statement, Finley's sympathies were from the beginning for the Allies, and especially France. The record of his publications in the years between the oubreak of war and U.S. entry into the conflict betrays the development of his allegiances. *The French in the Heart of America,* based on the lectures Finley delivered in France in 1910–11, appeared in book form in mid-1915 at the author's own expense. It received enthusiastic response in France, where the suggestive title was particularly appreciated. But even in the United States, historians of the stature of J. Franklin Jameson and Frederick Jackson Turner praised the volume. French Ambassador Jules Jusserand discreetly suggested in early 1916 a French translation in order to promote understanding between the two nations. Such a translation did appear later that year, further contributing to the Franco–American rapprochement.

It should not be thought that the evolution of Finley's French sympathies was simply due to some internal political reorientation on his part. The whole record of his life reveals a man who excelled in taking on the social and political coloration of the milieu. The years 1914 to 1917 were no different. As the nation as a whole, under political leaders known and respected by John Finley (even if he as a Republican did not vote for them), swung to the support of the Allies against Germany and Austria–Hungary, he too readied himself to endorse American entry into the war when it finally did come.

As Finley accommodated his convictions to American participation in the world war, he took extraordinary pains to develop a preparedness program for New York State. One of the options was a thoroughly militaristic program, complete with armed drill in the schools. Demand for such a program arose from various quarters of the state. Such organizations as the National Security League and the National Guard Association called for an all-out, compulsory program. A proposal to this effect was introduced in the legislature in the fall of 1915. Finley opposed the bill. Though he recognized the value of martial spirit, he could not countenance the transformation of schools into barracks, nor did he believe in making "that which implies a perpetuation of international hatreds and brutish warfare a purposeful feature of the education of our children."

The plan that Finley preferred took shape in 1916 and finally issued in legislative action in the spring of 1917. It was a preparedness program full of the spirit of public service and devotion to the higher collectivity, the state. There was no provision for military drill, with guns, in the secondary schools. Instead, a program of universal *physical* training for all boys and girls over eight years in both public and private schools was instituted. State grants of money would cover the costs. Finley involved in this plan his former handball partner and colleague, Professor Thomas A. Storey of the Department of Physical Instruction at CCNY. Storey drew up a comprehensive syllabus of physical training, which was sub-

sequently accepted by the regents. The plan provided for
a thorough statewide system of medical inspection,
supplemented by instruction in hygiene and cleanliness, and
outdoor recreational programs with hiking, camping, wall scal-
ing, swimming, and gardening—truly an all-around program.

Instruction in the use of firearms could not be altogether
ruled out, since the impetus for the universal training program
came after all from the threat of actual war. But Finley resisted
proposals favored by some educators who wished that such
instruction be made part of the regular school curriculum. He
succeeded in getting the purely military side of his universal
preparedness program transferred to summer camps on the
Plattsburgh, New York, pattern, a model of military and civic
preparedness that he much admired. It was even possible to
substitute vocational training, or some other type of approved
service activity, for the military drill in the summer camps.

Some in New York did not see the same danger that Finley
perceived in military training in the schools. One newspaper
did not believe it likely that New York youngsters would
"want to run amuck and kick some Belgian infant to death
from any practice in 'counting by fours' or 'about face'."
Another newspaper agreed with Finley that it was better to
have students "fight with all their wits and minds for a better
world tomorrow," but gently reminded him "that when the
time comes the order to clear ship for action, to serve artillery,
to entrench, must be obeyed 'today' not 'tomorrow'." These
carping criticisms did not amount to any serious challenge of
Finley's plan for a moderate preparedness program, which he
was able to carry through according to his own design.

This design drew much nourishment (as had his earlier
espousal of the cause of public service) from William James's
1910 essay "The Moral Equivalent of War." James had called for
the preservation even "in the midst of a pacific civilization [of]
the manly virtues which tend to . . . disappear in peace"—
"intrepidity, contempt of softness, surrender of private interest, obedience to command." Finley wholeheartedly agreed.
He stood for an educational experience that would reproduce
the "regimen and hard discipline of an army." The New York
State plan of universal training had this intention. It was "ser-

viceable for war and peace alike, a program which requires every boy to prepare himself to offer *some* services in the case of need."

Finley was not the only one to recognize the increasing relevance of James's ideas on the moral equivalent of war, as war itself approached. In response to the demands of the "wildest patriots" for "military service, flag-reverence, [and] patriotic swagger," notions of a truer "national service" occurred to many who abhorred war. For example, Randolph Bourne, in the summer of 1916, appealed for a "sublimation" of militarism into a broad, unifying national movement centering in the schools.

> This national service could do the things which need to be done, but which are not now being done. It could have for its aim the improvement of the quality of our living. Our appalling slovenliness, the ignorance of great masses in city and country as to the elementary technique of daily life—this should be the enemy of the army of youth. I have a picture [Bourne wrote to Finley] of a host of eager young missionaries swarming over the land, spreading the health knowledge, the knowledge of domestic science, of gardening, of tastefulness, that they have learned in school.

Like Bourne, Finley also considered it a marvel that James's idea, "which only a few years ago seemed rather utopian should . . . [have] prospect of coming true, in a practical, universal way."

Temporally, in the months just before the United States abandoned neutrality, Finley and Randolph Bourne occupied the same intellectual terrain, charted seven years earlier by William James. What course James himself (who died in the same year his "Moral Equivalent of War" was published) would have taken thereafter cannot of course be known. Bourne moved into the camp of those who opposed American involvement, and wrote bitterly of the American intellectuals who claimed to convince the nation of the rectitude of that involvement. John Finley for his part moved easily from support of the moral equivalent of war to the support of war itself.

Chapter 26

Mobilization for War and
Its Aftermath, 1917–20

Having been as a child a conventional admirer of the glories of war (which I saw of course in cinematographic terms), I can pretty precisely locate the source of my later antimilitarism. It was a weekend spent in a Quaker work camp in Philadelphia where, in my freshman year at college, I experienced my first serious, extended political discussions. The sentiments that surfaced then, in 1952, have animated me ever since, even though I am now committed to what I like to think of as a broader and more coherent attitude than simple pacifism.

The extraordinary vigor of Finley's activity in the summer and following months of 1917 was in sharp contrast to his previous genial and somewhat passive style of educational administration. The war released vast energies, and this vigor is reflected in the very first *Bulletin to the Schools* Finley issued after the United States entered the war. President Wilson's war message to Congress was printed, and the commissioner ordered that it be read in all classrooms in the state. In a spirit of solemn exhilaration, Finley announced that "Mobilization of the school army has begun." He indicated that in later issues he would spell out in detail what this mobilization meant for each New York schoolchild.

The subsequent *Bulletins* did indeed serve as Finley's major tool to help mobilize the state. Through them he publicized American involvement in the war as the example of a nation "carried away by irresistible idealism." In October of 1917, after he had returned from a second wartime visit to Europe, he elaborated the tasks imposed upon the schools by war. Their practical responsibilities include the fostering of physical fitness and thrift, supplying of health data to the draft board, acting as centers for the sale of Liberty Bonds (teachers, he said, must "teach bonds"), contributing to Red Cross activities, and aiding in food production. This last program became a major effort of the education department, which provided guidance in raising pigs and poultry, and tending gardens.

Finley also charged the schools with political and ideological tasks. They were urged to enter into the spirit of the universal training program by fostering among students the desire to become conscripts in the cause of the greater collectivities—the state and nation.

> This is an adult's war [Finley wrote], but the schoolhouse doors cannot shut its sounds away from the ears of our children. We must tell them what it means and guide their interest through tangible forms of service in the high cause to which we are committed as a nation. I have [he added] opposed giving the gun end of preparation. . . , but I have for years been advocating a conscription . . . that would lead every youth to realize his obligation to the community, the State, the nation, which together with the family, make his free development possible.

The teachers' responsibilities were clear; they must tell "this truth about the war without malice"—that America stands for right, while the German enemy is evil and out to conquer the world.

And what of any dissenter who might entertain a notion different from the commissioner's of what the "truth" about the world war really was? Such a person would receive little satisfaction from John Finley, who was no staunch champion of civil liberties, especially when the nation was indulging in an orgy of repression. He stated his view boldly and in terms consistent with his conception of education as sublimated militarism. Addressing the New York State Teachers Association in November, 1917, he urged that his fellow educators—

> must do with our mind and daily speech what the soldier does with his body and in his daily training in fighting; that is support our country in the cause to which it is committed in its own defense and that of human freedom. The same degree of loyalty is asked of a teacher or a soldier. If a teacher cannot give that unquestioning support to the country that makes his own individual freedom in time of peace possible, his place is not in the school. I will not say where it is, but of all places in the world, he should *not* be in the school of the representative of his country.

A few months later Finley wrote in the *Bulletin to the Schools* that if a man "does not thrill at the sight of the flag, there is

something wrong with his spirit and we do well to . . . challenge
. . . the right of any teacher to a place on the payroll if [his] . . .
teaching . . . does not function in fidelity, in patriotism, in
loyalty."

> More than once when engaged in the antiwar struggles of the sixties I
> encountered the thoughtless imperatives of fidelity, patriotism, and loy-
> alty. So threadbare were the arguments for continuing the murderous
> struggle against the Vietnamese that it was not hard to master the
> relevant data to refute these arguments. Supporters of U.S. government
> policy quickly exhausted the rational weapons at their disposal and
> were often reduced to insinuations that we ought to be silenced because
> our position was so convincing. I must admit that I was at first stumped
> by this position, but I soon came to see that, as America's earliest
> antiimperialists held, one of the consequences of imperialism is erosion
> of democracy in the "mother country."

All of the cases the commissioner heard relating to the right
of New York teachers to dissent from the government's war
policy were decided against the appellants. It does not reduce
Finley's responsibility for these decisions to point out that he
was absent from Albany when many of them were rendered.
His subordinates decided as he would have done, occasionally
quoting him in their verdicts. And when such cases came to
his personal attention, he similarly came down on the side of
order, not liberty.

As exhilarating and uncommonly forceful as his wartime
administration of the state education department was, it was
not the task that Finley preferred. He would rather have taken
up arms. He wrote to ex-President Theodore Roosevelt on
April 17, 1917:

> I am with you. We must go to France. We must make the supreme offer. I
> wish to be of those who go. And I should be proud to go with you if you
> go, and in whatever capacity I can best serve. Perhaps I can recruit a
> company at least.

Roosevelt, however, was rebuffed by the Wilson administration, which never did grant him the commission he pleaded
for. But Finley did manage to get to France in 1917, even if not
in military capacity.

Toward the end of the previous year he had been turning
over a plan in his mind. He wrote about it in November to the
French ambassador in Washington, his friend Jules Jusserand.

I have thought [he told Jusserand] that if one could see sympathetically
the schools of France . . . while the fathers and brothers of the children
are at the front, there might be found something that would be of
peculiar value in teaching patriotism in our own schools.

The time became ripe to raise the plan officially only in the
spring of 1917. At the first meeting of the regents after the U.S.
declaration of war (and before his eager letter to Theodore
Roosevelt), Finley "spoke of a plan long in his thought and
known to the regents, to visit the schools of France in wartime." This trip was intended as "an especially pertinent and
patriotic service" that would both bring "cheer to France and
also [prove] of practical value to our own State in meeting the
new educational problems which the war has brought."

The regents authorized Finley's trip "with unanimity and
enthusiasm of spirit." President Wilson also endorsed it. From
the outset, the ceremonial aspect predominated; Finley bore
the greetings of the University of the State of New York and
many other schools, colleges, universities, and distinguished
individuals. He sailed on May 5, this time without his family.
A letter from the French ambassador in Washington, Jules
Jusserand, "opened all official doors" to Finley. On May 19 he
had an audience with Raymond Poincaré, president of the
Third French Republic. Each spoke in his own native tongue,
but they had no difficulty understanding each other. Finley
expressed the warm sympathy for the French cause among
Americans. At the conclusion of the visit, Poincaré personally
escorted Finley "down the red-carpeted main steps . . . in the
court and out past the sentries into the Faubourg St. Honore."
The commissioner of education also visited in Paris with Gen.
John J. Pershing, commander of the American Expeditionary
Forces, who immediately remembered Finley as the man who
made the commencement address at Wellesley College in
1914.

Finley, who in his college presidencies had grasped the
possibilities inherent in academic ceremonies, also exploited
to the full ceremonial opportunities presented by the trip to
France in 1917. He visited Dijon, Lyons, Potiers, and other
provincial university centers (except Lille, which was behind
German lines). His visits touched off enthusiastic rallies in

honor of Finley, his country, and Franco–American friendship. At these richly sentimental events, Finley solemnly presented the letters of greeting from American schools and received the French greetings in return. School children sang
"The Star Spangled Banner" in French and concluded with
choruses of "Vive l'Amèrique!" Distinguished French citizens
such as the philosopher Henri Bergson spoke appropriate
words at these meetings. The significance or effect of Finley's
trip was hard to gauge, but it certainly involved a projection of
his academic style in an international context.

The trip had, in addition to its patriotic and ceremonial
sides, an educational aim. Finley also came in search of lessons
that could be drawn from the French wartime educational
experience. To this end he visited the Ministry of Public
Instruction in Paris, talked with officials, and kept his eyes
open throughout his travels in France. He was told, for example, that many teachers and older students were in the armed
forces, that retired teachers and refugees from German-held
areas were filling the vacancies in the classrooms, that girls
were knitting and sewing in their schools for the war effort. No
halt was made in German-language instruction in the French
schools, nor was any specifically military training provided,
although teachers were charged with the responsibility of
aiding the national loan subscription. Nonsubscribers were
branded as deserters who abandoned their brothers at the
front.

Finley could find little outward preparation for or adjustment to the war in the French educational system. Nevertheless France was able to teach America valuable lessons. First
there was impressive testimony to the value of education, as
the process of teaching children was not halted or curtailed
even when the nation was under attack. Finley stressed this
point in the published *Report* of his visit to France, although
seemingly he would have been at least as pleased to find the
war had done away with all nonpatriotic study. No less important was the unifying effect the war had on French society, an
effect that Finley hoped would be reproduced in the United
States. He perceived that in France a veritable *union sacrée*
had been forged. "Selfishness, strife and bitterness have been

lost in the supreme devotion to the nation's suffering." The
war effort brought the possibility that Americans too might
join in a "sacred union" around the religion of democracy.

> *In these times of rampant and often self-destructive individualism,
> the value of group loyalties is apparent mostly by its absence. Family,
> community, meaningful work no longer supply the support they once
> offered to individuals, especially in the industrial, capitalist societies.
> People often float uncomfortably in the culture of these societies, linked
> to each other by bonds of consumerism or ties equally tenuous. The
> comradeship of a political movement, engagement in collective struggle
> for human betterment, are all-but-unknown experiences for most
> Americans who, absorbed in themselves, hardly know what a collective
> movement can be. The danger is that the need for community will be
> filled by some organization or cult that mobilizes anomic recruits
> into a sacred union based upon atavistic xenophobia or some irrational
> devotion to a leader. If these observations have any validity, they impose a
> double burden on the political left in America. Not only must we struggle
> fiercely against nationalistic perversions of the impulse to community,
> which have in cases like Vietnam led to such barbaric butchery. But on the
> positive side, the American left must transcend its characteristic sec-
> tarianism and build a broad socialist community that, even in its opposi-
> tional tasks, displays within its own ranks the kind of comradeship,
> democracy, and mutual support that we wish to be part of our rough
> working model for a new society.*

Back in Albany Finley began to apply the lessons learned
during his trip to France. The Liberty Loan drive was pushed
forward with greater vigor. The *Bulletin to the Schools* included ever more urgent patriotic appeals. The commissioner
himself on public occasions called for renewed consecration
to the nation's cause by those who did not go abroad to fight.

> And what an army this is; this unseen mighty army which is helping to
> make a democracy worth saving by the other army! We who must remain
> at our posts . . . cannot let these momentous days in the world's history
> pass without doing our part to help bring in our own day that peace which
> will make the world a safe place hereafter for those whom we teach.

But the most noteworthy thing about Finley's utterances and
actions after American entry into the world war was how
consistent they were with what he had said and done before
1917, and even before 1914. His visit to France confirmed him
in his previous course, which as we have seen had been
directed toward the ideal of public service more than toward
any other, subsidiary goal. Thus the coming of the Great War,

instead of dashing Finley's hopes for a spiritual purpose in education, brought him to where he virtually embraced the conflict as making possible the fulfillment of these ideals.

While the war effort did make some contribution to national unity and a sense of patriotism, in time it became clear that the conflict had not brought in its wake the full realization of Finley's idealistic visions. After his return from France, in the fall of 1917, he was handed a humiliating defeat in the repeal of the Township Law to consolidate the rural schools of New York State. Evidence that skepticism about America's war aims, and possibly even disloyalty, were spreading among even schoolteachers in New York came to Finley's attention then too. The *Bulletin to the Schools* in 1918, even after the war was over, carried ominous warnings about "destructive propaganda" and "foreign enemies . . . trying to undermine our system of government." Manifestly, the dream of a nation united in its pursuit of High Ideals was not to be fulfilled by the world war.

It may be that these accumulated frustrations of his efforts at Albany in the months after April, 1917, made Finley begin to think about leaving the office of commissioner of education. Another factor in his willingness to leave the Albany post may have been his involvement with larger schemes of international benevolence. In 1918 various offers came to him to head educational and philanthropic expeditions abroad. One of these involved work with the U.S. Army Educational Division in France; another, which he eventually accepted, brought Finley to Palestine with Red Cross relief commissions in 1918 and 1919. He went out to the Near East, witnessed the victories of British General Allenby's armies, and wrote a stirring account of his adventures in the Holy Land, *A Pilgrim in Palestine* (1919). When in the fall of 1920 an attractive offer of a distinguished journalistic post was made, Finley did resign as commissioner of education and president of the State University of New York. Before vacating his Albany office, he drafted a "Last Word" to the audience of teachers, administrators, and students who received the *Bulletin to the Schools*. He remembered all the "shadows of time" that had receded into the past. But he thought more hopefully of the procession that had passed going in the opposite direction—into the future. These were the 2 million school pupils who had passed through the jurisdiction of Finley's department in those seven years. He expressed the hope that a substantial number of these had undergone the subtle spiritual "transmutation" that he considered the essence of education.

Chapter 27

Education and Journalism Combine:

The New York Times, *1920–40*

What satisfaction it would be to discover and broadcast to the world the importance of hitherto neglected figures whose significance was little suspected until my researches! Aside from the boost to an author's ego from uncovering a major aspect of historical reality, there comes into play the underdog syndrome: a nonentity suddenly becomes a celebrity, and all of us who are to one extent or another nonentities applaud. (That applause must also generate some ambivalence as well: resentment that our own hidden and unrecognized achievements remain uncelebrated.) But what if our candidate for posthumous heroism does not play the game? What if by temperament and choice his role amid the major institutions of his era, and among its leading figures, was genial acceptance of a background part? What then of John Finley? His biographer clearly must overcome the sense of disappointment in not having chosen a great mover and shaker and avoid making inflated claims. However, since a man is a man for all that, the writer must delineate the uniqueness of his subject and place that uniqueness against the backdrop of the era. Finley brushed closest to greatness during the last two decades of his life, a period spent, not exactly at the New York Times, *but in close connection with the great metropolitan daily. And that period also measures the limitations of the man, and limitations of the era as well.*

One of the casualties of the great depression of the 1890s, which so plagued Finley's fund-raising efforts at Knox College, was the New York City daily newspaper, the *New York Times*. Nearly bankrupt, the *Times* was acquired in 1896 by the man who twenty years earlier had revitalized a tottering newspaper in Tennessee, Adolph Simon Ochs, son of a German–Jewish immigrant. Ochs carried out a similar transformation at the *Times*. Refusing to descend to the sensationalistic journalism in his contemporaries, Hearst and Pulitzer, Ochs instead dedicated the *Times* to full, accurate, and reliable reporting; he chose as the paper's masthead motto "All the news that's fit to print," and on the basis of a cautious, conservative editorial policy built the *Times* into America's (and possibly the world's) most respected daily newspaper. Ochs's "business statement," which appeared on the editorial page of August 19, 1896, over his signature and has since been reprinted many times, reads:

> It will be my earnest aim that *The New York Times* give the news, all the news, in concise and attractive form, in language that is parliamentary in good society, and give it as early, if not earlier, than it can be learned through any other reliable medium; to give the news impartially, without fear or favor, regardless of party, sect or interests involved; to make the columns of *The New York Times* a forum for the consideration of all questions of public importance, and to that end to invite intelligent discussion from all shades of opinion.

Not always able to meet the lofty standards Ochs set down in 1896, the *Times* nevertheless became one of the world's great newspapers. Often, the justifiable criticisms levied against the *Times* were based upon the very principles Ochs had set up; people just expected more of the *Times,* and that expectation was itself the most eloquent testimony to Ochs's original vision. More than a mere newspaper, the *Times* became an institution, a formidable sovereignty in its own right. When its distinguished publisher summoned them, people responded. Finley had frequently, when president of CCNY, or state education commissioner, journeyed to midtown Manhattan in response to Ochs's requests. In 1920, on the retirement of editor Rollo Ogden, Ochs had a more weighty matter to take up with Finley: in August, at the Lake George, New York, summer estate of CCNY trustee Edward Morse Shepard, Ochs offered Finley a senior editorship at the *New York Times.*

> *The* Times's *awe-inspiring reputation first came to my attention during my high school years, as part of my obligatory revolt against parental authority. For me, this revolt took many forms (as I, now a father myself, experiencing similar behavior from my sons, vividly remember): one was a campaign to purge the reactionary* New York Daily News *from the house and substitute the more high-toned* New York Times. *Part of this campaign was based upon sheer adolescent snobbery, and sometimes I was secretly glad that the* News *was available, since the* Times *had no comic strips. Yet the fact that I made such*

efforts bespoke a budding political consciousness. Ironically, in later years the same political concerns that originally prompted me to read the Times *generated the sober awareness of the weakness of* Times *coverage of such topics as revolutionary Cuba and the war in Indochina.*

Although journalistic ambitions had been among Finley's earliest impulses on the Illinois prairie, and his subsequent educational posts had included such journalistic efforts as the Albany *Bulletin to the Schools,* he was not a newspaperman when Ochs called him to the *Times.* Yet most of Ochs's men on the *Times* had extensive prior newspaper experience, most of it gained in copy-editing offices, as *Times*man Turner Catledge observed in his insightful memoir. But by the early 1920s the newspaper had reached full maturity and, as an imposing institution in American society, and even as a formidable force on the world scene, it needed a tangible public presence. Speaking to an audience of *Times* employees in 1925, Ochs admitted that the newspaper's staff included "many men better qualified than I to make its speeches, so I leave that to others. When their remarks cause pleasant things to be said about the *Times,* I share in the benefits, and it is best that I keep in the background." It was the foreground, ambassadorial role that Ochs intended Finley to fill. As a perceptive journalist put it some years later, the *Times* required "a graceful public speaker, a representative at all sorts of gatherings—in short, what Britain expects of royalty."

Whether Finley would be willing to leave what he described to Ochs as "the best position in the American field of formal education" to come to the *Times* was no foregone conclusion. He got powerful negative advice from Chicago attorney Edgar A. Bancroft, an old Knox College friend, who warned that the *Times* position would involve Finley in disagreeable political contests and demand of him that he play the courtier to the venerable Adolph Ochs. "Remember also," Bancroft cautioned, "that you are not of the same race." But a liberal brother-in-law advised that Finley disregard Bancroft, since his counsel was "tinctured by . . . racial prejudice." Supportive letters came to Finley in Albany from his wife, Martha, from the family's summer home in Tamworth, New Hampshire. Mrs. Finley saw the key issue as her husband's freedom to exercise his personal influence in his work, which she perceived as his greatest contribution. "I do not believe," she wrote in the summer of 1920, "you could be hidden even under such a *bushel* as the Times." Moreover, the Albany post was becoming more and more an administrative job, and Mrs. Finley urged her husband to follow his sense of adventure and take the *Times* position.

The "Jewish question" was not to be a problem for Finley. Although the *Times* was dominated by a Jewish dynasty organized in a tight-knit clan of Ochses, Adlers, and eventually Sulzbergers, the new Anglo–Saxon editor felt he could negotiate a position for himself in its midst. Bearing extraordinarily little of the genteel anti-Semitism that was endemic in the contemporary white American Protestant milieu, Finley had also a solid decade of success in dealing with the ambitious, upwardly mobile, largely Jewish student body at CCNY. By the fall of 1920, nothing stood in the way of acceptance of the *Times* position.

Finley began his acceptance letter to Ochs with a Biblical reference—from the Old Testament. As Ecclesiastes distinguishes ordinary days from those consecrated to the Lord, so Finley distinguished October 18, when he felt entirely ready "to follow the appeal of the opportunity" Ochs had opened to him.

> I have reached this conclusion [Finley wrote] because I believe that with your ideal for the *Times* it offers the greatest opportunity that could come to me for usefulness in one's "own day and generation."

Unable to give an official acceptance until the regents had approved his resignation as New York State commissioner of education, Finley hoped to be ready to assume his new duties at the *Times* before the end of the year. Gingerly, Finley raised the question of his salary.

> I should be happier in making the venture—and I think I could be of greater value to the *Times*—if I did not have to require continuing sacrifices on the part of my family—sacrifices which they have willingly made with me through many years because I have been serving directly the City and State (as one serves in the Army).

Ochs assured him that he would "have no cause to regret" the decision to come to the *Times* and invited him to come around

to the *Times* office on election day to hear the returns. Finley
was about to become a newspaperman.

> *In past years I sometimes felt the urge to dash off a letter to the*
> Times. *The last such occasion was the publication on April 21, 1965, of
> an attack on the teach-in movement by* Times *columnist James Reston.
> Begun on the campuses in the spring of that year in response to the
> escalating Vietnam war, teach-ins were often all-night debating ses-
> sions, attracting a high level of political discussion. For some reason,
> Reston wrote of the teach-ins as if they were crude hate-America rallies,
> which was not the case since supporters of U.S. government policy were
> free to present their positions, and often did. I concluded my letter to the*
> Times *with the unduly gloomy observation, "Attacks on the conclusions
> that academics reach after seeking to inform themselves on the issues is
> another melancholy sign that the Vietnam crisis is beginning to put out
> the lights here at home." The* Times *did not print my letter, but it did
> appear in the splendid documentary volume* Teach-ins: U.S.A. *(1967),
> edited by Louis Menashe and Ronald Radosh. Soon after drafting my
> unpublished letter to the* Times, *I began work on my book* Vietnam,
> *published in December, 1965.*

Finley entered, and quickly became part of, a congenial
community at the *Times.* He moved into an office on the tenth
floor of the *Times* building on West Forty-third Street, filling
it with books and with a certain academic aura that distinguished the former educator from the other *Times*men. He
participated with the other editors in the noon editorial board
meeting and usually drafted one of the next day's editorials.
(He clipped these editorials and filled scrapbooks with them,
permitting a biographer some assessment of his role at the
Times.) Finley wrote the editorials that reflected his own
interests—philanthropy and welfare, the League of Nations,
college life and education generally, archaeology, and the Near
East. When the *Times* wished to note the birthday of some
dignitary, or comment on the commencement address of some
academic figure, or commemorate the achievements of a
noteworthy explorer, it usually turned to its learned
editorialist, Dr. Finley. Changes of season, the blooming of
crocuses, and Nature in general also called for his special
editorial gifts. The resulting products were not thundering
pronouncements on major policies, nor were they intended to
chart any fresh perspectives on the contemporary world. No,
Finley continued as he had for at least the three preceding
decades, as a purveyor of conventional homilies on the essen-

tial soundness of American life, leavened as it might sometimes be by wholesome reform efforts.

Finley's position at the *Times* suited him perfectly. He meshed gracefully with the Ochs/Sulzberger dynasty, which was a precondition for viable tenure at the newspaper. One of the most useful services he rendered was to intercede with the principals and headmistresses of some of New York's fashionable private schools to accept Ochs grandchildren and nieces in their exclusive establishments. Respectable cranks, like the dowager woman inventor of "the Mecha-Hormonogram," who made claims on the *Times*, were sometimes referred to Finley, who would then be hard pressed to manage a courteous brush-off. But his main function at the *Times* was to be what Arthur Krock in his *Memoirs* called the paper's "incarnation," its envoy to that influential portion of the public "that attends banquets, listens to baccalaureate addresses, lunches at the regular feasts of civic clubs and associations, and participates in the meetings of learned societies." Finley was appointed, Krock remembered, "as *The New York Time's* Public Presence." It was a role that he had been rehearsing for thirty years.

Although much of the last two decades of Finley's life was spent on the banquet circuit (a role he shared at the *Times* with business manager Louis Wiley), representing the newspaper to the outside world, there was an inner world at the *Times* that Finley also found congenial. Part of this congeniality was expressed in the house paper, the *Little Times*, of which Finley was literary coeditor. His appearances in the *Little Times* included a suggested text for the ritual of asking grace in the staff dining room: "What we find fit to print, O Lord/Is, after all, the pudding's proof." Once he spoke for the editorial department at a luncheon to celebrate the achievement of 25 million agate lines of advertising copy reached by December, 1924. "We editors could not exist without this wonderful foundation of 25,000,000 lines that has been built under us," Finley said.

As a Republican on a newspaper that styled itself "independent Democratic," Finley had another set of duties to discharge for the *Times*. These related to the succession of Republican presidents who occupied the White House during most of his *Times* years. These men had to be guided and gently prodded about the ceremonial responsibilities of their high office, especially in connection with the various philanthropies that expected some sort of presidential endorsement. On some occasions Finley's connections with the White House brought him some political tasks, as in 1932, when President Herbert Hoover's administrative assistant suggested that the *Times* criticize the Democratic president-elect, Franklin Roosevelt, more strongly for his refusal to participate in consultations on economic policy with the outgoing Republicans. Finley reminded the official of the *Times*'s generally Democratic orientation and passed the correspondence on to Adolph Ochs, who scrawled a marginal denunciation of the Hoover aide.

The major world and domestic events during Finley's years at the *Times*, the closely linked development of the Great Depression and the rise of fascism, brought little in the way of serious, adequate response either from the newspaper or from its gentle, scholarly editor. The *Times*'s attitude toward the appearance of fascist government in Italy in the early twenties was a minor journalistic scandal, so superficial and biased were the reporting and editorial policy; the best thing that can be said of Finley in this connection is that he seems to have written nothing himself on Mussolini's regime. He did write, however, on pre-Nazi Germany, interviewing Walther Rathenau in 1922, just before the liberal minister's assassination by right-wing, anti-Semitic forerunners of the Nazis. Writing with sympathy about Rathenau's visionary idealism, Finley never took careful measure of the groups and forces that were soon to rise with ferocity and plunge the world into war. On the domestic side, the *Times* moved in the 1930s from support of Roosevelt's candidacy to growing distaste for the welfare policies of the New Deal. Now widely recognized as an inadequate governmental response to economic distress, the New Deal welfare program came under increasing fire as unduly radical from the *Times*, with apparently no demurrer from editor Finley.

For many the twin crises of fascism and economic collapse impelled a leftward commitment in the thirties, which often culminated in joining the Communist Party. My current researches on the academic units of the U.S. Communist Party have often brought me into contact with vigorous men and women in their mid- and late sixties who peer inquisitively into my eyes as I interview them for my study, wondering if they can ever make it clear to a person who was born in 1933 what a burning perception of social injustice led them into the Communist movement. If I had been born fifteen or twenty years earlier, it was the path I probably would have followed.

Instead of dealing with weighty political and economic matters in his *Times* writing, Finley dealt mainly with other issues, which he doubtless thought just as important: the opium traffic, the League of Nations, attempts to despoil New York's Central Park, the *Dictionary of American Biography,* even Motherhood, and many, many other topics. If any thread linked his diverse utterances in this period, it was the creed that he imbibed on the prairie and from his ancestors: idealistic men and women, acting from generous motives, can redeem (if anything can) mankind. His very last piece in the *Times,* written just a few days before his death in March, 1940, was a homily in praise of heroism, courage, and sacrifice. Finley's own life did not often demand dramatic exhibitions of these qualities, which he may have had in abundance, but rarely displayed. So completely identified was he with his milieu that it is sometimes difficult to separate Finley's public life from its background.

This characteristic, which makes the subject of this biography so elusive, increased with time, so that during the final years of his life, spent at the *New York Times,* Finley was virtually indistinguishable from the dominant institutions of genteel, respectable America. Yet, there were and are other Americas; and it is from one of these variant viewpoints that perhaps the clearest vision of John Finley can be achieved.

Appendix

Table 1

**Percentages of Students (Both Graduates and Nongraduates)
Choosing Careers in the Ministry**

	Harvard College	Yale College	Oberlin College	Cross-Section of U.S. Colleges	CCNY	Knox College
1846–50	12	22	40	23	—	52.4
1851–55	7	18	22	22	—	20.9
1856–60	7.5	18.5	38	22	9.0	27.8
1861–65	8	15	19	20	5.0	27.6
1866–70	6	12	32	17.5	7.8	38.2
1871–75	7	11	22	17	3.2	32.6
1876–80	5	7	19	14.5	3.8	19.4
1881–85	5	7	25	12	3.3	14.2
1886–90	4	7	21	12	1.1	20.4
1891–95	7	5.5	18	10	3.0	14.6
1896–1900	3	4	9	5.9	1.7	9.6

The data in this table are taken from Bailey B. Burritt, "Professional Distribution of College and University Graduates," U.S. Bureau of Education, *Bulletin,* 19 (1912); *Knox Alumnus* [Directory Number], 20 (June 1937); and Donald A. Roberts, ed., *Alumni Register: The College of the City of New York, 1853–1945* (1946). The record is one of general decline all through the nineteenth century for all schools, but less so for Knox. CCNY is wildly atypical. Beginning in 1891, rabbis make up a significant portion of the clergymen there.

An Elusive Presence

Table 2
Knox College Finances, 1891–1900

Year	Income	Expenses	Deficit
1891–92	$23,489.41	$34,833.35	$11,343.94
1892–93	20,938.23	37,183.44	16,245.21
1893–94	19,551.32	35,780.10	16,228.78
1894–95	18,034.87	37,637.53	19,602.66
1895–96	17,688.45	39,645.45	21,957.00
1896–97	18,665.65	41,562.66	22,897.01
1897–98	19,278.98	43,260.41	23,981.43
1898–99	18,578.73	40,716.56	22,137.83
1899–1900	17,840.66	37,902.42	20,061.76

Source: Knox College Archives. I gratefully acknowledge the aid of Mr. Matthew Cyrelson, once an accountant in New York City, who helped me understand the significance of these figures, which to one more adept in financial matters, would be virtually self-evident.

Bibliographical Notes

Since little of value has ever been published on John Finley, with the exception of his son's biographical introduction to Finley's *Poems* (1941) and Harry J. Carman's brief sketch in the *Dictionary of American Biography*, this book is based exclusively on what historians call "primary" materials—diaries, letters, books, and articles by Finley himself. Most of this material is found in the Manuscript Division of the New York Public Library, where the Finley family deposited the papers of its most distinguished member. This material is used with the permission of the Finley family and the New York Public Library, Astor, Lenox and Tilden Foundations. Scarcely less important a source is the archival collections at Knox College in Galesburg, Illinois. Also useful have been materials in the Morris Raphael Cohen Library, CCNY; the library of The Johns Hopkins University, the New York State Library, Albany; the Library of Congress; and various letters and documents I have gathered in the course of researching Finley's life.

The original of the "letter of recommendation" cited in the preface is carefully preserved in a safe deposit box of a New York City bank. The letters cited in the introduction, as well as the great bulk of the Finley correspondence this book is largely based upon, come from the John H. Finley Papers, Manuscripts and Archives Division, New York Public Library. The Carnegie encomium is to be found in the Special Collections, Cohen Library, CCNY.

The genealogical data in chapter 1 are drawn from various local histories (Cecil County, Maryland; Fayette County, Pennsylvania; Westmoreland County, Pennsylvania) and *Torrence and Allied Families* by Robert M. Torrence (1938). Samuel and James Finley's sermons are listed in Evans's bibliography. Martha Finley's "Memories of My Married Life" (1950) and an article in the *Cleveland Plain Dealer* (February 14, 1909) are the best sources on John Finley's early life. (The latter item was brought to my attention by Professor Robert A. Huff of Hobart and William Smith colleges, for which I am very grateful.)

Finley's own memories of prairie schooling cited in chapter 2 are drawn from scattered letters and addresses in the Finley Papers, New York Public Library, from Knox College archives, and from Finley's *Poems*. The previously mentioned *Cleveland Plain Dealer* article of 1909 was also useful.

261

The first Knox College chapters (3 to 5) are based upon Knox College's printed *Catalogues,* the Knox college manuscript faculty record, trustee minutes, the *Coup d'Etat* (monthly student publication), the *Knox Student* (another undergraduate publication), minutes of the Adelphi Society, and correspondence in both New York and Galesburg libraries. Hermann R. Muelder's *Fighters for Freedom* (1959) is the indispensable guide to Knox's early history. Peter Lyon's *Success Story* (1963) is a biography of Finley's slightly older Galesburg contemporary, S. S. McClure. For the prize orations, see Charles E. Prather, ed., *Winning Orations of the Inter-State Oratorical Contests.* . . . (2 vols., Topeka, Kansas, 1909). My own heavily footnoted article, "Finley's Illinois Education," appeared in the *Journal of the Illinois State Historical Society* 42 (Summer, 1969), and I use portions of this article courtesy of the Illinois State Historical Library, Springfield.

The early Johns Hopkins University issued reams of documentary and promotional material, from which Finley's postgraduate experiences have been reconstructed in chapters 6 and 7. The Johns Hopkins *University Circulars,* the Johns Hopkins *Studies in Historical and Political Science,* the manuscript "Records of the Historical and Political Science Association and of the Seminary of History and Politics" have been the most useful. (With the assistance of the National Historical Records and Publications Commission [a division of the Archives of the United States], I am currently engaged in editing and publishing this important and neglected source, the Johns Hopkins seminary records.) The Herbert Baxter Adams Papers and the Daniel Coit Gilman Papers at Johns Hopkins are indispensable. The Baltimore years saw Finley's first nationally published writing, *Taxation in American States and Cities* (1888), done with Richard T. Ely, as was the article "Social Science in Colleges," *Christian Union* 38 (November 8, 1888). Finley's "Trading Companies" appears in successive issues of the *Chatauquan* 14 (January–February, 1892). Every historian of Johns Hopkins University follows humbly in the footsteps of Hugh Hawkins, whose book *Pioneer: A History of the Johns Hopkins University, 1874–1889* (1960) is a model of graceful scholarship. (The only shortcoming I have been able to find in Hawkins's work is his underestimation of the interest in "scientific philanthropy" at Johns Hopkins.)

Chapters 7 and 8, on the early history of American social work, are based on extensive studies I have been carrying out for over a decade. My relevant articles are: "Charity and Social Classes in the United States, 1874–1900," *American Journal of Economics and Sociology* 22 (April–July, 1963); "Philanthropy and Radicalism," *Science & Society* 29 (Fall, 1965); "The Whig Interpretation of Social Welfare History," *Smith College Studies in Social Work* 44 (June, 1974); "Philanthropy as Social Control in Late Nineteenth Century

America," *Societas* 5 (Winter, 1975). My "John H. Finley and the Academic Origins of American Social Work," *Studies in History and Society* (Bellingham, Washington) 2 (1969–70) is extensively excerpted here by permission of the editors of *Studies in History and Society*.

On the early social work milieu at Johns Hopkins, see Amos Warner's lecture "Charities" in notes supplementary to the Johns Hopkins *Studies in Historical and Political Science* 7 (1889), which was expanded in Warner's essay "Scientific Charity," *Popular Science Monthly*, 35 (August, 1889); Herbert B. Adams's "Notes on the Literature of Charities," Hopkins *Studies in Historical and Political Sciences* 5 (1887); the joint Charity Organization Society–Johns Hopkins *Report of a Conference on Charities and Other Subjects Pertaining to the Prevention of Suffering, Pauperism and Crime* (1887); Richard Ely's "Philanthropy," *The Chautauquan* 9 (October, 1888), reprinted in *Social Aspects of Christianity* (1889); and of course, Andrew Carnegie's famous essay "Wealth," *North American Review* 148 (June, 1889). All show the intense interest in philanthropic reform in the late 1880s, to which Finley was heir. A file of Finley's own early social work journal, the *State Charities Record*, is found in the New York Academy of Medicine Library. On the background of the State Charities Aid Association and its struggle for improved mental health care, see Albert Deutsch, *The Mentally Ill in America* (2d ed., 1949).

Much the same sources were used for chapters 9 to 11 as for 3 to 5. In addition, the *Exercises in Commemoration of the Founding of Knox College . . .* (1894) reveal the college's spirit. Material in Record Groups 94 and 159, U.S. Army records, National Archives, Washington, D.C., indicates problems with the cadet program at Knox. Finley's 1898 Union League Club speech is found in *Exercises in Commemoration of the Birthday of Washington, February 22, 1898* (1898). My own previous account of Finley's Knox presidency is to be found in "College President on the Prairie," *History of Education Quarterly* 9 (Summer, 1969).

Finley's abortive return to journalism in 1899, described in chapter 12, was reconstructed from materials in the Herbert Baxter Adams papers, Johns Hopkins; the Richard T. Ely papers, State Historical Society of Wisconsin; an article in the *Buffalo* (New York) *Illustrated Express* (August 27, 1899); and Peter Lyon's *Success Story* (1963).

Description of the Princeton years (chapters 13 to 15) is based on the Finley Papers, New York Public Library (as are all chapters thenceforth; the letter files begin in around 1902); the Francis Patton Letterbooks, Princeton University Library; Woodrow Wilson Papers, Library of Congress; Robert Bridges's "Princeton University," *The Outlook* 72 (August 2, 1902); Edwin M. Norris's "Some Writers of the Princeton Faculty," *Critic* 42 (June, 1903); Princeton University *Catalogues*. My study of Finley's role in early twentieth-century imperialism, with citations of all his articles and discussion of secondary literature, is in "John H. Finley y el Caribe, 1900–1903," *Revista de Ciencias Sociales* (Rio Piedras, Puerto Rico) 15 (Septiembre de 1971). The editors of the *Revista* have authorized my use of portions of this article here.

An especially important work was David F. Healey's *The United States in Cuba, 1898–1902* (1963). Finley's "Expansion" speech is in volume eighty-five of the Finley Papers, New York Public Library. On the tenets of "practical idealism," a creed that flourished in early twentieth-century America, see Henry F. May's *The End of American Innocence* (1959), especially chapter 2.

For the CCNY years, I have relied on S. Willis Rudy's *College of the City of New York: A History, 1847–1947* (1949), which is well researched but suffers from the filiopietism that vitiates much writing about higher education in America. For a good critique of this tendency, see Wilson Smith's "The New Historian of American Education: Some Notes For a Portrait," *Harvard Education Review* 31 (Spring, 1961). Unfortunately, reliance on Rudy's study is heightened by the subsequent loss of some of Finley's presidential correspondence that he had used. The Special Collections at the Morris R. Cohen Library, CCNY, contain some relevant official correspondence, although what survives of Finley's own letters from this period is in the New York Public Library. *The CCNY Quarterly* and the undergraduate periodical, *The Campus*, are essential sources. Stephen P. Duggan's *A Professor at Large* (1943) is a useful autobiography of a prominent CCNY faculty member. I have derived useful data from interviews with Professors Emeriti J. Salwyn Schapiro (1962) and Ephraim Cross (1963). New York City newspapers were also important, expecially the *New York Times*. For my own heavily documented essay on the CCNY years, see "Finley at CCNY, 1903–1913," *History of Education Quarterly* 10 (Winter, 1970), which I use here by permission of the editors of the *Quarterly*, which extends also important, especially the *New York Times*. For my own heavily

Finley's seven years as state commissioner of education in Albany have been reconstructed from manuscripts in the Finley Papers, New York Public Library (including his diary for these years), as well as the *Journals of the Board of Regents of the University of the State of New York (1913–20)*. "Proceedings of the Inauguration of John H. Finley . . . (New York State Education Department, *Tenth Annual Report* 4 [1914] and the article by Andrew ten Eyck in the *New York Tribune* (January 18, 1914) document the purposes discovered in Finley's approach to his Albany position. The extensive newspaper coverage of Finley's commissionership was collected and is conveniently available in University of the State of New York scrap books, New York State Library, Albany.

Finley's service as railroad arbitration commissioner has been reconstructed from materials in the *Congressional Record* (63d Cong.,

1st sess., 50, pp. 139–2442, passim and appendices); *Hearings before the House of Representatives Committee on the Interstate Commerce, June 20, 1913, on HR 2517.* . . . (63d Cong., 1st sess., August, 1913, pp. 144–46); J. N. Stockett, *The Arbitral Determination of Railway Rates* (1918); Fred Wilbur Powell, "Mediation and Arbitration of Railway Wage Controversies," *Quarterly Journal of Economics* 28 (February, 1914); and "Washington Notes," *Journal of Political Economy* 21 (December, 1913). The *Arbitration Award Between the Eastern Railroads and the Order of Railway Conductors and the Brotherhood of Railroad Trainmen* (November 10, 1913) is the outcome of Finley's work.

The unique manner in which Finley discharged the duties of New York State commissioner of education is evident in his personal journalistic brainchild, the *Bulletin to the Schools* (1914–20), a point that Frank C. Abbott (*Government Policy and Higher Education* [1958], esp. p. 127) misses with his bureaucratic complaint that Finley "wrote no Annual Reports . . . or documented works . . . concerning the functions of the state in respect to education. . . ." For Finley's judicial decisions, see the *Department Reports of the State of New York* . . . (1914–20) and John S. Brubacher's *The Judicial Power of the New York State Commissioner of Education* (1927). On the township struggle, see New York State Education Department, *Fourteenth Annual Report*, vol. I (1929). The 1915 Constitutional Convention left a *Revised Record* of its proceedings (4 vols., 1916).

The Finley Papers (vols. 84–88) include many addresses on national and international themes. The "Mobilization" address was widely reprinted; one reprinter was the *New York Times Magazine* (July 9, 1916). For Finley's ideas on preparedness, see his article "The New York State Plan of Universal Training," *The World Court* 3 (April, 1917). There are interesting differences between the manuscript "Memorandum of a Visit to France of John H. Finley (May–June, 1917)," New York State Library, and the official printed account, Finley, *Report of a Visit to the Schools of France in Wartime* (1917). For my own documented account of these Albany years, see "Romance and Educational Policy: John H. Finley's Inspirational Efforts as New York State Commissioner of Education, 1913–1920," *Paedagogical Historica* (Ghent, Belgium) 9 (1969): 2. I am indebted to the editors of this distinguished Belgian journal, not only for their authorization to reprint portions of my article, but for their helpful prepublication suggestions.

The view of Finley's admittedly negligible impact on the *New York Times* (1920–40) is derived, of course, from reading files of that newspaper, aided by Finley's own editorial scrapbooks (New York Public Library). Writing about the *Times*, especially by former *Times*men, has become a minor industry. Among the most helpful accounts are Meyer Berger's *The Story of the New York Times, 1851–1951* (1951), Arthur Krock's *Memoirs: Sixty Years on the Firing*

Line (1968), Gay Talese's *The Kingdom and the Power* (1961), and Turner Catledge's *My Life and the Times* (1971). Other useful sources are R. L. Duffus's oral history memoir (Oral History Collection, Butler Library, Columbia University), and articles in *Time* (May 3, 1937) and *Newsweek* (May 3, 1937). The Finley Papers, New York Public Library, document Finley's elusive editorial role as well as his intimacy with the Ochs/Sulzberger family.

The Author Tells a Bit
More about Himself

Born in New York City, which I used to think was the center of the universe, I was educated in the municipal schools and the city's (formerly) free college. At first I wanted to be some sort of artist. On my mother's side there is an artisan-craftsman tradition extending back to the Russian Ukraine, our old country. But at some point I got sidetracked and became a historian instead. After studying art at Temple University and Science at Los Angeles City College, I came back to New York and took a B.A. degree in philosophy from the City College of New York (CCNY). Married at a ridiculously young age, I then went on to the Johns Hopkins University, where I won an M.A. degree and (with some difficulty) a Ph.D. in history. My first marriage was the casualty of my educational progress, the final separation coinciding with the completion of the first version of this book. There was another, better marriage and more children afterward, but this too came to an end (just as the proof sheets of *An Elusive Presence* were being corrected). I vehemently resist the tendency, supported as it appears to be by some of the evidence, to consider the Finley project under some sort of jinx. Terminated marriages and divorces are not necessarily signs of failure; my wonderful children, Daniel, Todd, Eva and Rebecca were in no way offspring of "failure." My current employment is as professor of history at the Polytechnic Institute of New York, where I have been teaching for over a decade. Politically, I am a democratic socialist, a member of the fledgling socialist organization the New American Movement (NAM), and an editor of *Science & Society*, a quarterly journal of Marxian scholarship. In the recent past, I have been fortunate to have won research grants from the National Historical Publications and Records Commission (a division of the U.S. National Archives), the National Endowment for the Humanities, and the Louis M. Rabinowitz Foundation. My hobbies are athletics—especially fencing, swimming, and diving—and carpentry; I occasionally exhibit artwork and write fiction under the *nom de plume* Edward Antopol.

Index